MW01255093

THE
LIGHT EXTENDED
VOLUME 2

A JOURNAL OF THE GOLDEN DAWN

PRAISE FOR THIS BOOK

"When we talk about the Golden Dawn and its magick, we are quite often referring to the various Knowledge Lectures and Flying Rolls that form the backbone of the Tradition's philosophy. We speak of Pentagram and Hexagram Rituals, various Outer Hall arrangements and their officers, the Grade Rituals and their visible and invisible godforms, etc, etc. And while I in no way mean to diminish the importance of this material, I feel it is safe to say we've seen it all before. It's been published, republished, analyzed, re-written, discussed, debated, and then published again for the last one hundred and thirty years (give or take). However, in *The Light Extended: A Journal of the Golden Dawn, Vol. 2*, we are given the opportunity to explore some more obscure pathways through the Western Hermetic Mysteries; to dive down some rabbit holes we (perhaps) haven't recognized before. That, after all, is what a journal such as this should do!

Yes, there are some common Golden Dawn sites to visit herein: discussions of the four elements and their implements, psychology and magick, the making of simple tools and furnishings for your own home, and even astrology as introduced in the Neophyte Knowledge Lecture. But you will also find in this volume many side-roads to attractions that only the locals know about, because they aren't listed in the tourist brochures. Here are little-known rituals, explorations of obscure symbols, uncommon astrological tidbits, Greek Gods, and even the ancient Jewish Work of the Chariot (Merkavah). So, if you are looking for something a bit different, a bit deeper, a bit more unusual than the standard Golden Dawn fare, this is certainly one safari worth the price of your ticket."

— Aaron Leitch,
author of *Secrets of the Magickal Grimoires*

MORE PRAISE FOR THIS BOOK

"*The Light Extended* is a scholarly research journal of the Occult Sciences and, in particular, the Hermetic Order of the Golden Dawn. Frater Yechidah, the editor of this journal, has a high standard and nonpartisan approach to the occult research and ceremonial ritualistic dramæ of the Western Mystery Tradition and the Golden Dawn. Within the hallowed chamber of this esoteric journal, we find well known authors and researchers from the various Golden Dawn communities working for a common good. A place to come and learn in a peaceful space. I enjoyed reading this issue and the narrative that is reflected upon these pages. Read, Think, and Expand."

— Darcy Küntz,
editor of *The Golden Dawn Source Book*
and founder of the Golden Dawn Research Trust

The
LIGHT EXTENDED
VOLUME 2
A Journal of the Golden Dawn

Tony Fuller,
Frater Yechidah,
Samuel Scarborough,
John Michael Greer,
Jaime Paul Lamb,
Soror DPF,
Jayne Gibson,
J.P. Feliciano,
Chic Cicero and S. Tabatha Cicero,
Frater D,
Frater Manu Forti,
Frater A.R.O.

KERUBIM PRESS

DUBLIN 2020

Copyright © 2020 Tony Fuller, Frater Yechidah, Samuel Scarborough, John Michael Greer, Jaime Paul Lamb, Soror DPF, Jayne Gibson, J.P. Feliciano, Chic Cicero, S. Tabatha Cicero, Frater D, Frater Manu Forti, Frater A.R.O.

All rights reserved. No part of this publication may be reproduced, stored in a retrieval system, or transmitted, in any form or by any means, electronic, mechanical, photocopying, recording or otherwise, without the prior permission of the publisher.

Any person who makes any unauthorised act in relation to this publication may be liable for criminal prosecution and civil claims for damages.

The Moral Rights of the Authors have been asserted.

Cover design by Kerubim Press

First Edition 2020

ISBN 978-1-908705-17-4

Published by Kerubim Press
Dublin, Ireland

www.kerubimpress.com
enquiries@kerubimpress.com

CONTENTS

PREFACE

The members of the original Hermetic Order of the Golden Dawn were well educated men and women, and amongst their number were many scholars distinguished in their own fields of endeavour: these included scientists, medical doctors, clergymen, university teachers, authors, lawyers, poets and artists of various description. Given their intellectual calibre, it is hardly surprising that a large volume of literary, artistic and academic works emanated from a comparatively small group of people. Nor is it remarkable that some, perhaps most, of them utilised their talents in their individual magical work within the Golden Dawn Order. Such work was, of course, predicated on the vast corpus of explanatory and practical material largely provided to them, as they progressed through the Grades of the Golden Dawn, by two of its founders, William Westcott and S.L. Macgregor Mathers.

Notwithstanding the strict secrecy surrounding membership of the Golden Dawn and the safeguarding of its documents, it is fortunate that the majority of its 'official' instructional curricula, and many of the papers written by individual members, have survived to the benefit of the Order's modern inheritors. A distinction should be observed, however, between the two categories of documents. For the most part, the work of individual members did not become part of the official Order curriculum, nor was ever intended to be so. Rather, the expectation of each member was that he or she should carry out individual magical work based on Golden Dawn methods but within the context of their particular experience of life. Hence, the specific written record of one member would not necessarily have any validity or application for another. The Golden Dawn was remarkably free of dogma or any ideology to be followed blindly and this latitude extended into the private work. The sole requirement was that a member, and especially one who had reached the Grade of Adept, would work with the material provided on a personal basis. Whatever experiences he or she might have as a consequence, or whatever conclusions might be reached, was entirely a matter for that individual alone. Such private records were not usually shared with fellow members and it is an accident of fate that many have survived for our later perusal. Inevitably, therefore, some of the surviving papers and personal rituals written by members of the Golden Dawn, and its successor organisations, need to be considered in that individual context. Despite this caveat, it remains the case that the written acounts of experienced and scholarly Adepts of the Order are of enormous interest to modern scholars and occultists, frequently containing material of great value to those today who follow in their footsteps.

The practice of personal and scholarly work within the Golden Dawn system did not cease when the last of the Temples linked directly to the Order closed its doors in 1978. Indeed, the impressive tradition has continued unabated, and nowhere is this better exemplified than in this second volume of *The Light Extended: A Journal of the Golden Dawn*, edited by Frater Yechidah. As with its predecessor volume, distinguished modern Adepts of the Order have contributed important papers which fall into both the categories observed above. All demonstrate a high degree of scholarship, erudition and deep experience with advanced Golden Dawn concepts, and all are highly recommended to the reader who pursues the Golden Dawn Path, whether as scholar or magician.

— *Tony Fuller*, November 2020.

THE EVIL TRIANGLE

THE ROLE OF THE INVERTED TRIANGLE IN THE GOLDEN DAWN

by Frater Yechidah

The Cross and Triangle are perhaps the most identifiable Symbols of the Golden Dawn tradition, emblematic of the Cross of Suffering and the Three Supernals in the Qabalah, representing the Divine Light. The White Triangle is called the "Sacred and Sublime Symbol," upon which the Candidate places their hand during the Obligation in the Neophyte Ceremony, marking the beginning of their journey in the Order.

Much has been written on these, both in the original papers and subsequent commentaries, but less has been written on the Inverted Triangle and how it has potentially affected Order teachings.

We know, of course, that the Symbol of Water is ∇, and the Symbol of Earth is ∇. Both are Inverted Triangles. We might think nothing more of this, and even employ them ritually, though this was specifically cautioned against in the original Order.

> "Remember also that the $\triangle$ if apex downward is an extremely evil and hurtful Symbol ∇ and for this reason is it that these Symbols of the Elements are not usually traced as Sigils but are replaced by the Cherubic Emblems of ♌.♏.♒.♉."[1]

It is not difficult to see why the Order teaches this. With the Triangle representing the Supernal Triad, the inversion of this naturally represents the opposing force (the Supernals of the "Averse and Evil Sephiroth"), in much the same way the upright Pentagram

---

1 Ritual C, Ritual of the Hexagram (Private Collection). Another version explicitly gives the symbols $\triangle\nabla\triangle\nabla$ after "Symbols of the Elements."

represents "the rule of the Divine Spirit,"[2] while the inverted form is an Evil Symbol, "affirming the empire of matter over that Divine Spirit which should govern it."[3]

The significance of this cannot be overstated, as many today employ and recommend the use of the Alchemical Symbols of the Elements for ritual work, which, while understandable (and something I had at one time considered) may actually present a potential danger.

This may also be why the Order recommended using the Eastern Tatwas for skrying the Elements and not the more familiar Western Symbols. Indeed, this may partly explain the apparent incongruence of using the Tatwas in an otherwise Western system of esoteric teaching, and why the Tatwas should thus not be discarded in place of other seemingly more fitting Symbols. That said, while the Elemental Triangles for Water and Earth may be potentially dangerous to work with, Mathers considered the Tatwas themselves to be risky for uninitiates "as quickly leading to a dangerously passive condition."[4] Yet they were considered "perfectly safe" for the Zelator Adeptus Minor.[5] No such qualification was given for the use of the Alchemical Symbols of the Elements.

Ritual C also refers to a fifth form of the Hexagram, employing two interlocked Inverted Triangles, which is classified as "of a more Evil nature."[6] The Adept was cautioned against using this Symbol. References to it, and to the Inverted Triangle in general, were omitted from Regardie's The Golden Dawn, and thus many are unaware of the Order's teachings on these Symbols.

---

2 Ritual B, Ritual of the Pentagram (Private Collection).
3 Ibid.
4 Flying Roll XXVI, "Planets Expressed in Tatwic Symbols," Suplement to Flying Roll XII (Private Collection).
5 Ibid.
6 Ritual C, Ritual of the Hexagram (Private Collection).

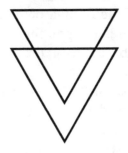

Figure 1: Fifth Form of the Hexagram

Of course, the Order never shied away from using the Inverted Triangle in its papers, particularly in relation to Water, so the mere presence of it was not considered problematic. Indeed, the Order also provided Qlippothic names and other Evil Symbols throughout its papers, and in the Initiation Ceremonies themselves. Yet there are no examples of the practical use of the Inverted Triangle outside working directly with an evil force, which I think is somewhat revealing.

We do, of course, see the ▽ Symbol employed for Water on the walls of the Vault, though it is accompanied by (and arguably balanced by) the Symbols of △ and ⏃. The Vault is also not free of Evil Symbols, for the very floor is filled with them. Indeed, the floor employs an Inverted Triangle, explicitly referred to in the 5=6 Ceremony as "the Inverted and Evil Triangle," in the centre of which is the "rescuing Symbol of the Golden Cross united to the Red Rose."[7] This is further balanced by the upright Triangle upon the ceiling.

The above might bring to mind the Cross and Triangle as employed in the Initiation Ceremonies of the Outer Order, particularly in the 2=9 Grade, where the Cross is placed inside the Inverted Triangle (in much the same manner as the floor of the Vault), and the 3=8 Grade, where the Cross is placed above the Inverted Triangle.

We can perhaps gain some insight into these from the explanation of the placement of the Cross and Triangle in the 0=0 Grade:

> "The Symbols which be upon the Altar represent the forces and manifestations of the Divine Light con-

---

7 5=6, Ritual of the Adeptus Minor (Private Collection).

centrated in the White Triangle of the Three Supernals as the Synthesis; wherefore upon this Sacred and Sublime Symbol is the Obligation of the Neophyte taken, as calling therein to witness the Forces of the Divine Light.

"The Red Cross of תפארת (to which the Grade of ⑤=⑥ is referred in the attribution of the Grades unto the Sephiroth) is placed in the ⓪=⓪ of Neophyte above this White Triangle—not as dominating it—but as bringing it down and manifesting it unto the Outer Order, as though the Crucified One, having raised the Symbol of Self-Sacrifice, had thus touched and brought into action in matter the Divine Triad of Light."[8]

We further see the Cross placed inside the upright Triangle in the 1=10 Grade, and below the upright Triangle in the 4=7 Grade. In all cases, even when the Inverted Triangle is used, there is an accompanying balancing force (*within* or *above* it).

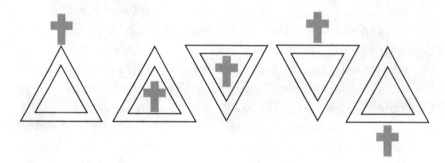

Figure 4: Cross and Triangle Placements in Grades

What is interesting about this is that there is one more possible variant, which is the Cross placed below the Inverted Triangle. While never explicitly labelled as such, nor even referred to, this is clearly an Evil Symbol, representing the inversion of the 0=0 placement, and thus an inversion of its symbolism. Yet this Symbol is never employed by the Order.

---

8 Ritual Z Part One, "Book of the Voice of Ⲑⲱⲟⲧⲉ," A Portion of the "Enterer of the Threshold" (Private Collection).

Figure 3: Unused Cross and Triangle Placement

Likewise, whenever the Inverted Triangle is used elsewhere, as in three of the forms of the Hexagram, it is always used with (and balanced by) the upright Triangle. It is never employed alone. Further, even when the Inverted Triangle is used as part of these, the upright Triangle is always traced first, in both Invoking and Banishing.

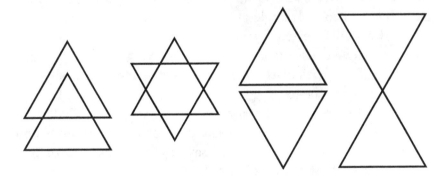

Figure 4: Standard Forms of the Lesser Hexagram

Even more interestingly, the two directions that relate most to Evil in the Golden Dawn tradition are North, "the place of greatest symbolic darkness,"[9] which corresponds with the Element of Earth (and thus ▽), and West, "at the borders of the Qlippoth,"[10] against which the Hiereus guards, and the direction of which corresponds with the Element of Water (and thus ▽). Given the teaching on the evil nature of the Inverted Triangle, I would argue that these assignments are no accident.

---

9 Ritual Z Part Three, Containing Symbolism of Admission to Neophyte Grade, Closing, Oration and Equinox (Private Collection).
10 Ibid.

It is important to note that the Order never completely prohibited the use of Evil Symbols, but rather strongly cautioned against it (and suggested such use be reserved for higher Grades, of which, of course, 6=5 seems appropriate).

> "And see that thou workest not with Evil forces save in a very few instances, as if thou art endeavouring to heal another from Sickness and Misfortune and thou art thus obliged to deal with the Evil force which is injuring him. And even so it will be better for thee not to do even this until thou hast arrived at a higher Grade than that of a Zelator Adeptus Minor."[11]

The above caution is vitally important, and it is with this in mind that we may perhaps look again with some reservation at the ritual use of the Elemental Triangles.

To draw an Inverted Triangle in ritual work may cause unintended negative consequences. Likewise, skrying this Symbol may seem harmless, particularly in relation to the Elements, but such would in actuality be fixating for a time on an Evil Symbol. I would argue that this could, in fact, awaken or strengthen the Evil Triad and the magician's own Evil Persona, perhaps in a very subtle and insidious way. As Ritual B would say regarding the use of Evil Symbols, "see that thou doest it not."[12]

---

11 Ritual C, Ritual of the Hexagram (Private Collection).
12 Ritual B, Ritual of the Pentagram (Private Collection).

ABOUT THE AUTHOR

Frater Yechidah is a magician and author.

He has written on many occult topics, including articles for *Hidden Spirit, Hermetic Virtues, The Gnostic,* and *The Light Extended.* He also blogs about topics related to the Golden Dawn and Gnosticism.

He established the occult publisher Kerubim Press and wrote two books on the Enochian system entitled *Enochian Magic in Theory* and *Enochian Magic in Practice.*

He has been involved with a number of esoteric groups, including the Order of the Sons and Daughters of Light, the Hermetic Order of the Golden Dawn, and the Ancient and Honourable Order of the Golden Dawn.

He lives in Dublin, Ireland.

The Equilibration of the Four Winds

by Samuel Scarborough

There are many Initiation Ceremonies within the Golden Dawn Tradition; five in the Outer Order, followed by Portal which is a sort of probationary Inner Order Grade, and of course there is the Adeptus Minor Initiation Ceremony for those who are invited into the Inner Order proper. For those lucky enough and who are willing to do the requisite work of the Adeptus Minor, there are the further Initiation Ceremonies for Adeptus Major and Adeptus Exemptus. These latter two where utilized in both the Stella Matutina and the Rosicrucian Order of the Alpha et Omega, though the ceremonies of the latter were different for these grades.

Outside of the Initiation Ceremonies, there were very few additional ceremonies, and of those the Equinox Ceremony, the Consecration of the Vault of the Adepti, the Consecration of a Temple, the Installation of Temple Chiefs, and a Ceremony for Peace (utilized by the Stella Matutina during World War II) are known. There is also one notable example of an Inner Order Ceremony utilizing the Evocation formula from the Inner Order's Ritual Z2 Magical Formulæ in which several adepti of the original Golden Dawn participated.

It was up to the adepti of the various temples and Orders to come up with these sort of workings, whether for an individual (a ritual more than ceremony) or with a small group of fellow adepti (a ceremony proper).

What is presented here is a ceremony designed for the invocation and communion of the Elements, Directions, and Winds associated with each Quarter within the Hall. This is to create a better understanding of the Directions, Elements, and Winds themselves, as well as to invoke their Forces in Equilibrated form into the Sphere of the Temple and the Sphere of Sensation of those present. These names and symbols associated with the Directions, Elements, and

Winds are integral to the understanding of the Forces represented therein.

The following Ceremony contains elements from various Initiation Ceremonies, notably the Neophyte, the Zelator, and the Theoricus. This Ceremony is an example of what can be done within a Temple setting for the benefit of the Temple, Order, and its members.

Explanation of Some of the Symbolism

The Hall is laid out as in the Opening of the Theoricus with a couple of exceptions. These are noted at the beginning of the Ceremony itself. The Ceremony is based more upon the Stella Matutina version of the Theoricus Ceremony than those of the original Golden Dawn or the later Alpha et Omega.

The regalia of the Officers is essentially that of the Stella Matutina, though any other Golden Dawn group, temple, or Order can substitute their own regalia with no ill effects.

Arrangement of the Elemental Representations on the Altar are to be placed at their corresponding edges of the Altar, as per the Theoricus Ceremony, with the Cross and Triangle placed on the center of the Altar, arranged as in the Neophyte Ceremony. The reasoning here is that the Elemental Representations correlate to the Four Winds as well and thus the edges of the Altar are more appropriate. The Cross and Triangle in the center of the Altar is a balanced focal point to further equilibrate the forces of the opposites represented by the Quarters and Elemental Representations.

Think of the Cross and Triangle in this arrangement mediating the union of opposites as given in speeches in both the Neophyte and Equinox Ceremonies, and the Forces of the Winds and their emblems upon the Altar.

Use of Godforms

The use of Godforms in Golden Dawn Ceremonies is a common occurrence, and they are used both in Initiation Ceremonies as well as personal rituals. The techniques for creation and assumption of Godforms are published in several books on the Golden Dawn and its magical practices, and are not discussed in this article.

Ideally, for this Ceremony, the Officers on the Floor are all adepti, that is of at least the 5=6 Adeptus Minor Grade, and are familiar with the techniques for assuming Godforms.

The Godforms for this Ceremony are named in the Ceremony itself. The Godforms are those from the Stella Matutina Theoricus Initiation Ceremony. Some of the Godform names and locations within the Hall may seem unfamiliar, particularly some of the Invisible Stations, yet are the names and locations as used by the original Stella Matutina.

The Hierophant is primarily Osiris, but is also Nu and Hormaku. When doing the primary work of invoking the East Wind, the Hierophant takes on the Godform of Henkhisesui, which is the Egyptian God of the East Wind and was used traditionally as a Godform in the Stella Matutina Theoricus Ceremony.

The Hiereus is primarily Horus, but is also assuming the Godform of Toum and Heka, and when invoking the West Wind is Hutchaiui.

The Hegemon is primarily Thmaa-est (Ma'at), but also the Godform of Ra and Mau, and represents the South Wind as Shehbui.

Finally, the Kerux is primarily the Godform Anubis of the East, and also Satem and Kephra, but represents the North Wind as Qebui.

The Sentinel who is outside the Hall takes on the Godform of Anubis of the West.

The Dais Officers, other than the Hierophant, take on their usual Godforms; Imperator (Imperatrix) is Nephthys, Cancellarius (Cancellaria) is Thoth, Past Hierophant (Past Hierophantia) is Aroueris (Horus the Elder), and the Demonstrator[1] (Demonstratrix) is Isis.

Herein the traditional Stella Matutina Dais Officer titles are utilized.

There are additional Invisible Stations associated with Golden Dawn Ceremonies, and many of these also are used in this Ceremony.

---

1 Demonstrator is the name of the Officer that in the original Golden Dawn is known as the Praemonstrator. Demonstrator is the traditional Stella Matutina name of this Officer whose role is primarily education within a Temple or Order.

These include the following:

- Ahathor = the ultimate East.
- Tharpesh = the ultimate South.
- Tho-oom-mo-oo = the ultimate West.
- Ahapshi = the ultimate North.
- Ameshet (Son of Horus) = Northeast corner.
- Toumathph (Son of Horus) = Southeast corner.
- Ahapi (Son of Horus) = Southwest corner.
- Kabexnuv (Son of Horus) = Northwest corner.

If the Enochian Elemental Tablets are used, and unveiled in particular, then behind these the appropriate Archangel would be built up and visualized; i.e. Raphael in the East, Michael in the South, Gabriel in the West, and Auriel in the North.

Before each of the Tablets should be the Elemental King drawn from the Tablet.

All of these Godform shells should be created and placed in their appropriate locations by the Hierophant prior to the Opening of the Temple as part of the work of the Hierophant in setting up the Hall. The Officers will then assume their Godform (the primary one), and the additional Godforms will "step up," as it were, during the appropriate course of the Ceremony when they are named.

The traditional descriptions and coloration of the above Godforms will not be covered in this article so as to leave some openness for others using this Ceremony. The traditional description and images of the Godforms of the Four Winds will be treated in some detail further in this portion of the article.

The Officers should take a moment at the Cardinal Points to allow the Godform of the appropriate Wind settle upon them before continuing with the Ceremony.

Descriptions of the Gods of the Four Winds

The Godforms of the Four Winds are very similar to the Kerubim in appearance, in that they are winged human figures with animal heads.

These Godforms are formulated in their appropriate Quarters. The below descriptions are a modern interpretation of these Godforms.

East Wind: Henkhisesui

Henkhisesui is a Ram-headed god wearing a belted kilt, and a solid nemyss on his head. His arms are outstretched to the sides holding an Ankh by the base with the loop upwards. Henkhisesui has two pairs of wings similar to those of the Kerubim. The nemyss is surmounted by a pair of wavy horns which are horizontal. These are further surmounted by four crowns which resemble feathers. Henkhisesui is facing left (the viewer's left).

The coloring for Henkhisesui is in violet and yellow.

South Wind: Shehbui

Shehbui is a Lion-headed god wearing a belted kilt, and a solid nemyss. His arms are outstretched just like Henkhisesui and are also holding Ankhs in the same manner. Shehbui has two pairs of wings as well. Shehbui's nemyss is likewise surmounted just as Henkhisesui's. Shehbui is facing left same as Henkhisesui.

The coloring for Shehbui is in red and green.

West Wind: Hutchaiui

Hutchaiui is a Serpent-headed god wearing a belted kilt and a solid nemyss. His arms are outstretched just as the above two god-forms, holding Ankhs in the same manner. Hutchaiui also has two pairs of wings. His nemyss is surmounted in the same manner as the above god-forms. Hutchaiui is facing right.

The coloring for Hutchaiui is blue and orange.

North Wind: Qebui

Qebui is a little different from the above Godforms. He too is Ram-headed, but has four heads, two facing right and two left. Qebui wears a belted kilt and a solid nemyss which is surmounted as the above god-forms. Qebui's arms are likewise outstretched and holding an Ankh in each hand in the same manner as the previous god-forms. Qebui has two pairs of wings.

The coloring for Qebui is black and white.

Basic images of these gods can be found in E.A. Wallis Budge's *The Gods of the Egyptians*.

For those who are interested, below are images of the Stella Matutina Godforms of the Gods of the Four Winds. These images come from the Smaragdum Thalasses H.O. 49 Temple of the Stella Matutina in Havelock North, New Zealand. *Smaragdum Thalasses*, meaning "Emerald of the Seas," is often referred to as Whare Ra (pronounced Phair-ray Rah), which properly was the name of the house wherein the Temple was located.

The below images of the Godforms of the Four Winds are the only known surviving examples. According to Golden Dawn scholar Tony Fuller, "uncoloured images of the godforms containing the 4 Winds, was issued to the Adepti."[2] The images shown here are from the papers of the last Demonstrator of Smaragdum Thalasses, Frank Salt, known as Greatly Honoured Frater Fiat Lux.

The following sequence for the Godforms of the Four Winds from Smaragdum Thalasses Temple will be East = Hierophant, West = Hiereus, South = Hegemon, and North = Kerux. Each image will be followed by a detailed color description.

---

2 Conversation with Tony Fuller on 15 February 2020 by the author.

East = Hierophant:

Description of the East Godform:

The Stella Matutina Godform of the East Wind used by the Hierophant (Hierophantia) in the 2=9 Theoricus Ceremony is a Man
standing with his arms outstretched in a Cross. Under his outstretched arms he has two pair of wings, one pair above another; the
upper pair on both sides is Green, while the lower pair of wings is
Purple (Violet) on both sides. He has Yellow skin and wears a Purple
(or Violet) nemyss (Egyptian style headdress) that is surmounted
by Green ram's horns which have four Purple (or Violet) feathers
above the horns. He wears a striped kilt with what is presumably a
Green belt. The kilt has alternating diagonal stripes of Yellow and
Purple (Violet). In each hand he holds a Red Crux Ansata (Ankh).
He stands on a floor that alternates Yellow and Purple.

West = Hiereus:

Description of the West Godform:

The Godform of the West Wind, as used in the Stella Matutina by the Hiereus (Hiereia) in the 2=9 Theoricus Ceremony, is a Serpent-headed Male figure standing with arms outstretched in the form of a Cross. Under the outstretched arms there are two pairs of wings, one above the other in similar manner to the Godform described previously; the upper pair on both sides of the body is Orange, while the lower pair is Green. The figure has Blue skin and wears an Orange nemyss surmounted by a pair of Green ram's horns that have four Blue-Green (Teal) feathers above the horns. The figure wears a diagonally striped kilt that alternates Orange and Blue. In the figure's outstretched hands, he holds a Red Crux Ansata (Ankh) in each hand. He stands on a floor that alternates Blue and Orange.

South = Hegemon:

Description of the South Godform:

The Godform of the South Wind, used in the Stella Matutina by the Hegemon (Hegemone) in the 2=9 Theoricus Ceremony, is a Lion-headed Male figure standing with arms outstretched in cruciform. Under the outstretched arms are two pairs of wings, one above the other in the same manner as the previous Godforms. The upper pair of wings is Purple (Violet) and the lower pair of wings is Yellow. The figure has Red skin and wears a Green nemyss surmounted by Yellow ram's horns that have four Violet or Dark Purple feather above the horns. The figure wears a diagonally striped kilt, with the top stripe being Yellow (presumably to indicate a belt), and the other other stripes alternating Green and Red. In the figure's outstretched hands, he holds a Red Crux Ansata (Ankh) in each hand. He stands on a floor that alternates Red and Green.

Note: In the original figure, the Red looks rather like Brick colored than Red, and the four feathers above the ram's horns appear darker than the other Purple used on this or the other figures. Of course, these variations in color could be from the use of watercolor paint and the paper, particularly as it has aged.

North = Kerux:

Description of the North Godform:

The Godform of the North Wind, used by the Stella Matutina by the Kerux (Kerukaina) in the 2=9 Theoricus Ceremony, is a Four-headed Bull-headed Male figure with outstretched arms in a cruciform stance like the previous three Godforms. Under the outstretched arms are two pairs of wings, one pair above the other pair. Both pairs are

Russet (Brown) on the left side (as facing the figure) and both wings on the right side (as facing the figure) are Green (possibly Olive), The figure has Yellow (possibly Citrine) skin on the upper portion of the body and heads, while the legs have Black skin. Each of the Bull heads appears to wear a different colored nemyss; the lower right (as looking at the figure) wears an Olive nemyss, the lower left head (as looking at the figure) wears a Black nemyss, the upper right head wears a Yellow (possibly Citrine) nemyss, and finally the upper left head wears a Brown or possibly Russet nemyss. The top of the figure is surmounted by a pair of ram's horns that are half Brown or Russet and half Olive, left and right halves of the ram's horns respectively. The ram's horns have above them four Yellow feathers. The Figure wears a diagonally striped kilt that alternates Black, Yellow, Brown, Green. This figure holds a Red Crux Ansata (Ankh) in each hand, and stands on a floor that is colored in the Black, Yellow, Brown, Olive (Green). This sequence of alternating colors repeats on the floor and the kilt.

Note: The colors in the original figure can be somewhat difficult to judge. There are instances where the Green is clearly darker and more like Olive, and places where it appears to be simply Green. Brown appears to be used on the original, but the colors of the Quarternary of Malkuth, whose colors would be Citrine, Russet, Olive, and Black, seem to fit in relation to the other Godforms in this set, and Olive is clearly indicated in places on the figure. It stands to reason that the nemysses, striped kilt, and floor follow this rule of Citrine, Olive, Russet, and Black.

While the coloration in this Godform using the Quarternary colors of Malkuth is purely supposition on my part, it does match with many of the teachings in relation to the Northern Quarter. The Brown being used for Russet, a color sometimes used to visualize the Elemental Earth Pentagram, makes sense due to the difficulty in creating it with the medium of watercolor paints. The same applies to Citrine and Olive.

Again the age of both the paint medium and the paper has caused some issues determining actual color.

Notes Concerning the Format of the Ceremony

In the following Ceremony the spoken words of the Officers is given in regular font, that is unitalicized. Stage directions, that is actions of the Officers, is given in *italics*. In a traditional Ceremonial Rubric the titles of the Officer to the left would be in red, as would be the stage directions for the actions of the Officer and others in the performance of the Ceremonial.

It will be noted that some words are capitalized or fully capitalized (all letters in the word in capitals). This is done to show importance or emphasis. Such as saying the name HORMAKU, spoken by the Hierophant or Hierophantia during the Ceremony, and activating that Godform in the Ceremony.

In other places, a word will be fully capitalized, but with all letters in **bold**. This is meant to indicate words to be vibrated by the Officer and normally refers to Divine Names used in the course of the Ceremony.

The Officers are listed in the following manner in the script for the Ceremony as:

> Hierophant (Hierophantia) = Hiero.
> Hiereus (Hiereia) = Hiereus
> Hegemon (Hegemone) = Hege.
> Kerux (Kerukaina) = Kerux.
> Sentinel = Sentinel.

No Floor Diagram—that is, a diagram showing the arrangement of the furniture and Officers within the space of the Ceremony—is given. There are several published Floor Diagrams which can be used, or should an existing Temple wish to use this Ceremony, then they can utilize the particular 2=9 Theoricus Opening Diagram normally used and modify that according to the instructions given below in the full rubric of the Ceremony.

A note concerning the use of the Invoking Spirit Pentagrams and the Elemental Pentagrams as given in the following rubric is in order. The Stella Matutina used the sequence of the Spirit Pentagrams, both the Active and Passive Pentagrams before the Elemental Pentagram, and this same sequence of Spirit Pentagrams preceding the Elemental Pentagram was used during the Banishing during the course of Ceremonial. This sequence appears in any number of original unpublished versions of the Stella Matutina Ceremonials from Amoun Temple (1903-1923), Smaragdum Thalasses Temple (1912-1978), and Hermes Temple (1916-1962). The sequence of action in the Stella Matutina tracing the Pentagrams differs from that used in the original Golden Dawn Ceremonials and later Rosicrucian Order of the Alpha et Omega Ceremonials, which followed the original Golden Dawn methods, in that Active and Passive Spirit Pentagrams precede the Elemental Pentagram in the Invoking but supersede the Elemental Pentagram during the Banishing.

Names and regalia of Officers are given in Stella Matutina terms. If any other Golden Dawn Temple uses the following Ceremony, the regalia and names of Officers follow suit for the Temple.

The Feminine names of the Officers is the traditional ones used by the Golden Dawn and which are normally found throughout the unpublished versions of the Ceremonials and in Ritual Z1 of the Inner Order in the original Golden Dawn, Alpha et Omega, and Stella Matutina, and may be somewhat different from what is used in many modern Temples of the Golden Dawn.

EQUILIBRATION OF THE FOUR WINDS CEREMONY

OFFICERS:

On Dais:

Imperator	White Robe, Red Mantle, Red and Green Nemyss, Yellow Slippers, Lamen suspended from Green Collar, Sword.

Cancellarius	White Robe, Yellow Mantle, Yellow and Violet Nemyss, Yellow Slippers, Lamen suspended from Violet Collar, Scepter.
Demonstrator	White Robe, Blue Mantle, Blue and Orange Nemyss, Yellow Slippers, Lamen suspended from Orange Collar, Scepter.
Past Hiero.	White Robe, Red Mantle, Red Nemyss, Yellow Slippers, Lamen suspended from White Collar, Scepter.

On Floor:

Hierophant	White Robe, Red Mantle, Red and White Nemyss, Yellow Slippers, Lamen suspended from White Collar, Scepter of Power, Banner of the East.
Hiereus	Black Robe, Black Mantle, Black and White Nemyss, Red Slippers, Lamen suspended from Red Collar, Sword, Banner of the West.
Hegemon	Black Robe, White Mantle, Black and White Nemyss, Red Slippers, Lamen suspended from Black Collar, Scepter.
Kerux	Black Robe, Black and White Nemyss, Red Slippers, Lamen suspended from Black Collar, Rod, Lamp.
Sentinel	(at door) Black Robe, Black and White Nemyss, Red Slippers, Lamen suspended from Black Collar, Sword.

ON ALTAR:

Cross and Triangle (Arranged as in Neophyte), Yellow Fan (East), Red Lamp (South), Cup of Water (West), Paten of Salt and Bread (North).

HALL:

> Banner of the East (East beside Hierophant), Banner of the West (West beside Hiereus), Pentacle (East), Pillars to the East of the Altar (with lamps veiled and on). Four small tables or side Altars in the Quarters, Appropriate colored candles in the Quarters. Thurible or Censer in the South, Cup of Lustral Water in the North.

> **NOTE:** If the Enochian Tablets are used in the Quarters, then they are either all veiled or all exposed.

MEMBERS:

> Robed and in their proper places within the Hall as per Grade.

The Hall is arranged as in the Opening of Theoricus with the following differences:

The Banner of the West is in the West to the left of the Hiereus. The Cross and Triangle are arranged on the Altar as in the Neophyte. The Elemental representations are arranged accordingly around the edge of the Altar, rather than around the arms of the Cross. The Thurible and Incense are in the South at the station of the Hegemon. The Cup of Lustral Water, also known as Holy Water, is in the North at the station of the Kerux. The Pentacle is in the East.

The incense used in this Ceremony can be any general incense, such as Olibanum, Frankincense, Sandalwood, or Lignum Aloes. Likewise, a blend of equal parts Olibanum, Myrrh, Galbanum, and Storax (bark) may be used. (This blend is ideally made at least 30-40 days ahead of time and allowed to cure and age in an airtight container away from direct sunlight). Other incenses or blends thereof may be used as well within this Ceremony, such as those utilized by many Orthodox, Roman Catholic, or Episcopal (Anglican) Churches, and which can be acquired through stores dedicated to supplying such churches.

A female who holds the Office of Hierophant is traditionally called the Hierophantia, but can, at her discretion, be called simply Hierophant. A female holding the office of Hiereus may be called Hiereia (at her discretion). A female holding the Office of Hegemon is known as a Hegemone, while a female Kerux, at her discretion is known as Kerukaina.

NOTE: If this Ceremony be the first to be performed at any meeting, the regulation with regard to the use of the Lesser Ritual of the Pentagram, and the Prayer of the East holds good, as laid down in the Rubric of the 0=0 Grade Ceremony.

The same applies to Purifying with Lustral Water and Consecrating with Fire, which are done as laid down in the Rubric of the 0=0 Grade Ceremony, performed in this case by the Kerux (Lustral Water) and Hegemon (Fire).

OPENING

When all Members are Robed and Assembled, Hierophant begins with a knock. Knocks are represented by ❧ in the following Ceremony.

Hiero: ❧ Fratres and Sorores of the _____ Temple of the _____ in the Outer, assist me to open the Temple.

Frater (Soror) Kerux (Kerukaina), see that the Temple is properly guarded.

Kerux (Kerukaina) rises with a Salute to the East, then goes to the Door and knocks once. The Sentinel checks that all is clear and properly guarded, then knocks once on the outer side of the door.

If there is no Sentinel, then the Kerux would knock once on the inner side of the door, open the door and look out into the pronaos, close the door and knock once after closing the Door.

Kerux: Very Honored Hierophant (Hierophantia), the Temple is properly guarded.

Returns sunwise to station, Saluting with 0=0 Signs when passing the East.

Hiero: Honored Hiereus (Hiereia), see that all present have beheld the Golden Dawn.

Hiereus (Hiereia) rises and salutes the East.

Hiereus: Fratres and Sorores, give the Signs.

All rise and give the Signs to the East.

Very Honored Hierophant (Hierophantia), all present have been so honored.

Hiereus (Hiereia) gives Signs to the East.

Hiero: I command that the Temple be Purified by Water and Consecrated by Fire.

Kerux and Hegemon rise with a Salute to the East. Kerux with Cup of Lustral Water and Hegemon with Thurible of Incense.
    They Purify and Consecrate as in the Neophyte Ceremony.
    When they return to their stations they Salute the East with the Sign of Silence.

Hiero: Honored Hegemon (Hegemone), to what is this particular Ceremony attributed?

Hege: To the Four Winds.

Hiero: Honored Hiereus (Hiereia), to what does this Ceremony especially refer?

Hiereus: To the Universe of Created things.

Hiero: Honored Hegemon (Hegemone), to what does this allude?

Hege: To the Universe of Creation as represented by the Twenty-first Trump of the Tarot. To the Four Directions or Winds, and to the Four Elements of Nature. It is also a reflection of the Sphere of Saturn.

Hiero: ¶ Let us Adore the Lord of the Universe and Nature!

All rise and face East.

Hiero: Holy art Thou, Lord of the Universe whom naught but Silence can express. Thou who art in all things and whom is all things. Thee we adore and Thee we invoke.

Holy art Thou who hast created the Firmament. Holy art Thou who hast shown forth the Throne of Thy Glory. Holy art Thou whose Countenance moved upon the Waters at the Beginning. Holy art Thou who hast the Earth as Thy footstool.

All perform Adoration to the Lord of the Universe.

All: Holy art Thou, Lord of the Universe! (Salute)
Holy art Thou, Whom Nature hath not formed! (Salute)
Holy art Thou, the Vast and the Mighty One! (Salute)
Lord of the Light and of the Darkness! (Sign of Silence)

All remain standing, facing East.

Hiero: Hierophant (Hierophantia) takes up the Pentacle and traces the Invoking Pentagrams of Spirit Active and Spirit Passive followed by the Invoking Air Pentagram within a circle in the East.

Hierophant (Hierophantia) Salutes the East, then moves sunwise to the South.

All face South.

Hierophant (Hierophantia) faces South and traces with the Pentacle the Invoking Pentagrams of Spirit Active and Passive followed by the Invoking Pentagram of Fire in a circle in the South.

Hierophant (Hierophantia) Salutes the South, then moves sunwise to the West.

All face West.

Hierophant (Hierophantia) faces West and traces with the Pentacle the Invoking Pentagrams of Spirit Active and Passive followed by the Invoking Pentagram of Water in a circle in the West.

Hierophant (Hierophantia) Salutes the West, then moves sunwise to the North.

All face North.

Hierophant (Hierophantia) faces North and traces with the Pentacle the Invoking Pentagrams of Spirit Active and Passive followed by the Invoking Pentagram of Earth in a circle in the North.

Hierophant (Hierophantia) Salutes the North, then moves sunwise to the East.

All face East.

Hierophant (Hierophantia) raises Pentacle on high.

Hiero: And the Elohim said, "Let us make Adam in our Image, after Our likeness and let him have dominion over the cattle and over all the earth, and over every creeping thing that creepeth over the Earth. Let him have dominion over the Fowl of the Air. Let him have dominion over the Fish of the Sea. Let us make Adam in our Image, after Our likeness, and let them have Dominion."

Hierophant (Hierophantia) makes a Cross with Pentacle, and then replaces Pentacle in the East.

In the Divine Name of **YHVH**, I declare that I have opened this Temple.

Hiero: יייי

Hege: יייי

Hiereus: יייי

Kerux: יייי

CEREMONY

Hiero: Fratres and Sorores, we are gathered here to celebrate the Creation of Nature as represented by the Four Elements which are analogous to the Four Winds or Directions and to Equilibrate their Forces within the Sphere of this Temple and the Spheres of its Members.

These Winds lie to the East, the South, the West, and the North and are thusly represented upon the Double Cubical Altar of the Universe as a yellow Fan for the East Wind, a Red Lamp for the South Wind, a Cup of Wine for the West Wind, and lastly a Paten of Bread and Salt for the North Wind.

יייי

The Hierophant (Hierophantia) quits the Throne of the East and moves directly to the East of the Altar, takes up the Fan and returns to his (her) station the way he (she) came.

The Hiereus (Hiereia) quits the Throne of the West and moves directly to the West of the Altar, takes up the Cup of Wine and returns to his (her) station the way he (she) came.

The Hegemon (Hegemone) moves directly to the South of the Altar, takes up the Red Lamp and returns to his (her) station the way he (she) came.

Kerux (Kerukaina) moves directly to the North of the Altar, takes up the Paten of Bread and Salt and returns to his (her) station the way he (she) came.

Hiereus: The Sphinx of Egypt spake and said, "I am the synthesis of of the Elemental Forces of Creation. I am also the symbol of Man. I am Life and I am Death. I am the Child of the Night of Time."

Hierophant (Hierophantia) stands holding the Banner of the East in his (her) left hand and the Fan in his (her) right hand.

Hiero: I am the Priest with the mask of OSIRIS and verily none may approach the Gate of the Eastern Heaven who hast not first been purified and consecrated.

I am also NU, the Goddess of the Firmament of Air, and HORMAKU Lord of the Eastern Sun.

I am the mighty letter ALEPH.

Hierophant (Hierophantia) faces East.

Hierophant (Hierophantia) traces the Hebrew letter Aleph with the Fan in the air before him (her).

I am the Kerub of the East, ADAM.

Hierophant (Hierophantia) traces the Sign of Aquarius with the Fan in the air before him (her).

I stand with the Banner of the Morning Light, which is the Banner of the East.

Hierophant (Hierophantia) traces with the Banner of the East an Equal-armed Cross in the air before him (her).

Hierophant (Hierophantia) faces as usual towards the central Altar.

I am HENKHISESUI, Ram-headed god of the East Wind. It is through me the Forces of the Eastern Wind flow in Equilibrated manner unto this Temple and its members.

Hierophant (Hierophantia) stands in the form of a Cross, holding the Banner of the East in the left hand and the yellow Fan (open) in the right hand, facing the central Altar.

Hiereus: I am Osiris, the Soul in Twin Aspect, united to the Higher by Purification, Perfected in Suffering, Glorified through Trial, I have come where the Great Gods are through the Power of the Mighty Name.

Hegemon (Hegemone) stands holding the Red Lamp in his (her) right hand.

Hege: I am the Priest with the mask of the Lion and verily none may approach the Gate of the Southern Heaven who hast not first been purified and consecrated.

I am also MAU, the Lion, very powerful and RA the Sun in his Strength.

I am the mighty letter SHIN.

Hegemon (Hegemone) faces South, holding the Red Lamp in the right hand and the Hegemon's Scepter in the left hand.

Hegemon (Hegemone) traces the letter Shin with the Red Lamp.

I am also the Kerub of the South, ARYEH.

Hegemon (Hegemone) traces the Sign of Leo with the Red Lamp before him (her).

Hegemon (Hegemone) then traces an Equal-armed Cross with the Hegemon's Scepter.

Hegemon (Hegemone) faces as usual towards the central Altar, Red Lamp in the right hand and Scepter in left hand.

I am SHEHBUI, Lion-headed god of the South Wind. Through me the Forces of the Southern Wind flow in Equilibrated manner unto this Temple and its members.

Hegemon (Hegemone) stands in the form of a Cross, holding the Red

Lamp in the right hand and Scepter in left hand, facing the central Altar.

Hiereus: I have passed through the Gates of the Firmament, give me your hands for I am made as ye, ye Lords of Truth, for ye are the Formers of the Soul.

Hiereus (Hiereia) rises with the Cup of Water in his (her) right hand and the Banner of the West in his (her) left hand.

I am the Priest with the mask of the Eagle and verily none may approach the Gate of the Western Heaven who hast not first been purified and consecrated.

I am also HEKA, Mistress of Hesur, Ruler of Water, and am TOUM, the setting Sun.

I am the mighty letter MEM.

Hiereus (Hiereia) faces West.

Hiereus (Hiereia) traces the Hebrew letter Mem in the air before him (her) with the Cup of Water.

I am also the Kerub of the West, NESHER.

Hiereus (Hiereia) traces the head of the Eagle in the air before him (her) with the Cup of Water.

Hiereus (Hiereia) traces with the Banner of the West an Equal-armed Cross in the air before him (her).

Hiereus (Hiereia) faces as usual towards the central Altar.

I am HUTCHAIUI, Serpent-headed god of the West Wind. Through me the Forces of the Western Wind flow in Equilibrated manner unto this Temple and its members.

Hiereus (Hiereia) stands in the form of a Cross, with the Cup of Water in his (her) Right Hand and the Banner of the West in the Left Hand, facing the central Altar.

Hiereus: Oh Lord of the Universe! Thou are above all things, before Thee the Shadows of Night roll back, and the Darkness hasteth away.

Kerux (Kerukaina) rises with the Paten of Bread and Salt in his (her) right hand and the Kerux's Lamp in left hand.

Kerux: I am the Priest with the mask of the Ox and verily none may approach the Gate of the Northern Heaven who hast not first been purified and consecrated.

I am also SATEM in the abode of SHU, the Bull of Earth, and I am KEPHRA, the Sun at Night.

I am the mighty letters ALEPH, MEM, and SHIN and the CROSS.

Kerux (Kerukaina) faces North.
Kerux (Kerukaina) traces the Hebrew letters Aleph, Mem, and Shin in the Air before him (her) with the Paten of Bread and Salt.

I am the Kerub of the North, SHOR.

The Kerux (Kerukaina) traces the sigil of the Head of the Ox with the Paten of Bread and Salt in the air before him (her).
Kerux (Kerukaina) traces in the air with the Kerux's Lamp and Salt an Equal-armed Cross.
Kerux (Kerukaina) faces as usual towards the central Altar.

I am QEBUI, Ram-headed god of four faces of the North Wind. Through me the Forces of the Northern Wind flow in Equilibrated manner unto this Temple and its members.

Kerux (Kerukaina) stands in the form of a Cross, with the Paten of Bread and Salt in his (her) Right Hand, facing the central Altar.
The Forces of the Four Winds flows through the Officers into the Hall concentrated onto the central Double Cubical Altar in the Hall.
Let the Officers hold these positions for a few moments while the Forces of the Four Winds gather within the Hall.

Hiero: (Knocks) יהוה

In the Divine Name **SHADDAI EL CHAI**, and through the Archangel of the East, **RAPHAEL**, and the Three Great Holy Secret Names of God bourne upon the Banners of the East, **ORO IBAH AOZPI**, let the Forces of the Eastern Wind be present here for us to commune with this day and hour.
Spirits of Air and the East adore your Creator.

Hierophant (Hierophantia) makes a fanning motion with the yellow Fan towards the Altar.

Hege: In the Divine Name **YHVH TZABAOTH**, and through the Archangel of the South, **MICHAEL**, and the Three Great Holy Secret Names of God bourne upon the Banners of the South, **OIP TEAA PEDOCE**, let the Forces of the Southern Wind be present here for us to commune with this day and hour.
Spirits of Fire and the South adore your Creator.

Hegemon (Hegemone) makes a waving motion with the Red Lamp towards the Altar.

Hiereus: In the Divine Name **ELOHIM TZABAOTH**, and through the Archangel of the West, **GABRIEL**, and the Three Great Holy Secret Names of God bourne upon the Banners of the West, **EMPEH ARSEL GAIOL**, let the Forces of the Western Wind be present here for us to commune with this day and hour.
Spirits of Water and the West adore your Creator.

Hiereus (Hiereia) makes a waving motion with the Cup of Water towards the Altar.

Kerux: In the Divine Names **ADONAI HA-ARETZ ADONAI MELEKH**, through the Archangel of the North, **AURIEL**, and the Three Great Holy Secret Names of God bourne upon the Banners of the North, **EMOR DIAL HECTEGA**, let the Forces of the Northern Wind be present here for us to commune with this day and hour.

Spirits of Earth and the North adore your Creator.

Kerux (Kerukaina) makes a waving motion with the Paten towards the Altar.

Hiero: (Knocks) ܢܢܢܢ

Hierophant (Hierophantia) stands in the form of a Cross facing the central Altar.

> The Forces of the East, MIZRACH, and the Eastern Wind who art HENKHISESUI which brings with it a Warm and Moist nature, a destroying force against the unrighteous and evil, an influx of Intellect, an Equilibrating Force, and the cleansing breezes of the Spring, be here that we might partake of thine Nature so that we might at length be Discerning, and as Prompt and Active as the Sylphs.

Hierophant (Hierophantia) remains standing facing the Altar in the form of a Cross.

Hegemon (Hegemone) stands in the form of a Cross facing the central Altar.

Hege: The Forces of the South, DAROM, and the Southern Wind who art SHEHBUI which brings with it a Hot and Dry nature, a destroying force against the evil and the darkness, an influx of Will, an Initial Fiery Force, and the purifying breezes of the Summer, be here that we might partake of thine Nature so that we might at length be strong of Will, and as Energetic and Strong as the Salamanders.

Hegemon (Hegemone) remains standing facing the Altar in the form of a Cross.

Hiereus (Hiereia) stands in the form of a Cross facing the central Altar.

Hiereus: The Forces of the West, MEARAB, and the Western Wind who art HUTCHAIUI which brings with it a Moist and Cold nature, a nurturing and fructifying force against the evil and the desolate, an influx of Intuition, the Creative Force, and the cleansing breezes of Fall, be here that we might partake of thine Nature so that wc might at length be Flexible and Attentive to Images as the Undines.

Hiereus (Hiereia) remains standing facing the Altar in the form of a Cross.

Kerux (Kerukaina) stands in the form of a Cross facing the central Altar.

Kerux: The Forces of the North, TZAPHON, and the Northern Wind who art QEBUI which brings with it a Dry and Cold nature, a purifying force in the heart of darkness and desolation, an influx of Strength and Fortitude, the Manifestation of Force, and the biting breezes of Winter, be here that we might partake of thine Nature so that we might at length be Laborious and Patient as the Gnomes.

Kerux (Kerukaina) remains standing facing the Altar in the form of a Cross.

Hiero: The Four Winds each have their own Natures, but are united in the Manifest by the Quintessence, that Force which is all things and in all things; the Spirit Divine, the **RUACH ELOHIM!**

Therefore, let the Four Winds be brought together in unison upon the Double Cubical Altar of the Universe, that central point wherein the **RUACH ELOHIM** dwells!

All four Officers move together directly towards the Altar.

Each stop and hold aloft their respective Elements so that they touch on high above the center of the Altar above the Cross and Triangle.

After a moment, they lower the Elements together and place them on their respective angles of the Altar.

Officers turn sunwise, facing their Quarter and return to their Stations the way they approached the Altar.

On reaching their Stations, they face as usual.

Officers take up their Implements as usual.

All stand and face the Altar as in the Opening.

Hiero: And lo! Upon the Double Cubical Altar of the Universe are the Emblems of the Four Winds in Harmony and Equilibrium, round the Cross and Triangle. These Forces have been separated, purified, and are bound back together under the Divine Breath of the RUACH ELOHIM in Perfection as images of the Material World bound by the Spiritual World.

Hierophant pauses briefly before continuing.

Nothing now remains but for us to partake together in Silence the Mystic Repast of the Four Winds that we might take within us the Equilibrated Forces of the Natures thereof, so that we might be Prompt and Active as the Sylphs, but avoid Frivolity and Caprice; be Energetic and Strong as the Salamanders, but avoid Irritability and Ferocity; be Flexible and Attentive to Images as the Undines, but avoid Idleness and Changeability; be Laborious and Patient as the Gnomes, but avoid Grossness and Avarice.

All this is brought together and bound by the Unifying Force of Spirit, the **RUACH ELOHIM**, that we might enter thus far into the Sanctuary of the Divine Mysteries and at length stand before the Throne of the Divine having accomplished the Great Work, the MAGNUM OPUS!

Let this Mystic Repast maintain us in our search for the QUINTESSENCE, the Stone of the Philosophers. True Wisdom, Perfect Happiness, the SUMMUM BONUM.

The Hierophant advances to the West of the Altar and gives the Projection Sign towards the Altar five times.

Hierophant (Hierophantia) takes up the Fan, and holds it upright over the center of the Altar.

To feel with me the Warm breeze of MIZARACH.

Hierophant fans himself (herself), then returns the Fan to the Altar.
Hierophant (Hierophantia) takes up Lamp, and holds it upright over the center of the Altar.

To feel with me the Hot breeze of DAROM.

Hierophant (Hierophantia) waves the Lamp thrice so that he (she) can feel the hot air, then returns the Lamp to the Altar.
Hierophant (Hierophantia) takes up the Paten, and holds it over the center of the Altar.

To feel with me the Cold breeze of TZAPHON.

Hierophant (Hierophantia) dips Bread in the Salt and eats it, then waves the Paten thrice before returning it to the Altar.
Hierophant (Hierophantia) takes up Cup, and holds it over the center of the Altar.

Finally, to feel with me the Cool breeze of MEARAB.

Hierophant (Hierophantia) traces with the Cup a Rose Cross as if standing upon the center of the Altar, then drinks from the Cup.
Hierophant (Hierophantia) waves the Cup thrice, then replaces it on the Altar.
Hierophant (Hierophantia) moves deosil to East of the Altar, faces West.
Starting with Dais Officers, Demonstrator (Praemonstrator) quits Dais and halts briefly at the White Pillar, the other Dais Officers line up silently behind Demonstrator (Demonstratrix) in Order; Imperator, Cancellarius, Past Hierophant.
Demonstrator comes to West of Altar, and receives in Silence the Mystic Repast of the Four Winds from the Hierophant (Hierophantia).
When completed, Hierophant (Hierophantia) returns to Station. Demonstrator moves to East of Altar with Sun, and faces West.
Demonstrator administers Repast to Imperator (Imperatrix).

Demonstrator returns to Station. Imperator moves to East of Altar with Sol, and faces West, and administers the Repast to the Cancellarius (Cancellaria).

The rest of the Dais Officers do the same in order leaving the Past Hierophant (Past Hierophantia) to administer the Repast to the Hiereus (Hiereia). Hiereus (Hiereia) administers the Repast to the Hegemon (Hegemone). Hegemon (Hegemone) administers the Repast to the Kerux (Kerukaina). The Sentinel comes into the Hall, and the Kerux administers the Repast to the Sentinel.

When all the Officers except the Kerux have partaken, the Inner Members in order of seniority of admission, partake but do not wait for instructions in this. If there is a pause, one comes forward. They line up next to the White Pillar to wait.

Hiero: Let all the Members below the Grade of Portal be seated.

5=6 Members then communicate in the order in which they happen to be seated in the Hall, commencing with the one nearest the left of Hierophant; and working round by S.W. & N. to the one nearest his right. Each lifts and hands the Elements to the one who comes after him and each returns to his place round the Altar with Sol and then sits down. When all 5=6 Members have partaken and the last is standing East of Altar:

Hiero: Let the Portal Members partake.

They rise and partake as the Officers before.

Hiero: Let all Members of the 4=7 Grade now rise.

They rise and partake as before.

Hiero: Let all Members of the 3=8 Grade now rise.

They rise and partake as before.

Hiero: Let all Members of the 2=9 Grade now rise.

They rise and partake as before.

Hiero: Let all Members of the 1=10 Grade now rise.

They rise and partake as before.

Hiero: Let the Neophytes now rise.

They rise and partake as before. When the last Member has partaken of the Repast, the Hierophant (Hierophantia) knocks.

ו TETELESTAI! IT IS FINISHED!

Hiero: (Knocks) וווו

Hierophant (Hierophantia) stands and spreads arms in benediction.

> Let that which we have partaken sustain us now and evermore in our search for the QUINTESSENCE and may we ever feel the Breath of the **RUACH ELOHIM** upon us.

CLOSING

Hiero: (Knocks) ו Assist me to close the Temple.

All rise.

> Frater Kerux (Soror Kerukaina), see that the Temple is properly guarded.

Done.

Kerux: (Knocks) ו Very Honored Hierophant (Hierophantia), the Temple is properly guarded.

Hiero: ¶ Let us Adore the Lord of the Universe and Nature!

All rise and face East.

Hiero: Holy art Thou, Lord of the Universe whom naught but Silence can express. Thou who art in all things and whom is all things. Thee we adore and Thee we invoke.

Holy art Thou who hast created the Firmament. Holy art Thou who hast shown forth the Throne of Thy Glory. Holy art Thou whose Countenance moved upon the Waters at the Beginning. Holy art Thou who hast the Earth as Thy footstool.

All perform Adoration to the Lord of the Universe.

All: Holy art Thou, Lord of the Universe! (Salute)
Holy art Thou, Whom Nature hath not formed! (Salute)
Holy art Thou, the Vast and the Mighty One! (Salute)
Lord of the Light and of the Darkness! (Sign of Silence)

All remain standing, facing East.

Hiero: Hierophant (Hierophantia) takes up the Pentacle and traces the Banishing Pentagrams within a circle in the East.

Hierophant (Hierophantia) Salutes the East, then moves sunwise to the South.

All face South.

Hierophant (Hierophantia) faces South and traces with the Pentacle the Banishing Pentagrams in a circle in the South.

Hierophant (Hierophantia) Salutes the South, then moves sunwise to the West.

All face West.

Hierophant (Hierophantia) faces West and traces with the Pentacle the Banishing Pentagrams in a circle in the West.

Hierophant (Hierophantia) Salutes the West, then moves sunwise to the North.

All face North.

Hierophant (Hierophantia) faces North and traces with the Pentacle the Banishing Pentagrams in a circle in the North.

Hierophant (Hierophantia) Salutes the North, then moves sunwise to the East.

All face East.

Hierophant (Hierophantia) raises Pentacle on high.

Hiero: And the Elohim said, "Let us make Adam in our Image, after Our likeness and let him have dominion over the cattle and over all the earth, and over every creeping thing that creepeth over the Earth. Let him have dominion over the Fowl of the Air. Let him have dominion over the Fish of the Sea. Let us make Adam in our Image, after Our likeness, and let them have Dominion."

Hierophant (Hierophantia) makes a Cross with Pentacle, and then replaces Pentacle in the East.

In the Divine Name of **YHVH**, I declare that I have Closed this Temple.

Hiero: יהוה

Hege: יהוה

Hiereus: יהוה

Kerux: יהוה

All Members are now led out by the Kerux starting with the Portal (and above Members), followed by 4=7 Philosophi, then 3=8 Practici, then 2=9 Theorici, 1=10 Zelatores next, and finally 0=0 Neophytes.

Officers remain, and banish the Hall again before disrobing and leaving.

FINIS

ABOUT THE AUTHOR

Samuel Scarborough is a Senior Adept with the Ordo Stella Matutina, a modern Golden Dawn Order following the work of the original Stella Matutina. He has been interested in the occult and esoteric
for the last 30 years and a practitioner of the Golden Dawn tradition
and system for nearly as long. His interests include Alchemy (both
Practical and Spiritual), Tarot, Astrology, Geomancy, Qabalah, and
Ceremonial Magic. Historical research, particularly into the Golden
Dawn Tradition, coupled with his passion for Ritual and Ceremonial
work, have led him to study much of the original Golden Dawn and
Stella Matutina materials giving him a better understanding of the
Golden Dawn through his studies.

Over the years he has contributed to numerous esoteric and oc-
cult publications, including *The Alchemy Journal*, *The Journal of the
Western Mystery Tradition*, *Hermetic Virtues*, and *The Hermetic Tab-
let*. He has also contributed material to *Commentaries on the Golden
Dawn Flying Rolls*, *The Light Extended: A Journal of the Golden Dawn*,
and the *Philosopher's Stone: Spiritual Alchemy, Psychology, and Ritual
Magic* by Israel Regardie with additional material edited by Charles
"Chic" Cicero and Sandra Tabatha Cicero.

THE VIBRATION OF THE DIVINE NAME

by John Michael Greer

The sheer mass of instructional papers produced by the Hermetic Order of the Golden Dawn between its founding in 1888 and its fragmentation after 1900 is one of the great obstacles to the prospective student of magic. It is thus not surprising that for a century after that time, most of the inheritors of the Golden Dawn teachings focused on sorting out a manageable collection of practical techniques from the profusion of alternatives. As the twenty-first century approaches its third decade, though, a case can be made for plunging back into the profusion to salvage neglected technical methods of magic and put them back into common use.

This is what I have tried to do in this paper. The Golden Dawn papers include a powerful ritual of self-initiation that makes use of telesmatic images of the Divine Names attributed to the Sephiroth. Most of it appears in Books Five and Seven of Israel Regardie's collection *The Golden Dawn*, while a simplified version may be found in Regardie's early book *The Middle Pillar*. While individual Golden Dawn practitioners and temples may well have made use of the ritual of Vibration of the Divine Name, I know of no publicly available source that presents it as a coherent technique and explores its role in Golden Dawn magical training.

The Vibration of the Divine Name is a theurgic working—that is to say, it aims at attuning the microcosm of the practitioner with the powers of the macrocosm. It can be practiced alongside a course of temple initiation or on its own, as a method of self-initiation. It should be preceded by at least two years of daily practice with the Middle Pillar exercise. Given that preparation, however, I have found it to be a powerful and effective ingredient in the mage's toolkit.

The Sources

In *The Golden Dawn*, most of the ritual framework and some of the inner work for the Vibration of the Divine Name can be found on pages 619-620 of the seventh edition, under the heading "Example: The Vibration of Adonai ha-Aretz." More of the inner work appears on page 613, under the heading "The Vibratory Mode of Pronouncing the Divine Names," and still more on pages 435-437, in the Z-2 paper "The Symbolism of the Opening of the 0=0 Grade of Neophyte." The practice depends on a working knowledge of the art of constructing telesmatic figures, which is explained on pages 612 and 614-618. A simplified version of the whole technique can be found in Chapter Five of Israel Regardie's *The Middle Pillar*.

The Image

A telesmatic image corresponding to each Divine Name must be worked out and imagined in detail before the ritual itself can be practiced. The example given, Adonai ha-Aretz, is described in the original papers as follows:

> "ADNI makes the figure from head to waist; HARTZ from waist to feet. The whole name is related to Malkuth, matter, and Zelatorship.
>
> "Aleph—a winged, white, radiant crown.
>
> "Daleth—head and neck of woman, beautiful but firm, hair long, dark, and waving.
>
> "Nun—arms bare, strong, extended as a cross. In the right hand are ears of grain, and in the left a golden cup. Large dark spreading wings.
>
> "In addition a broad gold belt on which Adonai ha-Aretz is written in Theban or Hebrew characters.
>
> "The feet are shown in flesh color with golden sandals. Long yellow green drapery rayed with olive reaches to the feet. Beneath are black lurid clouds with

patches of colour. Around the figure are lightning flashes, red. The crown radiates white light. A sword is girt at the side of the figure."

The figure for Shaddai El Chai can be constructed easily enough on the same principles. It provides the image for Yesod, the etheric plane, and the Theoricus grade:

Shin—a crown of red gold shaped like flames.

Daleth—head and neck female, with long golden hair. Bare arms, beautiful and feminine, extended downward at an angle as though bestowing blessings.

Yod—a grass green robe covering small breasts and a maiden's slender body.

Aleph—wings outspread, luminous white in color.

Lamed—a slender belt of gold on which Shaddai El Chai is written in Hebrew or Theban characters. A sword is girt at the figure's left side.

Cheth—behind the figure a crescent moon the color of amber is rising in a clear sky.

Yod—delicate beautiful feet, bare, standing on green grass.

Telesmatic images for the other Divine Names from Hod to Tiphareth at least should be constructed by each student along the same lines given here, using the material from *The Golden Dawn* as a guide. Some degree of creative imagination will be necessary, but this is hardly a disadvantage. Since it works best to practice the ritual with one Divine Name exclusively until some degree of success is achieved, and then move onto the next, all the telesmatic images need not be created at once.

The Ritual

1. Stand facing East in the center of the ritual space, robed, and with the Lotus Wand if you wish. Begin by performing the complete Lesser Banishing Ritual of the Pentagram.

2. Go to the east. Make the signs of Isis, Apophis, and Osiris, speaking the letters L, V, X while making them. Extend your arms in the form of a cross and vibrate the Divine Name IAO. Then draw in the air before you, with the Lotus Wand or the first two fingers of your right hand, the symbol of the Rose Cross, exactly as you would in the Rose Cross Ritual (see Diagram 1).

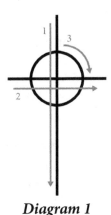

Diagram 1

3. Do this also in the South, West, and North, and then return to the center and face East.

4. Turn your attention to the Divine White Brilliance of the Kether center above the crown of your head. Contemplate that brilliance for a time, and recognize it as your link with the Infinite.

5. Draw in a deep and full breath, and as you do so, bring down a ray of the Divine White Brilliance into the Tiphareth center (in your heart or solar plexus, whichever you habitually use for Tiphareth in the Middle Pillar exercise). Imagine the light taking shape as the letters of the Divine Name you are about to vibrate. On the outbreath, vibrate the Name, either by speaking the Name itself or pronouncing its letters one at a time; these have different effects, which are best learned through experience. The vibration should be centered in

the heart and should be felt as radiating outward through the entire universe to its uttermost limits.

6. Repeat this as many times as there are letters in the Name, bringing down light from the Kether center on the inbreath, formulating the letters of the Name there, and vibrating the Name on the outbreath. This establishes the invoking whirl in the heart.

7. Now extend the arms to the sides in the form of a cross. Draw in another deep and full breath and imagine it charging the letters of the Name in the Tiphareth center. Then imagine the Name descending along the Middle Pillar from the Tiphareth center to the Yesod center at the genitals and then all the way down to the Malkuth center between the feet.

8. Pause, visualizing the Name in the Malkuth center. Then bring it rushing back up the Middle Pillar through the Yesod center to the Tiphareth center. Make the Sign of the Enterer, and vibrate the Name strongly, sending the Name and the breath in a single ray to the uttermost limits of the universe before you.

9. Make the Sign of Silence and remain still, contemplating the force you have invoked. When you feel a returning ray of energy from the uttermost East, visualize the Name taking shape in the air in front of you in the form of a cross of letters, with each letter drawn in brilliant white light. (See Diagram 2, which gives the example of the Name Shaddai El Chai.)

Diagram 2

10. Vibrate the Name again, and see the letters of the Name radiating white light throughout the universe, until all things dissolve into it. This establishes the expanding whirl in the aura.

11. Once all things have dissolved into white light, formulate the telesmatic image of the Name standing before you as clearly and precisely as you can, starting with the crown (which derives from the first letter of the Name) and proceeding from there. Once you have visualized the image clearly, imagine it expanding outward so that it becomes the universe, and you and all other created things are within it. See and feel yourself surrounded by its radiance. You may visualize this as white light, or as light of one of the four color scales attributed to the same Sephirah as the Divine Name; these also have different effects, which are best learned through experience.

12. Now draw in a breath, and with it bring the radiance of the Name in through your nostrils to your Tiphareth center. Still breathing in, send it from that center to your left side and down from there, down the outside of the left leg to the feet, and thence to the Malkuth center. Breathing out, bring it up the outside of the right leg and the right side, thence to the Tiphareth center, and thence out through the throat and nostrils into the universe. Do this four times in all, to the rhythm of the Fourfold Breath.

13. Recite a prayer to the divine manifestation expressed by the Name, giving thanks for the blessing and empowerment you have received.

14. Perform the complete Lesser Banishing Ritual of the Pentagram. This completes the ritual.

Commentary

The Vibration of the Divine Name is an effective method for attuning the Sphere of Sensation and the subtle bodies generally to the divine energies of each of the Spheres. It may be practiced daily for this purpose. In my experience the effects are strongest if the ordinary Middle Pillar exercise is also practiced daily, and some time elapses between these two workings—for example, doing the Middle Pillar exercise in the morning on rising and the Vibration of one of the Divine Names in the evening had excellent results.

In a working Golden Dawn temple working along traditional lines, this ritual would be well suited to the sub-grades of the Adeptus Minor grade. Thus initiates of the sub-grade of Zelator Adeptus Minor could be set the Vibration of Adonai ha-Aretz as part of the work of that sub-grade; when they advance to Theoricus Adeptus Minor, they would pass on to the Vibration of Shaddai El Chai, and so on through the sub-grades.

For solitary practitioners, as already mentioned, practice of the ritual of Vibration of the Divine Name should be taken up only after at least two years of daily practice of the Middle Pillar exercise, so that the necessary centers and channels in the subtle body will have been opened, strengthened, and purified adequately to make best use of the influx of divine energies. Regular practice of the Rose Cross ritual is also important as a preparation, since this strengthens the effect of the IAO formula in the ritual. Once these preparations have been made, however, this ritual may be used as part of a more extensive set of practices for self-initiation. For example, for one year, the practitioner might perform the Vibration of Adonai ha-Aretz daily, while performing once each week a full ceremonial working of the powers of Earth, in which the same Divine Name is invoked and the archangel, angel, ruler, elemental king, and elementals of Earth are called upon. The next year would go to Yesod and Air, and so on. Such a course of self-initiation is at least as effective as temple initiation.

This ritual also has a marked positive effect on the place where it is performed, and on the world generally. (This seems to be brought about partly by the use of the IAO formula in the opening, partly by the practice of sending the vibration from the heart out to the limits of the universe, and partly by the establishment of the expanding whirl in the aura.) When it has been practiced regularly, this can approximate to a minor exorcism—the divine presence invoked by the ritual appears to be capable of chasing off many types of noxious spirit and unwelcome energetic conditions. It may be possible to develop a formula of spiritual healing based on it, but I have not yet pursued that line of research.

References

Regardie, Israel, *The Golden Dawn*, ed. John Michael Greer (Woodbury, MN: Llewellyn, 2015).

-----, *The Middle Pillar* (St. Paul, MN: Llewellyn, 1970).

ABOUT THE AUTHOR

John Michael Greer began his occult studies in 1976 with a cheap paperback introduction to Golden Dawn magic, and began serious training a few years later with his first copy of Israel Regardie's *The Golden Dawn*.

Since then he has published more than 70 books on subjects ranging from ceremonial magic and nature spirituality to unexplained phenomena and the future of industrial society, with a dozen novels, half a dozen translations of magical texts, and the editing work on the seventh edition of Regardie's *The Golden Dawn* in there as well.

He served for 12 years as Grand Archdruid of the Ancient Order of Druids in America (AODA) and currently heads a hybrid Druid/Golden Dawn order, somewhat unimaginatively titled the Druidical Order of the Golden Dawn.

He lives in Rhode Island with his wife Sara.

ON THE LUNAR OCCULTATION OF VENUS

AND PLANETARY INTEGRATION THROUGH THE HERMETIC ARTS

by Jaime Paul Lamb

INTRODUCTION

The lunar occultation of Venus is an astronomical event during which the Moon conceals the planet Venus from our view. This phenomenon occurs with some regularity, due to the circuit of both celestial bodies being roughly on the same orbital plane, particularly at the Moon's nodal points when intersecting the ecliptic. What is especially thought-provoking, however, is that this macrocosmic, astronomical phenomenon is hermetically mirrored at various microcosmic scales: from the redox reaction of copper in a silver nitrate solution in chemistry to the star and crescent glyph in religious symbolism; and from the sequence and inherent motifs in Tarot symbolism to the arrangement of the *sephiroth* ("emanations") and their connecting paths on the qabalistic *Etz Chaim* ("Tree of Life"). Of the various microcosmic correspondences to the lunar occultation of Venus, the feminine reproductive system seems to be the most striking example of cosmic sympathy, in that an astronomical event is mirrored in a natural and recurring process in the human body.

Both literally and metaphorically, the lunar occultation of Venus is a ubiquitous schema encountered across several domains. The symbolic material constellated around this event, as well as its multidisciplinary scope, uniquely lends itself to investigation from the perspective of the Occult Sciences, such as those prescribed by the Hermetic Society of the Golden Dawn. In the following, we will first examine this phenomenon as it occurs in its domain-specific context; then we will assemble an interpretation of this mechanism vis-à-vis the accepted modalities of the Hermetic Arts (viz., Western Astrology, Qabalah, Tarot, alchemy and ceremonial magic), resulting in a synthesized theoretical perspective with further implications in the integration of archetypally feminine influences—those of the Moon and of Venus.

Obviously, one need not be a female in order to consider the influence of, say, the Moon and Venus in their astrological chart, or to experience a personal resonance with the feminine symbolism employed in the High Priestess or Empress Tarot cards—as these represent archetypal concepts occurring in the mind of both men and women. Much in the manner of Jung's contrasexual theory of the *anima* in men and *animus* in women, certain complimentary psychological qualities may be embodied by the opposite gender. That being said, the mysteries of the lunar occultation of Venus hold just as much integrative potential for men as for women.

IN ASTRONOMY

In astronomical vernacular, an occultation is an eclipse-like event occurring when a nearer celestial object completely blocks a further object from the perspective of an observer.[1] This phenomenon differs from an eclipse in that the latter is contingent upon one body casting its shadow upon another; whereas, during occultation, one body merely obscures another from view. Since the Moon is the closest celestial body to the Earth, and because its orbit is within 5° of the ecliptic, crossing it twice per month at its nodal points (*caput et cauda draconis*), it frequently occults other stellar and planetary objects from our observational vantage point.[2] During the lunar occultation of Venus, the Moon conceals, or veils the direct light of Venus.[3] This macrocosmic astronomical event is hermetically mirrored at various microcosmic scales—all of which may be seen to symbolize a certain dynamic between these archetypally feminine influences.

---

1 "An Eclipse by Any Other Name: Doing Science with Transits and Occultations," *NASA*, 2017, retrieved at: nasa.gov
2 Howell, "What is Occultation?", *Space*, 2016, retrieved at: space.com
3 Urrutia, "Disappearing Act: Venus Hides Behind the Moon Before Dawn on Thursday," *Space*, 2019, retrieved at: space.com

IN CHEMISTRY VIA MYTHOLOGY

The association of silver with the Moon is well-established in classical mythology (e.g., the "silver bow" of huntress and lunar goddess, Artemis; Hecate's association with silver and currency, etc.), medieval alchemical symbolism, and has even been reaffirmed by modern astronomy, as quantities of this precious metal have been discovered on Earth's lone natural satellite.[4] Known as *lunar caustic* by medieval alchemists, Silver nitrate was discovered by Albertus Magnus in the 13th century. This solution is *lunar* because of its association with the metal, silver, and was deemed *caustic* in that it can corrode organic tissue.[5] It is made by dissolving silver in nitric acid and is highly soluble in water.

Similarly, the English word *copper*, which comes from the Latin *cuprum*, also has an etymology with mythological implications. Cuprum was the Latin name of the Greek island Cyprus, a major cult center and birthplace of Aphrodite (Venus), the Cyprian.[6] The association of the planet Venus with the color green is reinforced in other domains, such as the oxidation of copper, a process during which a *verdigris*, or greenish patina, forms on the metal's surface and the color green in chlorophyll being associated with vegetal fertility. Interestingly, it has been found that women have approximately 20% more copper in their blood than men.[7] In Hermetic, Qabalistic and Alchemical philosophy, as well as in the Queen Scale of the Golden Dawn, the color green is associated with the planet Venus.

In a relatively dramatic example of a simple redox reaction, copper is introduced to an aqueous silver nitrate solution, causing fractal-like silver precipitates to form on the copper, thereby *concealing* it; the silver appears to *grow* on the copper in crystalized

---

4 Than, "Moon's Silver Hints at Lunar Water Origins," *National Geographic*, 2010, retrieved at: nationalgeographic.com
5 Szabadváry, *History of Analytical Chemistry*, Taylor & Francis, 1992, p. 17
6 Entry: "Copper", *Online Etymology Dictionary*, retrieved at: etymonline.com
7 Quinn, et. al., "Gender Effects on Plasma and Brain Copper," *International Journal of Alzheimer's Disease*, U.S. National Library of Medicine, 2011, retrieved at: ncbi.nlm.nih.gov

structures.[8] Metallic elements such as copper (Cu), like all metallic atoms, are insoluble in water; however, the silver ions in a lunar caustic, or silver nitrate ($AgNO_3$) solution, are water soluble. The copper atoms become ions and dissolve into the solution, causing it to turn bluish; the silver ions become atoms and fractally precipitate on the dissolving copper—*obscuring it*—while the nitrate ions are spectator ions and stay in solution.[9] The result of this single replacement reaction is the *occultation* of the copper (Venus) by the silver precipitates (the Moon), a striking example of this venereo-lunar dynamic in the realm of chemistry.

IN ISLAMIC SYMBOLISM

The star and crescent is commonly employed as a symbol of Islam and has been used in that context since at least the Ottoman Empire.[10] While the crescent is relatively easy to interpret as a lunar symbol, the five- or eight-pointed stars accompanying the crescent Moon require further elucidation. Venus' apparent path, from the perspective of the Earth, forms a five-petalled rosette against the firmament; this figure is completed over a period of 583.9211 days, which is referred to as Venus' synodic period. This formation was not lost on the astronomers of the ancient world, who long ago conflated the pentagram with the planet Venus. Periodically, an eight-pointed star is used in place of the five-pointed, *but the venerean symbolism is not lost*, as the eight-pointed star has long been associated with the goddess Inanna (Sumerian) and later by Ishtar (Akkadian),[11] both of whom were associated with the planet Venus and eventually subsumed by Aphrodite (Venus).

---

8 Bell-Young, *What Happens When You Put Copper Wire in Silver Nitrate?*, 2018, retrieved at: reagent.co.uk
9 "A Redox Reaction: Copper in Silver Nitrate Solution," *Honors Physical Science*, retrieved at: honorsph.startlogic.com
10 Glassé, *The New Encyclopedia of Islam*, Entry: "Moon", p. 314
11 Black & Green, *Gods, Demons and Symbols of Ancient Mesopotamia: An Illustrated Dictionary*, The British Museum Press, 1992, pp. 169-170

The Star and Crescent of Islam and the Ottoman Empire

Furthermore, in Islam, the *Jumu'ah* prayer (*Salaat-ul-Jumu'ah*, or "Friday Prayer") is performed at equinoctial noon (*Dhuhr*) every Friday.[12] Not only is Venus the planetary ruler of Friday but, according to Agrippa's table of planetary hours, equinoctial noon on a Friday is a solar hour, which may be interpreted to signify the highest "concentration" or "luminescence" of venerean influence. Green is considered the most revered color in Islam, due to its associations with Paradise, the turban and cloak of Muhammed, and al-Khidr, the "Green One."

Taken astronomically, the star and crescent of Islam depicts the lunar occultation of Venus—a phenomenon which is particularly striking during a waxing or waning crescent Moon, as it appears in its Islamic context. During this event, Venus seems to disappear as it is occulted by the shadowed portion of the Moon. In Islamic symbolism, the waning crescent is generally depicted and, in the shadowed area finishing the sphere implied by the crescent, the five- or eight-pointed star is visible.

---

12 "Hashemi, Kamran," *Religious Legal Traditions, International Human Rights Law and Muslim States*, vol. 7, Brill, 2008

IN THE REPRODUCTIVE SYSTEM

The average length of a complete menstrual cycle is 28 days,[13] which is just under the length of a lunar month (29.53059 days)— although, a 29-day cycle is more common in women under the age of 25. Generally, women are most fertile a three to five days before, during, and one to two days after ovulation—this five to eight day period is known as the *fertility window*. It is worth noting that, not only are five and eight members of the Fibonacci sequence—which was discerned by Leonardo of Pisa during a study on rabbit fertility —but they are also represented as the pentagram of Venus and the octagram of Inanna, both fertility deities.

The pentagrammic rosette created by Venus' synodic orbit

Ovulation, from the Latin *ovulum*, meaning "little egg,"[14] occurs when a mature ovum, or "egg," is discharged from the ovary, within which it was generated. Eggs are, of course, associated with Easter, a celebration of the vernal equinox—the onset of spring and fertility. Etymologically, the word *Easter* is related to the Northumbrian *Eostre* (or *Ostara*), the goddess of spring and fertility, and an Anglian syncretism of Inanna, Ishtar, Aphrodite and Venus.

---

13 Chiazze, Macisco, Parker & Duffy, "The Length and Variability of the Human Menstrual Cycle," *JAMA*, 203 (6), 1968, pp. 377-380
14 Entry: "Ovulation", *Online Etymological Dictionary*, retrieved at: etymonline. com

Other cognates of the word *Easter* are *Eos* (goddess of the "rosy-fingered dawn") and the Proto-Indo-European root *aus*, meaning "to shine," especially of the dawn.[15] Estrus, which is defined as "a regularly recurrent state of sexual receptivity during which the female of most mammals will accept the male and is capable of conceiving,"[16] comes to us from the Latin *oestrus*, meaning "frenzy, gadfly" and alludes to one being bothered by stinging sexual impulses. The menstrual cycle is metered by the ebb and flow of estrogen,[17] which is so named because of the hormone's ability to inspire the state of estrus.[18]

With this in mind, we see that the menstrual cycle's cyclical operation may be seen as a sort of clock regulating the duration during which the door (Hebrew: *daleth*) of fertility shall remain accessible —the temporal element of the menstrual cycle being decidedly lunar, while the spatial element, being materially represented by fertilization and procreation, satisfies the venerean influence. Together, the lunar and venerean components of the female reproductive system culminate in a representation of time and space in the act of creation. In summary, the lunar component (menstruation) veils and regulates the venerean component (fertilization/conception); therefore, the female reproductive system may be seen as yet another microcosmic scale of the lunar occultation of Venus.

METHODS OF INTEGRATION

As we have illustrated, the redox reaction in chemistry, the star and crescent of Islam and ancient Mesopotamia, and the female reproductive system may be interpreted as various microcosmic scales of the macrocosmic astronomical event known as the lunar occultation of Venus. In the following, we will outline how this dynamic is manifested in various sub-systems of the Hermetic Arts—particularly Western Astrology, Qabalah, Tarot and cer-

---

15 Entry: "Easter," *Online Etymological Dictionary*, retrieved at: etymonline.com

16 Entry: "Estrus," *Merriam-Webster Collegiate Dictionary*, retrieved at: merrian-webster.com

17 "Menstruation and the Menstrual Cycle Fact Sheet", *Office of Women's Health*, USA. 23 December 2014

18 Entry: "Estrogen," *Online Etymological Dictionary*, retrieved at: etymonline. com

emonial magic—and how these occult modalities may facilitate the identification and integration of lunar and venerean influences. Again, the concepts and images we have been discussing, while being archetypally feminine, are no more confined to the experience of women than martial or jovial influences are to the experience of men—each sex having its contrasexual compliment in the psyche.

ASTROLOGY

It should first be mentioned that the sciences of astronomy and astrology are essentially the same, in that they both study the movements and relative positions of celestial objects; what separates astrology, however, is the accompanying Hermetic belief that these astronomical events exert an influence on the Earth and mankind. Venerean influences become veiled or otherwise mediated by the saline and aquatic lunar forces, *just as fertility is governed by the menstrual cycle*. This, again, is representative of the lunar occultation of Venus. Astrologically, certain qualities are assigned to the Moon and Venus which, when considered, point to a particular path toward their reconciliation. The planet Venus rules both Taurus and Libra in the classic attributes of Western Astrology. Her "night house" is Taurus and her "day house" is in Libra, the autumnal equinox and time of harvest. The Moon rules Cancer and is exalted in Taurus. Thus we find that the zodiacal sign of Taurus hosts both Venus, its ruler, and the Moon, which it exalts. Ergo, we may deduce that the zodiacal sign of Taurus (home of the Pleiades) holds for us a key to the integration of these two archetypally feminine influences. We will return to this key shortly.

QABALAH

According to the generally accepted body of Hermetic and qa-balistic correspondences,[19] the Moon is attributed to the Hebrew letter *gimel* (meaning "camel") and Venus is attributed to the

---

19 Küntz (ed. & trans.), *The Complete Golden Dawn Cipher Manuscript*, Holmes Publishing Group, 1996

letter *daleth* (meaning "door"). These letters inhabit the 13th and 14th paths, respectively, on the *Etz Chaim*. These intersecting paths correspond to the Moon and Venus. The lunar 13th path spans from the *sephiroth Kether* to *Tiphareth* (the Sun), down the middle pillar, which also includes the *sephirah Yesod* (the Moon). The middle pillar may be seen as the temporal axis of the Tree, since it contains both the Sun and the Moon, which regulate our diurnal/nocturnal cycles or circadian rhythm, making them the most conspicuous temporal indicators from the perspective of the Earth. Conversely, the 14th path, which is vertical and intersects the 13th path, may be seen as being spatial in nature, since it represents the yonic "door" through which the light of *Chokmah* is projected into *Binah* and brought forth into creation. This is akin the soul's entry into the gate of Capricorn, which is ruled by Saturn and representative of its sphere, in the Neoplatonic cosmological model.

Unlike the relationship between the Saturnal *Binah* and the telluric *Malkuth*, which share more of a Hermetic, micro/macro dynamic[20] wherein *Binah* is considered the Superior Mother and *Malkuth* is the Inferior Mother (akin to the positive and negative mother in Jungian psychoanalysis), there is a certain dissonance between the venerean and lunar expressions of femininity—Venus representing space and the concrete; the Moon representing time and the abstract. There is, however, an Aquarian path toward the reconciliation of these archetypes.

Qabalistically, the *sephirah* of *Yesod* (the Moon) and that of *Netzach* (Venus) are connected by the 28th path on the *Etz Chaim*. Fittingly, the color attributed to the venerean *sephirah*, *Netzach*, is green, which is the color of the *verdigris*, or patina, of oxidized copper. The mean between a lunar orbit (27.3) and a complete lunar phase (29.5) is 28.4,[21] which rounds to 28, the number of the path connecting the two *sephiroth*. This path is attributed to the Hebrew letter *tzaddi* and, thereby, to the Tarot card The Star XVII—and it is through this Aquarian key, in addition to its Taurian symbolic allusions, that we will develop our synthesis between the thesis of the Moon and the antithesis of Venus.

The 28th path, and the *sephiroth* it conjoins, may be travelled in a

---

20 Fortune, *The Mystical Qabalah*, Williams and Norgate, 1935, p. 162
21 "Moon Phase Calculator", *Star Date*, retrieved at: stardate.org

focused meditative, or astral process known as *pathworking*. Having its origins in the portal system of the Hermetic Order of the Golden Dawn, this process is akin to C.G. Jung's "active imagination," or what has more recently been referred to as "creative visualization." One somewhat simplified way in which this may be performed is by, first, sitting comfortably with both feet on the ground and hands palms down on the lap; practicing a simple breathing exercise such as the four-fold breath until relaxed but centered; imagining oneself standing in the purple light of *Yesod*, for example, or upon the surface of the Moon; peering through space in the direction of *Netzach/Venus*, notice a gate marked by the Hebrew letter *tzaddi*; while traversing the path leading through the gate, notice the Pleiades star cluster, Sirius and the constellation Taurus overhead, raining their transformational astral rays—*as if from pitchers of water*—down upon oneself; passing through the gate, continue into the sphere of green, venerean light, or imagine oneself being immersed in a field of tall, green grains; the pathworker should take as long as they like in this process and note any thoughts, entities, objects or other visions that arise.

TAROT

Tarotically, the High Priestess II and the Empress III represent the lunar and venerean feminine archetypes, respectively. The Priestess, with the crescent Moon at her feet, sits before the veil of fertility, which is emblazoned with pomegranates—a symbol of fecundity. She guards the door (*daleth*) to the *sanctum sanctorum* of procreation by imposing a system of temporal regulation, i.e., the menstrual cycle. The word *menstrual* is cognate with the words *month* and *Moon*,[22] thereby reinforcing its temporal and lunar cyclical natures. The Empress card, which is next in the sequence of the Major Arcana, is depicted seated on a couch in a field of grain with the planetary glyph for Venus on a heraldic crest by her side, encompassing a wealth of symbolism related to fertility—but access to this venerean space is limited by the Priestess.

---

22 Entry: "Menstrual", *Online Etymological Dictionary*, retrieved at: etymonline. com

The Star XVII Tarot is assigned to the 28th path on the *Etz Chaim*. The card depicts an Aquarian woman pouring out two pitchers of water—one onto the earth, as if as a libation to the fertile mother, the other back into the body of water from whence it came, as a tribute to the cosmic mother who reflects our memory and, as the *anima*, guards the portal to the unconscious. The eight-pointed star—symbolic of Inanna, the Venus of the Sumerians—hangs in the firmament among the "seven sisters" comprising the Pleiades. The Pleiades are a particularly important piece of this astrological symbol set in that the seven sisters' home is in the constellation of Taurus—*which is ruled by Venus and the sign within which the Moon is exalted.* Thus, the venerean star and the lunar crescent are synthesized by the 28th path of the *Etz Chaim*, and the Aquarian integration of the spatial (the fertile Venus) and the temporal (the cyclic Moon) is achieved.

Le Toille XVII ("The Star"), Tarot de Marseilles

PRACTICA UTILIZING THE HERMETIC ARTS

From the perspective of the Hermetic Arts, these lunar and venerean influences may be brought into equilibrium and integrated by the performance of adjacent practices such as astrological contemplation, qabalistic pathworking and Tarot meditation, as discussed above. Other methods are: the performance of simple alchemical operations, talisman and sigil construction, and ritualized invocations. We will presently address the latter three occult modalities, beginning with alchemy.

Alchemy, and her daughter chemistry, are both concerned with the interaction, combination and transformation of substances. Alchemy, however, differs from chemistry in that the alchemist believes that the processes and operations performed in the crucible or retort are simultaneously taking place within the alchemist. Like all Hermetic Arts, there is an emphasis on the sympathetic relationship between the microcosm and the macrocosm. Spagyric alchemy, with which we will concern ourselves for our example, is that which is performed in the vegetable kingdom, as opposed to metallurgic alchemy, which is confined to the mineral kingdom. It usually involves the separation (*solve*), purification and recombination (*coagula*) of a plant's basic salts and/or alkaloids (salt), essential oils (sulfur) and fermented alcohol content (mercury).

Using the simple method of this process for venereo-lunar integration, we will first select a plant, herb, root, seed or resin associated with the Moon and with Venus. For the Moon, we will use anise and, for Venus, we will use red rose petals, both of which reflect their planetary rulers. First, grind an equal amount (approximately 2 tbsp each) of the anise and dried rose petals to a powder in a mortar and pestle; transfer the powder to a small glass jar; slowly pour in grain alcohol (a universal vegetable mercury, identical to what would be produced by the fermentation of the anise and rose petals) until the ground material is covered by about one inch; cover the jar with plastic wrap, then the lid, and set aside in a cool, dark place for 40 days (an alchemical month); during this time, the essential oils (sulfur) will have leached out into the alcohol (mercury); pour the oils and alcohol through a muslin cloth into another small glass jar and set aside; put the alcohol-soaked powder into a baking dish and set alight; this should burn down to white ash; at this point, either add the white ash directly to the oil and alcohol tincture or further reduce it through evaporation with distilled water, then add to the tincture. At the end of this process, one will have performed a simple operation of spagyric alchemy in the vegetable kingdom. This particular operation—in which the salt, sulfur and mercury of plants ruled by the Moon and Venus have been separated, purified and reunited—is meant to have an effect on the alchemist, via the above-mentioned Hermetic, microcosm/macrocosm dynamic; as the three philosophical principles of the anise and rose petals are combined in one spagyric tincture, the lunar and venerean influences ruling these plants is also integrated within the body (salt), mind (sulfur) and spirit (mercury) of the alchemist.

Commonly employed in various magical traditions, sigil com-position and meditation is another method by which venereo-lunar integration may be achieved. In the practice of sigil magic, a glyph is composed which encompasses symbolic elements associated with the willed outcome. For our example, a glyph (see illustration below) representing a composite of the astrological symbols for the Moon, Venus, Aquarius and Taurus has been composed in an effort to synthesize the venereo-lunar influences via symbolism associated with the 28th path and the Star XVII Tarot card. A sigil meditation may be performed by, first, sitting comfortably with both feet on the ground, hands palms down on the lap and the sigil on a table, a music stand or taped to the wall in front of you; practicing a simple breathing exercise such as the four-fold breath until relaxed but centered; concentrate on the sigil, but not on its theoretical meaning; *meet the sigil on its terms*—this process is less about the meaning you want to actively project onto the sigil than it is about passively letting the sigil communicate with your unconscious mind; let the sigil project its meaning *into* you. Do this for as long as you feel you are still *downloading* information from the sigil. Theoretically, this process will aid in influencing the products of one's imagination, which emanate from the personal and collective unconscious and are then projected outwardly by the current of one's will, thereby creating a feedback loop affecting and integrating one's inner (microcosmic) and outer (macrocosmic) worlds.

Venereo-lunar sigil with integrative 28th path symbolism

Ritualized invocation offers another method of integration of the lunar and venerean influences. Invocation is defined as "the act or process of petitioning for help or support [...] a prayer of entreaty (as at the beginning of a service of worship) [...] a calling upon for authority or justification [...] a formula for conjuring".[23] In the magical sense, the practice of invocation has been used for millennia in efforts to obtain the intercession of divine, angelic, zodiacal, decanic, planetary and elemental entities or forces. When this practice is used in conjunction with other hermetically corresponding elements, it is said to be *ritualized*. For our venereo-lunar example, one might begin by clearing a space to perform the ritual; set the ritual area with the colors green (for Venus/*Netzach*) and purple (for the Moon/*Yesod*), including candles of those colors; burn a lunar incense, such as myrrh resin; anoint oneself with the aforementioned venereo-lunar tincture; perform the invoking form of the Lesser Pentagram Ritual (or some similar preparatory ritual); facing West, trace an enneagram in the air with a dagger or fingers and recite the following hymn, loudly and clearly:

23   Entry: "Invocation", *Merriam-Webster Collegiate Dictionary*, retrieved at: merriam-webster.com

HEAR, Goddess queen, diffusing silver light, Bull-horn'd and wand'ring thro' the gloom of Night. With stars surrounded, and with circuit wide Night's torch extending, thro' the heav'ns you ride: Female and Male with borrow'd rays you shine, And now full-orb'd, now tending to decline. Mother of ages, fruit-producing Moon, Whose amber orb makes Night's reflected noon: Lover of horses, splendid, queen of Night, All-seeing pow'r bedeck'd with starry light. Lover of vigilance, the foe of strife, In peace rejoicing, and a prudent life: Fair lamp of Night, its ornament and friend, Who giv'st to Nature's works their destin'd end. Queen of the stars, all-wife Diana hail! Deck'd with a graceful robe and shining veil; Come, blessed Goddess, prudent, starry, bright, Come moony-lamp with chaste and splendid light, Shine on these sacred rites with prosp'rous rays, And pleas'd accept thy suppliant's mystic praise.[24]

Then, turning to the South, trace a heptagram in the air with a dagger or fingers and recite the following hymn, loudly and clearly:

HEAV'NLY, illustrious, laughter-loving queen, Sea-born, night-loving, of an awful mien; Crafty, from whom necessity first came, Producing, nightly, all-connecting dame: 'Tis thine the world with harmony to join, For all things spring from thee, O pow'r divine. The triple Fates are rul'd by thy decree, And all productions yield alike to thee: Whate'er the heav'ns, encircling all contain, Earth fruit-producing, and the stormy main, Thy sway confesses, and obeys thy nod, Awful attendant of the brumal God: Goddess of marriage, charming to the sight, Mother of Loves, whom banquetings delight; Source of persuasion, secret, fav'ring queen, Illustrious born, apparent and unseen: Spousal, lupercal, and to men inclin'd, Prolific, most-desir'd, life-giving, kind: Great sceptre-bearer of

---

24 Taylor (trans.), *The Hymns of Orpheus*, London: White & Son, 1792, pp. 124-126

*the Gods, 'tis thine, Mortals in necessary bands to join;
And ev'ry tribe of savage monsters dire In magic chains
to bind, thro' mad desire. Come, Cyprus-born, and to
my pray'r incline, Whether exalted in the heav'ns you
shine, Or pleas'd in Syria's temple to preside, Or o'er th'
Egyptian plains thy car to guide, Fashion'd of gold; and
near its sacred flood, Fertile and fam'd to fix thy blest
abode; Or if rejoicing in the azure shores, Near where
the sea with foaming billows roars, The circling choirs
of mortals, thy delight, Or beauteous nymphs, with eyes
cerulean bright, Pleas'd by the dusty banks renown'd of
old, To drive thy rapid, two-yok'd car of gold; Or if in
Cyprus with thy mother fair, Where married females
praise thee ev'ry year, And beauteous virgins in the
chorus join, Adonis pure to sing and thee divine; Come,
all-attractive to my pray'r inclin'd, For thee, I call, with
holy, reverent mind.*[25]

After reciting the hymns, one might perform the banishing form
of the Lesser Ritual of the Pentagram and close in their preferred
fashion. The regalia and paraphernalia involved in such ritualism
may be as simple or as elaborate as the operator chooses, so long
as Hermetic correspondences are taken into account. It is also
important to utilize magically efficacious times for rituals of this
sort, such as on a Monday during an hour ruled by Venus; a Friday
during an hour ruled by the Moon; any Friday during the zodiacal
sign of Cancer (which is ruled by the Moon), etc.; these temporal
considerations due much to strengthen the subtle cosmic sympathies
integral to Hermetic operations of this sort.

CONCLUSION

It has been the purpose of the present work to show that the lunar
occultation of Venus is a motif that may be identified across many
domains—such as astronomy, chemistry, religious symbolism and
the human reproductive system. We have also illustrated how the

---

25 Ibid., pp. 185-187

application of the practices associated with the Hermetic Arts—such as astrological contemplation, qabalistic pathworking, Tarot meditation, alchemical operations, sigil meditation and ritualized invocation—may help to facilitate the integration of these feminine archetypal influences in women as well as men.

ABOUT THE AUTHOR

Jaime Paul Lamb is the author of *MYTH, MAGICK & MASONRY: Occult Perspectives in Freemasonry* (The Laudable Pursuit, August, 2018) and *APPROACHING THE MIDDLE CHAMBER: The Seven Liberal Arts in Freemasonry and the Western Esoteric Tradition* (The Laudable Pursuit, 2020).

He is a member of Old Well-Saint John's Lodge no. 6, F.&A.M., Norwalk, CT, USA; a charter member of Ascension Lodge no. 89, F.&A.M., Phoenix, AZ, USA; a Frater of both the Arizona College of the Societas Rosicruciana in Civitatibus Foederatis and the Hermetic Society of the G ∴ D ∴, and is a Past Master of Arizona Research Lodge no. 1.

GREEK GODS IN THE GOLDEN DAWN

by Soror DPF

When people hear the name Order of the Golden Dawn they immediately think secret society involving the occult, whereby it can more accurately fall under the *syncretic* label, as it tends to blend Jewish Mysticism with Christian Mysticism, and ceremonially, ancient Egyptian Mysteries—this later becoming termed *Western Mystery Tradition*.

Where, then, does that leave the Greek influence, the Greek pantheon, or Hellenic mysteries?

As a Hermetic Order, we can see reference to the God *Hermes* —the Greek counterpart to the Egyptian God Thoth, as the Golden Dawn teachings include the magic of *Hermes* through the writings of *Hermes Trismegistus*, found in *The Emerald Tablet* [Tabula Smaragdina].

Hermes Trismegistus is considered the personification of the Greek God *Hermes* and the Egyptian God Thoth, enabling communication and wisdom to merge and therefore teach. (Although, Trismegistus is thought not to be any one person.)

Hermes, an ancient Greek (Ionian-Attic) name, stems from the word Herma, [Herm in English] which began as a monumental pile of stones, later descriptive male sculptures, and Phallic stones. In modern times, the word is used as slang (as a shortened version of Hermaphrodite, which is the amalgam of Hermes and Aphrodite) to represent a person with both Male and Female body parts. This points to his duel nature (balanced forces) and of his transgressions regarding boundaries; *Hermes* can even traverse the boundaries of the living and the dead, accurately termed Psychopomp [psycho-pompos], as recorded in the *Hymn to Demeter*,[1] and is notedly the 'Messenger of the Gods' carrying the Herald's Staff [Kerykeion] according to the Greeks.

---

1 Homer, *Homeric Hymn to Demeter.*

He is represented in the Golden Dawn's *'Lamen of the Kerux'*, as explained in the *Grade of Theoricus*:

> *"The Tree of Life and the Three Mother Letters are the Keys wherewith to unlock the Caduceus of Hermes."*[2]

Again, he is mentioned in the work entitled *The Golden Dawn Journal - Book 3: The Art of Hermes.*[3]

An account of *Hermes* can be read in the book *Greek Religion* by *Walter Burkert.*[4]

Hermes is considered the Greek counterpart to the Roman God Mercury, who we find mentioned in the *ThAM Heptagram Ritual*[5]

As Mercury, we can also find him paired with Vesta, the Roman counterpart of the Greek Goddess *Hestia,* in another side lecture (which we will come to later).

In 1888, the Temple named *Isis-Urania* was founded in London, a Graeco-Egyptian title, incorporating both Greek and Egyptian Deity.

Urania [Ourania] is one of the nine *Mousai* [Muses]. She was the Greek Goddess of Astronomy and Astronomical writings. She was also a daughter of the great God Zeus by Mnemosyne.[6]

In the *'Homerica'* it is written:

> *"Ourania (Urania) bare Linos, a very lovely son: and him all men who are singers and harpers do bewail at feasts and dances, and as they begin and as they end they call on Linos (Linus)."*[7]

---

2 Ritual of the 2=9: Grade of Theoricus, Private Collection.
3 Chic Cicero, Sandra Tabatha Cicero, *The Golden Dawn Journal - Book 3: The Art of Hermes.*
4 Walter Burkert, Greek Religion: pg. 156: 2.8; A German scholar of Greek mythology and cult; Professor of Classics at the University of Zurich, Switzerland.
5 Theoricus Adeptus Minor - The Order of the Ritual of the Heptagram Ritual, Part I, Private Collection.
6 Hesiod: Theogony. 78; Ovid. Fasti. v.55.
7 Homerica, Fragments of Unknown Position 1 (from Diogenes Laertius 8. 1. 26) - source: Theoi.com.

It is no surprise then to learn that W. Wynn Westcott of the Golden Dawn released his own edited version entitled '*Collectanea Hermetica.*'

From *Urania* we are led to her Father, *Zeus,* who appears in the 3=8 Ceremony.[8]

Zeus was the youngest child of the Titans Kronos and Rheia.[9]

Zeus was considered the Greek 'King of the Gods' and the God of the Sky, Weather, Law and Order. His attributes are far too many to mention in this article, yet include the *Lightning Bolt, Eagle* and *Bull:* of which, all three can be symbolically depicted within the papers and work of the Golden Dawn. *Zeus* married his sister, the Greek Goddess Hera—we will discuss both more fully further down.

Now, let us understand that the Greek divine names are frequently used as archetypes within the Order, the notion that Gods in the Golden Dawn do not exist as Gods themselves, but rather *Godforms,* as a representation of certain forces, powers, and potencies.

However, as seen in certain lectures, papers, and rituals, the names of myriad Gods, including the Greek Gods, do appear, even if as Spirit Personifications, or *Daemones,* of the human condition. The Greek Goddess *Sophia,* for instance, personifies *Wisdom.*

THE ELEUSINIAN MYSTERIES - (Hellenic Greater and Lesser Mysteries, reconstructed even today - in the procession from Athens to Eleusis each year), would appear to have been highly inspirational to the Initiatory processes of the Golden Dawn, being that the Eleusinian Mysteries were a tradition of Initiatory Rites, and that the Order continues the same formation and titles of their Officers, the Hierophant or Chief Officer, The Keryx [Hierocceryx], Dadouchos, being the most prominent examples.

The Mysteries in Eleusis were Initiations traversed through the Underworld, guided by Chthonic Deity (Gods of the Underworld) and themes, much like the Golden Dawn's use of the Egyptian pantheon and their Chthonic Deity, in their Initiation Rites; though

8 Ritual of the 3=8: Grade of Practicus, Private Collection.
9 The Titans were the Hellenic Deities that preceded the Olympians whom *Zeus* led.

as we are highlighting, the Eleusinian Mysteries too are as relevant to these ceremonies, therefore the tradition continues.

They were even discussed in a paper written by W. Wynn Westcott:

> "...the classic writings contain but faint glimpses of even the Eleusinian Mysteries, and these disclose the fact that the pupils were partly ignorant of the true mysteries, a notable example of which is seen in the use of the words Konx Om Pax, of which they knew not the meaning, the words being the Greek imitation or translation of really ancient Egyptian words, whose meanings has been kept secret for centuries."[10]

Manly P. Hall writes:

> "The secret exercises for spiritual unfoldment given to disciples of the higher degrees are unknown, but there is every reason to believe that they were similar to the Brahmanic Mysteries, since it is known that the Eleusinian ceremonies were closed with the Sanskrit words 'Konx Om Pax'."

Manly continues:

> "The Greater Mysteries (into which the candidate was admitted only after he had successfully passed through the ordeals of the Lesser, and not always then) were sacred to Ceres, the Mother of Persephone, and represent her as wandering through the world in quest of her abducted Daughter."[11]

In the *22 Atus of Thoth*, within the Golden Dawn's side lectures, we find reference to Ceres. Further references can be found later in the article.

---

10 V.H. Frater Sapere Aude (Dr. W. Wynn Westcott), Historic Lecture - Golden Dawn. This connection is also referenced in the Ritual of the 0=0: Grade of Neophyte.

11 Manly P. Hall, The Secret Teachings of All Ages: pg. 12, (Pacific Publishing).

Ceres

As pantheons tend to adopt counterparts, and where traditions oft conflate their Deity, we will find crossovers; for instance, where a Roman Deity is named, the Greek equivalent is also prominent in its nature, attributes of the forces, powers or potencies called.

The Latin version of the word *Pax,* by all accounts, means Peace, and the Greek Goddess *Eirene* (another listed under the names of *Daemones*) is the Greek Goddess of Peace, therefore, by using etymology the Golden Dawn essentially calls on this Deity—although this can read as pure conjecture. Westcott did allude to the meaning of the word *Pax* in Greek vs. Egyptian, Sanskrit or Latin in this case, to be separate, which is plausible, especially when we translate Konx Om Pax to the Golden Dawn use of the term, '*Light in Extension.*'

We can apply the same principle to the Greek God Adonis, whose name derives from the Phoenician word 'Adon', meaning 'Lord'. Adon is also at the root of the Hebrew word *Adonai,* which is invoked in the LRP before each Golden Dawn ceremony.[12]

In *The Tarot Trumps* [the 22 Atus of Thoth],[13] there are many Deities named, including the Egyptian Mother Goddess Mut [Maut]. In the lecture it depicts Mut thus: "*The Mother Goddess of All Ex-*

12 Lesser Ritual of the Pentagram.
13 The Tarot Trumps, 3=8 side lecture.

tended through the Universe," who we could naturally attribute to the energies of the Greek Mother Goddess Gaia [Gaea].

In the table below, we will note the Greek equivalents within the astrological attribution of the planets bearing the names of Gods and Goddesses to the signs:

Minerva and Vulcun
Venus and Mars
Apollo and Diana
Mercury and Vesta
Jupiter and Juno
Ceres and Neptune

The above table lists the Roman names how they are paired within the side lecture. Below are the Greek equivalents:

ATHENA [Αθηνη, Athenaia, Athênê] - the Greek counterpart to Roman **Minerva**; and Egyptian Neith; most noted for her Aegis [a shield, though some sources state it to be a cape] made from the skin of the giant Pallas (hence the epithet Pallas Athena; Pallas from the word *Pallô* meaning 'to brandish a spear') bearing the head of the gorgon Medusa; and *Athena's* birth from the head of *Zeus*, fully formed.

Athena was the Olympian Goddess of wisdom, good counsel, war, the defence of towns, heroic endeavour, weaving, and pottery, to name a few. She was highly regarded and involved in a multitude of myths, including the War of the Giants, and the Trojan War. She is connected to *Hephaestus* through his attempted advances on the Goddess.

Athena can also be found referenced in the paper on the *Cherubic Squares*.

"[Neith] said by Plato in Timaeo [sic], to be the same as the Greek *Athena*.

Translation of the passage is: *"The principal City*

of this one is Sais, whence also came Amasis the King. There is in this town a Goddess that passes for Chief; she is called Egyptian Neith, and in Greek according to what the Egyptians report, Athena. Athena is said by Diodorus Siculus to be the ruler of Air, with the Egyptians."[14]

We also find *Athena* in the paper 'The Hermetic Cross and the Via Lactea' (which from this point forward will be written as the acronym 'The Hermetic Cross')

HEPHAESTUS [Ηφαιστος, Hêphaistos] - the Greek counterpart to Roman **Vulcun**; who attempted to violate the Goddess Athena, which, as a result, his seed was absorbed into the Earth giving birth to Erichthonius. *Hephaestus* was the Olympian God of fire, forge, stonemasonry and sculpture. In Greek myth he is the son of *Hera,* with no Father, yet, as Vulcun it is stated he was fathered by Jupiter [Zeus] and Juno. He was married to Aphrodite.

APHRODITE [Αφροδιτη, Aphroditê] - the Greek counterpart to Roman **Venus**; was the Olympian Goddess of love, procreation, beauty and pleasure.

She was the wife of Hêphaistos,[15] though had many lovers. She was notedly born out of the castrated genitals of the Primordial [protegenos] God of the sky, Ouranos [Uranus] through the seafoam.[16] She had an adulterous affair with the Greek God Ares, and fell irrevocably in love with the youth of beauty Adonis.

Aphrodite was recounted as having been wounded during the Trojan War trying to save Aeneas, her son. She is also referenced as a counterpart to Lucifer.[17]

---

14 The Book of the Concourse of the Forces, Cherubic Squares (ThAM), Private Collection..

15 Odyssey. viii. 270.

16 Hesiod, Theogony 188, Cicero De Natura Deorum 3.21, Apuleius 6.6, Nonnus Dionysiaca 1.86, et al.

17 Source: Unknown

ARES [Αρης, Arês] - the Greek counterpart to Roman **Mars**; a God of War, in all its barbaric context, having an antagonistic rivalry with Goddess Athena, and in the Iliad, Zeus according to Homer, blasted to *Ares*: "*You are the most hateful to me of all the gods who hold Olympus; forever strife is dear to you and wars and slaughter.*" He had an adulterous, deep love affair with Aphrodite.

APOLLO [Απολλων, Apollôn, Apollon] - Likely the only God to hold one name across both Greek and Roman pantheons (though in late antiquity, Roman poets referred to him as Phoebus), with Greek myth predating the Roman by more than 1,000 years. *Apollo* was one of the most revered of the Greek Gods, with a Temple in the Sanctuary at Delphi [Delphoi], (in which held a *Hestia* [hearth]). He was the God of prophecy, oracles, poetry and music, and known both for his healing and causation of plague and disease.

The twin brother of Artemis, he was known for the revenge killing of Cyclopes, who destroyed his son Asklepios [Asclepius]; the slaying of the serpent Python at Delphi; and his birth (*Apollo-Helios*) on the Island of Delos,[18] where Leto, after journeying far, arrived and petitioned the Island: "*Delos, if you would be willing to be the abode of my son Phoibos [Phoebus] Apollon and make him a rich temple.*"

An epithet most applied to him is Phoibos [Bright] and Hekatos [Far-Shooter].

Homer attributed the Homeric Hymn 3 to Pythian Apollo.[19]

Apollo appears in the Golden Dawn 3=8 ceremony, and in the ThAM Heptagram Ritual.

---

18 Ibid.
19 Homeric Hymns: trans. Evelyn-White - Greek epic C7th to 4th B.C.

Delos Lions, Temple of Apollo

ARTEMIS [Αρτεμις] - the Greek counterpart to Roman **Diana**.[20] She is Apollo's twin. On the Island of Delos, it was the earliest Temple, named the *Artemision*, constructed circa 700, that belonged to *Artemis (Artemis-Selene)*,[21] along with the Horn Altar. The most noted Sanctuary, however, was the Temple in honour of her twin brother Apollo, which was constructed far later.

An epithet of *Artemis* is *Potnia Theron* [Lady of the Beasts]. She is also known as a Goddess of childbirth, from the myth where she acted as midwife to her Mother Leto, during Apollon's birth.

Her distinctive attributes were the bow and arrows of the hunt. She drove a chariot drawn by deer. *Artemis* was a virgin Goddess.

The *Karyatides*, which translates as 'maidens of Karyaï', an ancient town of Peloponnese. Karyai had a temple dedicated to the goddess *Artemis*, where maidens honoured *Artemis* in their dancing rituals.

Artemis is referenced directly in *'The Hermetic Cross.'*, as are the *'The Nymphs of Artemis'*, *Celaenô*, *Eurybia* and *Phoebe*.

Artemis can also be considered the *'Amazon Goddess of Ephesus'*[22] as the Temple of *Artemis*, also called Artemesium, is the temple at Ephesus, which is now in western Turkey, and that once was one of

20 Diana, The Tarot Trumps, 3=8 Side Lecture; Ephesian Diana, The Hermetic Cross and the Via Lactea; as Triple Diana, The Hermetic Cross and the Via Lactea.
21 Strabo.
22 Ritual of the 12 Gates, The Hermetic Cross and the Via Lactea, as Diana.

the Seven Wonders of the World.

Zeus, Leto, Apollo, Artemis

HERMES [Ερμης, Hermês] (referenced here again due to the table of paired gods above) - the Greek counterpart to Roman **Mercury**; most recognised for bearing the Herald's Wand: [kerykeion] the *Caduceus*, his *Golden Sandals*, and the symbol *Herma* [Hermae]. The Sandals (Greek: Pedila, meaning Sole) were apparently winged; it is written in the Orphic Hymn 27: "*With winged feet, 'tis thine thro' air to course.*" As *Kasmilos* [Casmilos] *Hermes* is considered the *Fourth Kabir*.[23] We will explore the Kabiri further below.

HE'STIA [Εστια, Ionian. Histiê, Hestia] - the Greek counterpart to Roman **Vesta**; *Hestia* means Hearth or Fireside, therefore the Goddess governs over the hearth, home, family, domesticity and the state. She is another virgin Goddess, whereby both Apollon and

---

23 Mnaseas, Sources for the Study of Greek Religion, David G. Rice/John E. Stambough.

Poseidon sought her hand in marriage, refused and requested of Zeus to allow her to remain a virgin.

Due to the hearth, and its prominent daily use, the cooking of both familial, communal and sacrificial feasts were *Hestia's* domain, as she received a share of every sacrifice to the Gods, prepared in it.

Hestia was the first born of the Titans Kronos and Goddess Rheia; the former swallowed *Hestia* at birth, only to be forced later by Zeus to regurgitate her.

She is depicted most often as veiled.

ZEUS [Ζευς] - the Greek counterpart to Roman **Jupiter**, and Jove; King of the Gods, of the Olympians; Husband and Brother to Greek Goddess *Hera*.

Zeus is God of the sky, thunder, law and order, destiny and fate.

The Fates [Moirai, Moirae - Roman: *Parcae*] (*Daemones* personifying Destiny), were according to Hesiod the daughters of Zeus and Themis (though initially he wrote them to be fatherless and mothered by Nyx).[24]

Zeus was the youngest child of Titans Kronos and Rheia, the former, as we have learned, devouring his children at birth. However, *Zeus* escaped this fate when his Mother deceived Kronos by handing him a stone wrapped in swaddling. *Zeus* was then raised secretly in Crete [Krete] by Nymphs, and protected by the mighty *Kouretes*.[25]

Zeus is referenced multiple times in *'The Hermetic Cross.'*, including the following:

> *"It is a symbol of a whirling Force, of a revolving Flail, the Weapon of Zeus and Thor..."*

Additionally, *Labrandian Zeus* is mentioned in the *'Ritual of the 12 Gates.'*

---

24 Hesiod, Theogony.
25 The KOURETES DAKTYLOI (Curetes, Dactyls) were three, five, or nine rustic daimones (spirits) appointed by Rheia to guard the infant god Zeus in a cave on Mount Ida in Krete (Crete). Source: Theoi.com.

HERA [Hêra, Ἥρη, Hêrê] - the Greek counterpart to Roman **Juno**. More importantly, the Egyptian Mut [Maut] (whom, as we previously pointed to, in the Golden Dawn is considered a Mother Goddess) is Zeus' wife and sister.

Olympian Queen of the Gods, Goddess of marriage, women, the sky and stars of heaven. She can be depicted as being accompanied by a Lion. In the Golden Dawn the Lion represents the *Fire of Netzach*, the *blood of the lion*.[26] The lion is also mentioned in the Ritual of the 3=8.[27]

Hera is also heavily referenced in *'The Hermetic Cross.'*

Hera is Mother to Hephaistos [Hephaestus] whom she produced alone and cast him from heaven, for his disability. She assisted the Argonauts in their search for the Golden Fleece, and the Greeks in the Trojan War.

Hera Lions

DEMETER [Δημητηρ, Dêmêtêr, Damater,[28] Deo] - the Greek counterpart to Roman **Ceres**; was the Mother of Persephone [Kore] - Roman: Proserpine [Proserpina].

---

26 Israel Regardie, pg. 217, The Golden Dawn: A Complete Course in Practical Ceremonial Magic.

27 Ritual of the 3=8: Grade of Practicus, Private Collection.

28 In Dorian, and Aeolic dialects.

She is the Olympian Goddess of agriculture, grain, bread, the harvest, fertility and sacred law.

Attributes include the Cornucopia (Horn of Plenty), Sceptre, Sheaf of grain, and Torches [though the latter is predominantly an attribute of Hekate].

Described as 'Lady of the Fruits' by Nonnus, the Orphic Hymn to Ceres, and the Homeric Hymn to Demeter.

Demeter presided over the prominent ancient mystery cults of the Hellenic lands, and was a prime focus of the Eleusinian Mysteries.

Homer wrote: "*...when blonde Demeter separates fruit and chaff in the rushing of the winds.*"[29]

The myth that speaks the most of *Demeter* is the 'Abduction of Persephone by Hades'.

As Ceres, she appears in the 3=8.

As *Demeter,* she is referenced in the '*Ritual of the 12 Gates*' (AO) "*Callimachus in his Hymn to Demeter sings...*"

Again, she is mentioned in '*The Hermetic Cross.*'

Axieros is identified as *Demeter*, in '*Sources for the Study of Greek Religion*'.

POSEIDON [Ποσειδων, Poseidôn] - the Greek counterpart to Roman **Neptune**; Olympian God of the sea, earthquakes, drought, floods and horses.

His most familiar attribute is the three-pronged *Trident*, crafted by Cyclopes [Kyklopes].

Another child devoured by his father Kronos, and with Zeus calling on the aid of the Goddess Metis [Mêtis], who fed Kronos a magical elixir, *Poseidon* and his siblings were disgorged.

Poseidon, during the War of the Gigantes, crushed Polybotes [Polybôtos] beneath the Island of Kos [Cos].

He was part of the contest with Athena for dominion over Athens, producing the very first horse as a gift.

One of his many conquests, was seducing the Gorgon Medusa [Medousa] (who was the only mortal of the Gorgones), where the mistake was made of doing so in Athena's Shrine, leaving Athena

29 Homer, *Iliad.*

raining down revenge on the once beautiful Medusa, causing her to turn Medusa's hair to snakes.

OTHER GREEK GODS APPEARING IN THE GOLDEN DAWN

SELENE [Σεληνη, SELE'NE, Selênê, Mene, Luna] - was the goddess of the Moon, or the Moon personified into a divine being.

She is called a daughter of Hyperion and Theia, and accordingly a sister of Helios and Eos.[30]

As the Titan Goddess of the Moon, she has close connections to Artemis, *(Artemis-Selene)* and Hekate *(Hekate-Selene)*.

Selene is found in *'The Hermetc Cross'* paper from ThAM.

HELIOS [Ηλιος, Hêlios, Helius, Êelios] - The Greek counterpart to the Roman Sol, and the Sun personified, and a brother of Selene and Eos.[31]

In the Homeric hymn to *Helios*, he is called a son of Hyperion and Euryphaëssa, and is the god who sees and hears everything, which we can see regards the myth of Persephone, where Demeter and Hekate ask his assistance.

Helios is mentioned in *'The Hermetc Cross'*.

PALLAS [Παλλας] - Titan God of battle and warcraft, who was slain by the Goddess Athena. "Pallas: A great virgin. It is an epithet of Athena; from brandishing (pallein) the spear, or from having killed Pallas, one of the Gigantes (Giants)."[32]

We also find reference to Pallas in the paper on the *Cherubic Squares*.[33]

---

30 Hes. Theog. 371, &c.; Apollod. i. 2. § 2; Schol. ad Pind. Isthm. v. 1, ad Apollon. Rhod. iv. 55.

31 Hom. Od. xii. 176, 322, Hymn. in Min. 9, 13; Hes. Theog. 371, &c.

32 Suidas s.v. Pallas, trans. Suda On Line, (Byzantine Greek lexicon C10th A.D).

33 The Book of the Concourse of the Forces, Cherubic Squares, Private Collection.

PERSE'PHONE [Περσεφονη, Persephonê; Kore] - The Greek counterpart to Roman **Proserpine** [Proserpina].[34]

Daughter of Demeter, and Queen of the Underworld, ruling with her Husband the Chthonic [Khthonios] God Hades [Haides], who, according to Hesiod, abducted her.[35]

As Goddess of Spring growth, she was honoured alongside her Mother Demeter in the Eleusinian Mysteries; *Persephone* represented the cycles of life, death and rebirth, with her descent to and returning ascendence from the Underworld, whereby she will spend one third of each year in Hades, with her husband, and the remaining two thirds, with her Mother and the Gods above.

Persephone had her own mysteries which were celebrated in Athens in the month of Anthesterion (modern day February/March).

Her Father was Zeus: *"He [Zeus] came to the bed of all-nourishing Demeter, and she bare white-armed Persephone whom Aidoneus [Haides] carried off from her mother; but wise Zeus gave her to him."*[36]

As *Axiokersa*, she is included in the Ritual of the 3=8,[37] representing the *Third Kabir*, though this title is shared, it would appear, with Anael, who is mentioned, as is *Proserpine* [Persephone] in the same ritual.

HADES [Ἀιδης Haides; Aidoneus; Ploútōn] - considered the Greek counterpart to Roman **Pluto**, (though 'Dis Pater' was more accurately the Roman equivalent, as the name Pluto [Ploútōn] was later adopted as the name of *Hades*, with the latter being termed the name of the Underworld itself).

Hades appears in the Ritual of the 3=8 in multiple instances, each bearing a differing title: the first as '*Hades*' himself, while elsewhere

34 Ritual of the 3=8: Grade of Practicus; The Hermetic Cross and the Via Lactea. Private Collection.
35 Ibid. Theog.
36 Ibid. 912 ff - trans. Evelyn-White.
37 3=8.

we are introduced to *Axiokersos*, the *Second Kabir*, who is depicted as both '*Hades*', and then Samael, where we also find Pluto referenced.

HEKATE [Εκατη, Ἑκατα, Hekatê] - whose origin is largely unknown, though scholars are forming a connection to Samothrace, with evidence of her Cult across Hellenic lands having been recorded, noting her Sanctuary in Athens, and the Temple at Lagina (modern day Turkey). Hekate was, however, adopted by the ancient Greeks, and often worshipped in the Sanctuaries of other Gods: Hesiod wrote, "*Hekate whom Zeus the son of Kronos (Cronus) honoured above all.*"[38]

We can find multiple references to *Hekate* in the Golden Dawn, most notably in the Ritual of the 3=8, where it is written: "*...because it filleth the life producing bosom of Hecate...*"[39]

She is further mentioned in the Ritual: "*...storm enrolled bosoms of the all-splendid strength of Hecate Father-Begotten.*"[40]

And further: "*... Strophalos of Hecate ...*"

She is also referenced as '*Triple Hecate*' in '*The Hermetic Cross*'.

Hekate in myth is noted as aiding Demeter in her search for her daughter Persephone, guiding Demeter by night with her twin flame torches, which gives *Hekate* the epithet *Dadoukhos* [Dadouchos]: A term which we recognise in the Golden Dawn as the "*Consecrator of the Temple, its members, and its candidates.*"[41]

Nonnus states[42] "*...that the Cabeirus Alcon brandished Hekatês Diasôdea purson, so that we may draw the conclusion, that the Samothracians and Lemnians worshipped a goddess akin to Hecate, Artemis, Bendis, or Persephone, who had some sexual connexion with Hermes, which revelation was made in the mysteries of Samothrace.*"[43]

---

38 Hesiod, Theogony 404 ff - trans. Evelyn-White.
39 3=8.
40 3=8.
41 Frater Yechidah, The Dadouchos: Mishkan ha-Echad - Golden Dawn Blog.
42 Dionys. xxx. 45.
43 Source: Theoi.com.

Lagina Hecate Temple

KRONOS [Κρονος, Cronus] - the Greek counterpart to Roman **Saturn** [Saturnus].[44]

King of the Titans, and God of time, *Kronos* was considered the same as Chronos [Khronos], the Primordial God of time, appearing in the Orphic Theogonies.

He ruled the cosmos after castrating his Father the God Uranus [Ouranos], deposing him, and from the blood arose the *Erinyes* [The Furies].

Kronos was considered a force to be reckoned with, as he had a destructive energy.

He is most noted as the Father who consumed his own children at birth.

During the war between the Olympians and the Titans, Zeus eventually sent *Kronos* into the pit of Tartarus.

Kronos' wife was the Goddess Rheia [Rhea].

Kronos is largely referenced in '*The Hermetic Cross*' paper.

Chronos, as time, is mentioned in the *Cherubic Squares*.[45]

RHEA [Ρεια Ρεα, Rheia, Ops, Opis] - was Titaness, Mother of the Gods, Goddess of female fertility, motherhood (*Meter Magale*) and

---

44 ThAM Heptagram Ritual - relating to the planet. Private Collection.
45 The Book of the Concourse of the Forces, Cherubic Squares. Private Collection.

generation. Married to the God Kronos, and Mother to Hestia, Demeter, Hera, Hades, Poseidon, and Zeus.

Some mythographers consider Rhea to be merely another form of 'era', the earth, while others connect it with 'rheô', *I flow*.[46]

This is also noted by G.H. Frater S.R.M.D. (MacGregor Mathers) in the *Cherubic Squares* paper.[47]

Rhea is referenced further in '*The Hermetic Cross*'.

OURANOS [Ουρανος, Uranus, Caelum] - was the primordial god (protogenos) of the sky. He had 12 sons, and 6 daughters with the Goddess Gaia, of the twelve sons, 5 rebelled and Kronos castrated *Ouranos* with an adamantine sickle.

Ouranos prophesied the fall of the Titanes, which came to pass when Zeus cast the five brothers into the pit of Tartaros.

Ouranos is referenced directly in '*The Hermetic Cross*'.[48]

ANTEROS [Αντερως, Anterôs] - God of both reciprocated and unreciprocated love, was the Son of Ares and Aphrodite. In the *Cherubic Squares* paper, it reads: "*Later on Sanchoniathon speaks of a second 'love' the Son of Astarte, who seems to be nearly the Greek Anteros; as he is said to be the brother of Eros.*"[49]

In other sources it is written: "*We must especially notice the connexion of Eros with Anteros, with which persons usually connect the notion of 'Love returned', but originally Anteros was a being opposed to Eros, and fighting against him. (Paus. i. 30. § 1, vi. 23. § 4.) This conflict, however, was also conceived as the rivalry existing between two lovers, and Anteros accordingly punished those who did not return the love of others; so that he is the avenging Eros, or a deus ultor. (Paus. i. 30. § 1; Ov. Met. xiii. 750, &c.; Plat. Phaedr. p. 255, d.)*"[50]

---

46 Plat. Cratyl. pg. 401.
47 The Book of the Concourse of the Forces, Cherubic Squares. Private Collection.
48 The Hermetic Cross and the Via Lactea, Private Collection.
49 The Book of the Concourse of the Forces, Cherubic Squares. Private Collection.
50 Source: Theoi.com

THEMIS [Θεμις, Thme] - the Greek counterpart to the Egyptian Maat [Meet].[51]

She was the Titan Goddess of divine law and order, held the art of prophecy, and presided over the ancient oracles, including the Delphoi [Delphi].

Aeschylus wrote: *"The first prophet, Gaia (Gaea, Earth); and after her to Themis, for she was the second to take this oracular seat of her mother."*[52]

Themis was an earlier wife of Zeus, and his initial counsellor.

She was Mother to the *Horai* [Horae], (The Seasons), and the *Moirai* [Moirae], (The Fates).

HERACLES/HERCULES [Δακτυλος Ἡρακλης, Daktylos Heraklês, Heracles, *Hercules*] - was the leader of the five *daemones* titled the 'Daktyloi' (Dactyls), who founded the Olympic Games in the age of Kronos (Cronus).

He is identified with the son of Zeus and Alkmene, the Hero *Hêraklês*.

He is referenced directly in *'The Hermetic Cross'*[53]

Heracles is the Greek for *Hercules*, who is also referenced more prominently in *'The Ritual of the 12 Gates'* and *'The Hermetic Cross'*.[54]

The Greek historian Herodotus writes that *Heracles* was an Egyptian god first, while the Romans called him *Hercules*.

ATLAS [Ατλας, Endures, Dares (atlaô)] - was a Titan God and

---

51 Ciceros, *Self Initiation into the Golden Dawn Tradition*, pg. 30; Lewis Spence, A Dictionary of Non-Classical Mythology.
52 Aeschylus, Eumenides 2 ff - trans. Weir Smyth. (Greek tragedy C5th B.C.)
53 The Hermetic Cross and the Via Lactea, Private Collection.
54 The Ritual of the 12 Gates; The Hermetic Cross and the Via Lactea. Private Collection.

Bearer of the Heavens. One of the leaders of the Titanes, after being defeated by the Olympians, *Atlas* was condemned to carry the world (Heavens) on his shoulders, also aiding mankind in the instruction of the art of astronomy.

Atlas is mentioned in 'The Hermetic Cross.'

CYBELE [Κυβηλη, Kybêlê] - Mother of the Gods in ancient Phrygia, a primal nature Goddess, worshipped across Anatolia. The Greeks identified her with Rhea.

Cybele is often depicted as riding a Lion. She is referenced in 'The Hermetic Cross.'[55]

LUCIFER [Εωσφορος, Eôsphoros, Luciferus, Lucifer] - Known as the Light-bringer, or Dawn-bringer, was a god of the star (aster planeta) Venus. References have his parents as Astraios and Eos.[56] *Lucifer* is also mentioned as a son of Jupiter.[57]

Noted as having Fathered Ceyx, Daedalion, Leuconoe and the Hesperides.

According to Ovid, in his Metamorphoses,[58] *Lucifer* was the God of Morning:

> "As Lucifer (the morning star) more brilliant shines than all the stars, or as golden Phoebe (the Moon) outshines Lucifer (the morning star)."
> "Brilliant in the dawn Lucifer (Morning-Star) had mounted high, the star that wakes the world to work."

Lucifer is referenced heavily in 'The Hermetic Cross'.[59]

---

55 Ibid.
56 Hesiod Theogony 378, Apollodorus 1.8, Nonnus Dionysiaca 6.18 & 37.70.
57 Servius on Virgil's Aeneid iv, 130.
58 Ovid, Metamorphoses (Latin C1st B.C. – C1st A.D.)
59 The Hermetic Cross and the Via Lactea, Private Collection.

When analysing the above references regarding the Deities, we can almost see a pattern depicting the symbolism, attributes and energies represented in the very Deities themselves, leading us back to the use of Godforms.

Godforms can be a most useful way to describe Deity, especially when it comes to the Cabeiri, where there are contradicting accounts of differential accuracies.

THE KABEIROI [Καβειρος, Καβειροι, Cabeiri; Kabeiros; Kabiri] - are an ancient cult of Thrakian [Thracian] deluge Gods of Samothrake [Samothrace]. The Cabeirian mysteries were not unlike the Eleusinian mysteries; in fact, Manly P. Hall wrote:

> *"The Cabiric Mysteries of Samothrace were renowned among the ancients, being next to the Eleusinian in public esteem."*[60]

Both traditions, according to accounts, include some of the same Deity.

Manly continues:

> *"Herodotus declares that the Samothracians received their doctrines, especially those concerning Mercury [Hermes]..."*

Mnaseas[61] wrote: *"They were four in number:—Axieros, Axiokersa, Axiokersos, Casmilus. It is there stated that Axieros is Demeter; Axiokersa, Persephone; Axiokersos, Hades; and Casmilus, Hermes,"* an account that was later quoted by Apollonius Rhodius i. 917.

Others have Hephaestus in place of Hades, while he is considered

---

60 Manly P. Hall, pg. 20, *The Secret Teachings of All Ages.* (Pacific Publishing).
61 Mnaseas of Patrae or of Patara, was a Greek historian of the late 3rd century BCE.

the Father of the Kabeiroi in other works.

In the 3=8, it reads: "... *Hear thou the voice of Axiokersos, the second Kabir ...,*"[62] then continues: "... *Axiokersa the third Kabir spake to Kasmillos the candidate and said ...*"[63] Followed by: "... *this Michael (Archangel) is also Axieros, the first of the Samothracian Kabiri ...*"[64]

Notice how Axieros is attributed to the Archangel Michael in the Golden Dawn paper, yet is widely depicted as being Demeter elsewhere; the latter being as the Cabirian Mysteries were claimed to have been held in honour of Demeter, Persephone and Hekate.

More can be read about Samothracian Gods and their mysteries in *Thracian Magic: Past & Present.*[65]

The title *Kabeiroi* stems from the Kabeira Mountains in Phrygia, with Greek Gods including Zeus and Dionysus being identified as Kabeiroi.

They were also closely connected to the Phrygian *Korybantes* [Corybantes], the Cretan *Kouretes* [Curetes] and the Trojan *Daktyloi* [Dactyls], also in the version of the *Kabeiroi* being but two, a set of twins, they are identified with the *Dioskouroi* [Dioscuri] in the myth of the Argonauts.[66]

Though most revered in the Samothracian region, the *Kabeiroi* were also considered a group of mystic divinities far across the ancient world.

The contradictions we see above in their identities exist even in antiquity.

"*Strabo in his discussion about the Curetes, Dactyls, &c. speaks of the origin of the Cabeiri, deriving his statements from ancient authorities, and from him we learn, that Acusilaus called Cadmilus a son of Cabeiro and Hephaestus, and that he made the three Cabeiri the sons, and the Cabeirian nymphs the daughters, of Cadmilus.*"[67]

62 3=8.
63 Ibid.
64 Ibid.
65 Georgi Mishev, Thracian Magic: Past and Present. (Avalonia).
66 Source: Theoi.com.
67 Strabo, x. p. 466, Source: Theoi.com

Burkert writes: *"It is said that the Tyrrhenians bring first fruit offerings to Zeus, Apollo, and the Kabeiroi."*[68]

The mysteries of the Kabeiroi, are continued even today in the Threskeia Initiations; Threskeia is the religion/faith, so named from antiquity, as it is said that 'Orpheus the Thracian' was the first to prescribe the Greek Mysteries.[69]

Mystai [Initiates] received *Myesis* [Initiation] during the Cabirian Mysteries, as did the initiates at Eleusis, and as do the members of the Golden Dawn.

THE CORYBANTES [Κορυβας Κορυβαντες, Korybas, Korybantes] - Were the Samothracian Corybantes, seven orgiastic *Daemones*. The korybas was an orgiastic dance performed by armoured men with clashing spear and shield, whilst devotees' cries danced along with the rhythm.

These Samothrakian *daemones* were also closely connected with the Phrygian Daktyloi (Dactys), the Kretan Kouretes (Curetes) and the Euboian Korybantes.

They are directly mentioned in *'The Hermetic Cross'*.

THE IDAIC DACTYLS [Δακτυλος Δακτυλοι, Daktylos, Daktyloi] - Translation: Fingers. Were the five *Daktyloi (Dactyls)* seen as identical to the Kouretes. *Daemones* who, along with the Hekaterides, represented all ten fingers, symbolising the finger to finger union of the human hands. The *'Dionysiaca'* lists two of the Telkhines, Damnameneus and Skelmis, which are names applied to the *'Daktyloi'* by Hesiod.

Referenced also in *'The Hermetic Cross'*.

68   Walter Burkert, Greek Religion, pg. 281; Myrsilos FGrHist 477 F 8.
69   Source: threskeia.webs.com

THE TELCHINI [Τελχις Τελχινες, Telkhis, Telkhines] - numbered four, were magician sea-gods of the islands of Keos (Ceos, Cos, Kos) and Rhodes. They created the art of metal-work. It said that the sickle used by Kronos to castrate his Father Ouranos was crafted by the *Telchini*.

They are directly referenced in *'The Hermetic Cross'*.

THE ANEMOI [Ανεμος Ανεμοι, Anemos, The Four Winds] - Gods of the four winds: Boreas the Northwind, Zephyros [Zephyrus] the West, Notos [Notus] the South, and Euros [Eurus] the East.

Sanchoniathon, Homer and Hesiod make mention of the connexion between the Four Winds and the Spirits of the Elements, according to Mathers in his *Cherubic Squares* notes.[70]

HARPOKRATES [Ἁρποκρατες; Harpocrates; Harparkrat; Harpacrat; Hoorpokrati; Harpa-Khruti] - The God of Silence. *Harpokrates* was the Greek interpretation of the Egyptian Harpa-Khruti (Horus the Child). Most recognised with the index finger held to his lips, in the Sign of Silence.

The 'Sign of Silence' or *Sign of Harpocrates*, is used often within the tradition of the Golden Dawn: In the *Assumption of Harpocrates*, the Godforms used are that of Harpokrates. Stavish wrote: "*Harpocrates is 'the god who is the cause of all generation, of all nature, and of all the powers of the elements' and as such he 'precedes all things and comprehends all things in himself'*."[71]

He also wrote: "*Harpocrates: Then vibrate his name - Hoor-po-krat-ist, while you imagine yourself emerging from the primordial waters of creation.*"

Ritual Z tells us: (Fourth, the Station of Harpocrates) "*The invisible Station of Harpocrates is in the Path of Samekh, between the Station of Hegemon and the Invisible Station of the Evil Triad. Harpocrates is the God of Silence and Mystery, whose Name is the*

---

70   The Book of the Concourse of the Forces, Cherubic Squares, Private Collection.
71   Mark Stavish, M.A. - Assumption of Godform.

Word of this Grade of Neophyte. He is the younger brother of Horus, Hoor-Po-Krattist."[72]

In the same work, it states: *"... the two green squares of HARPOCRATES,"* and *"HOORPARKRATI will be found to rule GEMINI PISCES..."*

Now what may be noticeable to Golden Dawn members here is the similarity of the name *Harpokrates* with 'The Grand Word' *Har Par Krat,* whispered mouth to ear in syllables, during the Ritual of the 0=0 Grade of Neophyte, as the Neophyte exchanges the word with Horus (Hiereus).

So, in conclusion, we find there to be just as much Greek influence as there are Egyptian in the ceremonial aspect of the Order of the Golden Dawn, and it's likely there are further references in later papers, or in papers yet to surface, that I have yet to gain access to or read.

END

---

72 Israel Regardie, Grade of the Neophyte, *The Golden Dawn: A Complete Course in Practical Ceremonial Magic.*

ABOUT THE AUTHOR

Soror DPF was born in the 'oldest recorded town in Britain', the Pre-Roman town of Camulodunum, now known as Colchester, in 1968. (The earliest record of the town's existence is a reference by the Roman writer, Pliny the Elder in AD77).

She has written a variety of media, for niche publisher's Anthologies, including Avalonia's *Hekate: Her Sacred Fires*; Magazines/ eZines, including *Isis Seshat, Mirror of Isis*, and *Isian News, Isian Voices*, as well as articles published online for the Fellowship of Isis International Symposium.

Soror DPF is also a consecrated Adept and Priestess in training, in the Fellowship of Isis, and was also a founding Torchbearer of the Covenant of Hekate, though since has inaugurated a Hierón dedicated to Hekate/Εκάτη Própolos.

Her interests are eclectic, delving into pre-Hellenic, Thracian, Ancient Greek with their Eleusinian Mysteries, Babylonian, Ancient Egyptian Mysteries, Western Mystery Traditions, and in more recent years the Qabalah and the Golden Dawn systems.

THE FOUR ELEMENTS
AND THEIR IMPLEMENTS

by Jayne Gibson

*For Osiris, who has been found perfect before the Gods
hath said:*
> *These are the Elements of my Body,*
> *Perfected through suffering, glorified through trial.*

— Excerpt from the Prayer of Osiris

INTRODUCTION

This paper will illustrate the multi-faceted aspects of the Elements and their corresponding Implements for their use in ritual magic. The Elemental Implements or Tools are the first talismans to be consecrated in the grade of Adeptus Minor, and their use will be continuous in the magical life of an Adept. You will find these Implements illustrated in the lower arcana of the Tarot through its suits: Wands (Fire), Cups (Water), Swords (Air) and Pentacles (Earth) and they are also illustrative of the Divine Name of Creation, YHVH,[1] that is, Yod (Fire), Heh (Water), Vau (Air) and Heh Final (Earth). They are the bare bones of a magical cosmos and represent the forces of Creation, for it is the Elements that give Magical Forces the ability to manifest.

The Magician must know and understand the Elements, not only in the images of their outward form, but also in their magical significance. This is important because of their association with most occult energies, and the Elemental Tools hold such an important place in the magical life of the Adept. The Magician must be able to distinguish and balance the properties of the Elements if he or she is to use these Tools to control Magical Forces.

As stated above, the Wand, the Cup, the Dagger and the Pentacle are conduits of the Forces from which all physical life proceeds, for they correspond to the Letters of the Divine Name YHVH. The Wand is indicative of the Power aspect or the Yod. The Cup represents the Maternity/Love aspect or the Heh. The Dagger is indicative of the Reconciling aspect or the Vau, and the Pentacle represents that aspect of the Divine concerned with the actual working out of the Divine Plan or the Heh Final. Whatever exists is what it is by application of the principles symbolized by these four Implements.

The Magical Tools owe a great deal of their potency to the fact that their use is so intimately harmonious with their symbolism, and the complete fitness for their intended purpose is their essential quality. The Wand directs, the Cup sustains, the Dagger liberates, and the Pentacle (a Shield) defends.

The Dagger and the Wand are distinctly masculine symbols, while the Cup and Pentacle are feminine. The Wand is the complementary partner for the Cup, as the Dagger is for the Pentacle. The masculine symbols are chiefly concerned with the intellect and action, while the feminine ones stand for emotive and protective instincts. In correct

---

1 *YHVH* is a Divine Name that may have originated as a descriptive term for the God El, whose name means "God who is present, who makes himself manifest." Taken from: McDermott, John J. *Reading the Pentateuch: A Historical Introduction.* Paulist Press. (2002).

combination, they make a complete circle of creative consciousness.

The Dagger and Cup can also be partners, like the Wand and the Pentacle, and this is illustrated by their microcosmic arrangement upon the altar. The Cup is opposite of the Dagger, indicating a connection between the two. Air and Water are both gases in differing stages of density—Air can be liquefied and Water made gaseous. Physically, Air and Water exchange natural energies with each other by atmospheric cycles of rainfall, and this concept can be applied metaphysically. In balancing Earth and Fire, bear in mind that Earth provides all the fuels for Fire and also the Fire-resistant properties which make it possible for Fire to consume fuel in a controlled way. Fire needs fuel fed to it from Earth's readily combustible materials in order to keep burning. Thus Earth and Fire act as controls upon each other.

According to Aleister Crowley in his book *777*, the Elemental Tools are vice-regents of the true Tools of the Sephiroth. The Wand is indicative of the Sephirah Chokmah, which is the Divine Will, the Father, while the Cup represents Understanding, the Mother, the Sephirah of Binah. The Dagger corresponds to Reason, the Son, the six Sephiroth of the Ruach (Chesed, Geburah, Tiphareth, Netzach, Hod and Yesod), while the Pentacle corresponds to Malkuth, the Daughter and the material world.

Therefore, the Cup is the heavenly food of the Magician and the Pentacle is the earthly food. The Cup is hollow to receive Divine influence, while the Pentacle is flat like the fertile plains of the earth. The Wand is Divine Force and the Dagger is human force. The Wand is the Will, the Wisdom and the Word of the Magician and the Cup is Understanding, the vehicle of Grace. The Dagger is Reason, and the Pentacle is the shell of the body, the temple of Divine Spirit.

The Wand, as the Will and representing the wisdom and spiritual presence within the self, is closely associated with the Chiah, the creative and inquisitive inner impulse. The Cup is a true symbol of the Neschamah, Intuition, and the seat of all the true psychic abilities in the human. The Dagger is of cold steel, hard, sharp and piercing like the Ruach, which is the human mind, the higher and moral aspects of which are shown in the Sephiroth of Chesed (mercy and compassion), Geburah (strength and justice) and

Tiphareth (the enlightened mind), and the lower aspects of which are given in Netzach (the emotions), Hod (the intellect) and Yesod (the unconscious). The round, inert Pentacle is a fitting symbol of Earth, which is the platform upon which Divine Forces manifest. The Pentacle is a token of the body about to receive the influx of Divine Light, and it is also the expression of a complete thought and an act of the will.

The Cup conveys a sense of companionship and sociability that make life worthwhile on a spiritual level and signifies our ability to receive and pour out love, just as its complementary symbol, the Wand, measures the extent of our will in action. The Pentacle indicates breadth and the area of coverage, while the Dagger marks the exact point where magical action and attention are concentrated.

These Implements can be seen collectively to represent the creative faculties of the Magician and in their perfect sense, the Purified Adept. The Wand represents the Spirit, the animating principle of each human individual which derives directly from the Divine. The Cup symbolizes the Soul, the purely emotional levels of love, hate and every condition of sentient consciousness between those extremes. The Dagger represents the Mind, the purely mental and intellectual nature and applied ideology conveyed mostly through the spoken or written word. The Pentacle symbolizes the Body, the container and outward manifestation of spirit, soul and mind.

These Tools conduct the forces of manifestation and with them the Adept can build endless operations of Magic. Nevertheless, these Implements are not automatic in their action, and they must be used consistently in order to get any practical results. Once the Magician has become skilled in their use, Divine energies will flow through the Magician, and magic will start to become a practical proposition. Every Magician is responsible for discovering the inner values and applications of these Implements by meditation and experience through ritual work. One must not only learn them but live them so that what they symbolize may be realized. Let us proceed to examine each of the Elements and their corresponding Implements in turn.

Altar Arrangement

(**NOTE:** In the following sections, the pronouns of "he" and "she" are used only to illustrate the qualities of the Elements, that is, he/active/projective/male and she/passive/receptive/female.)

THE ELEMENT OF FIRE – THE WAND

The Element of Fire – the emblem of Sprit

Fire is an aggressive and projective Element. The Element of Fire, the most transformative of the Elements, is the animating or life-giving principle in magic that is designed toward manifestation. It is the closest of the Elements to the Divine nature and is analogous to the magical will. Angels are said to be made of Fire or pure, radiant energy. Elemental Fire is Light and Illumination, the Divine Will projected forth into manifestation, and it is the control of this Element that will allow the magician to focus the will upon a central idea or goal.

Fire is both the creator and the destroyer, but unlike the other Elements, it cannot exist in physical form without consuming something else. Thus, Fire transforms all it touches into new forms. Controlled, Fire essentially transmutes; however, uncontrolled it devours all things and returns them to primal energy, to that Principle which gave them being.

Fire is a masculine Element, its aspects being passion, creativity, motivation, will power, drive and sexuality, both physical and spiritual. It is the Element of authority and leadership, a reflection of the Celestial Light, giving life to all things. Fire is a catalyst; it seems to devour but really transforms simply, and adopts nothing of what it touches to itself. This is the mystery of Fire, for though it may be fed by other materials, its flame remains unstained and incorruptible.

Fire is thought of as the force of life; it is light, illumination, clarity of consciousness, the focused will, inner sight, and the Divine Spark shining within an earthly vehicle. It is the Element of courage, determination, consecration and the mysteries of the Spirit. Magicians should work with Fire until they experience its radiance and clarity, allowing them to bring this Element through into the material plane.

The Archangel of Fire - Michael

In the Greek New Testament, the word *arch* means "chief, principle, greatest or highest," and the word *angel* means "messenger." Therefore the title of Archangel means the highest or greatest messenger. The Archangelic ideas in connection with the symbolism of the Elemental Implements are helpful because they aid in understanding the characteristics of the Tools to which they are associated. The Archangel of Fire is Michael, whose name means "Who is Like God," making this Archangel the greatest messenger whose nature is the closest the Divine. Michael was the first Angel created, and he veils the Light of the Divine by appearing in the form of an Angel, yet this being has the power, authority and attributes that belong to the Highest Divine.

In angelology Michael has four main roles. His first role is the leader of the Heavenly Army in their triumph over the powers of evil. He is viewed as the angelic model for the virtues of the spiritual warrior. In his second role, Michael is the angel of death, carrying the souls of all the deceased to heaven. In his third role, he weighs all souls on his perfectly balanced scales (hence Michael is often depicted holding scales). In his fourth role, Michael, the special patron of the Chosen People in the Old Testament (the Jews), is also the guardian of the Catholic Church, and it was not unusual for this angel to be revered by the military orders of knights during the Middle Ages. Michael is the patron of Chivalry and Knightly Orders, the Defender of Justice, and the Healer of Disease (not wounds).

Michael aids in the pursuit of truth, integrity and faith. He is also a healer of degenerative disease or terminal illness. One could work with Michael in rituals designed towards strength, courage, and defense. However, the most important aspect of Michael is his closeness to the Divine Light, and working with this Archangel can reveal some of the higher mysteries.

The Wand

The Wand is the archetypal implement of the will of the Magician, and it has always been considered a major transmitter of magical power. It rules, regulates and directs the Element of Fire. The Fire Wand resembles a rod or a staff; and staffs are associated with ruling powers and were once borne by kings and commanders to show their high office.

It is the Tool which governs Fire, the least governable of the Elements, and the one most emblematic of the dazzling potencies encountered in the Art of Magic. It represents everything in and around you with enough energy to arouse your capabilities of creative consciousness and also represents all that may be accomplished by applied will, intelligence and inspiration.

Correspondences for Elemental Fire

Divine Name	Elohim	אלהים	ALHYM
Archangel	Michael	מיכאל	MYKAL
Angelic Choir:	Ziqquqim	זקוקים	ZQVQYM
Angel	Ariel	אריאל	ARYAL
Ruler	Seraph	שרף	ShRPh
King	Djin		
Elementals	Salamanders		

- **Qabalistic World:** Atziluth
- **Letter of Tetragrammaton:** Yod
- **Hebrew Letter:** Shin ש (Sh/S)
- **Basic Nature:** Consecratory, destructive, cleansing, energetic, sexual, forceful
- **Energy:** Projective
- **Color:** Red
- **Part of the self:** Spirit
- **Direction:** Microcosmic: South; Macrocosmic: East
- **Sephiroth:** Chokmah, Geburah and Netzach

- **Planets:** Mars and Venus
- **Values and virtues:** Leadership, trust in self, sovereignty or royalty
- **Rituals:** Consecration, destruction, protection, courage, sex, energy, strength, and authority
- **Ritual Forms:** Burning, smoldering or heating
- **Herbs:** Stinging, thorny or hot such as thistles, stimulating such as coffee beans. Ashes, Allspice, Cactus, Chilli Pepper, Cinnamon, Clove, Ginger, Pepper, and Tobacco
- **Stones:** Any red or fiery stone. Ruby, Red Jasper, Lava Rocks, Bloodstone, Carnelian, Diamond, Flint, Garnet
- **Incenses:** Spicy and hot scents, such as Allspice, Cinnamon, Clove, Ginger, Dragon's Blood, and Tobacco
- **Metals:** Gold and brass
- **Season:** Summer
- **Time:** Noon (Zenith)
- **Tool:** Wand
- **Point in Life:** Youth
- **Astrological Signs:** Aries, Leo and Sagittarius
- **Tarot Card(s):** Judgment and the Suite of Wands
- **Sense:** Sight
- **Symbols:** Candle Flame or the Flaming Cauldron[2]

---

2 The Flame of the Cauldron can be achieved by placing a very small amount of 90% isopropyl alcohol into a censer or cauldron and lighting it. I caution the reader to use a very small amount to limit the height of the flame and the duration it burns. I also caution the reader to not move the censer or cauldron once it is lit because if the alcohol spills, the flame will follow the stream.

THE ELEMENT OF WATER – THE CUP

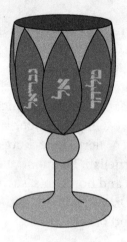

The Element of Water – the emblem of the Soul

Water comprises the bulk of our physical bodies and permits their mobility. As we emerged from the ocean primevally by the action of Light upon Water, so must we be reborn on inner levels through ocean equivalents. This is ritually symbolized by the rite of baptism. On inner levels, Water is a container or carrier of consciousness, linking up conscious energies between all life-forms. Hence, the Cup is a Communion symbol.

Water is a feminine element; it is the Element of intuition, dreams, the emotions, the subconscious mind, purification, and the mysteries of the soul. It is cleansing, healing, psychic, and represents love in its many forms. Contact with this Element engenders a passive state of consciousness, a meditative state, in which communication with spiritual forces can be achieved.

The Archangel Gabriel

Gabriel is the Archangel of Water, whose name means "The Strength of God," and this Archangel has several inter-linked functions. As a chief messenger, Gabriel is a consciousness-carrier between the Divine and the human. Therefore, this angel is considered to be the communicator and mediator between Heaven and Earth. Gabriel serves a triple function, Annunciator, Guardian and Guide. She is the divine messenger who relays information between the Divine and humanity and bestows the gifts of spiritual vision as well as the powers of life, procreation and equilibration. Gabriel is the angel of mercy while Michael is the angel of judgment.

She is also a principle fertility figure because she bears news on one level that fertilizes minds, and she bears seed on another level to fertilize bodies. Gabriel is the Life-bearer, powered by Love, and she helps force into form. She resurrects life from death and Water provides her with the life medium for its continuation. As Ruler of the Western Gate and Key-holder of the floodgates of Heaven, she links with Lunar Tides and all the ancient fertility attributes of the Moon.

Gabriel can bring messages from the Divine, aid in spiritual visions, give prophecies of the unknown, and she can help with dream and vision interpretation. It is also said that Gabriel will give guidance on the pathway of the soul.

The Cup

The Cup can be seen as a tool for conditioning the meditative consciousness of the Magician. This implement is associated with the Element of Water as it is a container of liquids, but it can also be seen as a receptacle of the fluid powers of the mind. Elemental Water is preeminently the means of freeing oneself from impurities, allowing spiritual vision to reveal the true nature of the self. The ability to reject the false and to preserve the truth is characteristic not only of Elemental Water but also, in another manner, of the Cup itself, as the function of the Cup is to preserve that which it contains.

The Cup is round (a circle) like the Pentacle, not straight like the Wand and the Dagger. Reception, not projection, is its nature. The circle symbolizes the infinite while the cross represents the finite. The Wand can be seen as an instrument of binding and limitation as a channel and director of energy, while the Cup can be perceived as an expansion of consciousness into the Infinite. This idea can be reversed, however, when one views the Cup as a container of consciousness and the Wand as expressing the rise of that consciousness into the purely Spiritual World (as indicated by the Yods painted on its tip).

As a control instrument of Water, the Cup has meanings as deep as the oceans themselves. Start finding Cups everywhere, from the hollow of your hands to the Space that holds the stars of Heaven.[3] All hollows are associated to the Cup—the cave, the cauldron, the well, the bowl—our minds are cups holding consciousness.

The Cup and Love go together. Love preserves, pours out, comforts, and cheers. It may also intoxicate, poison, embitter and even slay. The contents of the Cup may be anything at all in liquid (soulful) form. Life, death and resurrection come from and through the Cup; it is the womb as well as the tomb, and its circle represents the Eternal Spirit containing all. Thus, in the Cup should be seen the principle of a container, receptivity and the capacity for loving care.

The Cup symbolizes the Sangreal or vessel of every virtue possible. It especially indicates whoever bears the "Blessed Blood," which all souls relating themselves with the Divine can share in kinship with Creation. Its symbolism denotes the nearest condition to an ideal heaven that we are likely to find on earth because it signifies a spiritual state of love far beyond anything imaginable by the human mind. It is a symbol of Purity and the greatest bliss that may be experienced by humans in spiritual safety. It is the Cornucopia and the Magic Cauldron, and can be seen to contain the Elixir of Life. The Cup is most familiar as the Grail, the wonderful, mystic container of uncertain appearance but of surpassing spiritual sweetness and ineffable joy.

Correspondences for Elemental Water

Divine Name	El	אל	AL
Archangel	Gabriel	גבריאל	GBRYAL
Angelic Choir:	Mekhoroth	מכורות	MKVRVTh
Angel	Taliahad	טליהד	TLYHD
Ruler	Tharsis	תרשים	ThRShYS
Queen	Nichsa		
Elementals	Undines		

3 This holds true for all of the Elemental Tools - look for them in everyday life.

- **Qabalistic World:** Briah
- **Letter of Tetragrammaton:** Heh
- **Hebrew Letter:** Mem מ (M)
- **Basic Nature:** Flowing, purifying, psychic, healing, soothing and loving
- **Energy:** Receptive
- **Color:** Blue
- **Part of the self:** Soul
- **Direction:** Microcosmic: West; Macrocosmic: North
- **Sephiroth:** Binah, Chesed, Hod
- **Planets:** Jupiter and Mercury
- **Values and virtues:** Devotion, prayer, empathy
- **Rituals:** Receptivity, meditation, reflection, imagination, purification, love, psychic awareness, dreams, sleep, and peace
- **Ritual Forms:** Dilution, placing in water, libation and pouring, washing away such as bathing.
- **Herbs:** Aquatic such as Water Lilies, Seaweed. Water Flowers, African Violet, Chamomile, Eucalyptus, Hemlock, Lilac, Lotus, Morning Glory, and Poppy.
- **Stones:** Transparent or translucent such as Amethyst and Aquamarine. Blue, as in Blue Tourmaline. Azurite, Beryl, Blue Calcite, Chalcedony, Coral, Quartz Crystal, Lapis Lazuli, Moonstone, Mother of Pearl, Pearl, Sapphire, and Blue Tourmaline.
- **Incenses:** Dreamy, soft, sweetish scents, such as Chamomile, Cardamom, Gardenia, Hyacinth, Iris, Jasmine, Lilac, Lily, Lotus, Myrrh, Orchid, Violet, and Ylang-Ylang.
- **Metals:** Silver
- **Season:** Autumn
- **Time:** Dusk
- **Point in Life:** Maturity
- **Astrological Signs:** Cancer, Scorpio, and Pisces
- **Tarot Card(s):** The Hanged Man and the Suit of Cups
- **Sense:** Taste
- **Symbols:** Shells, Bowls, Wine, or a Cup of Water.

THE ELEMENT OF AIR – THE DAGGER

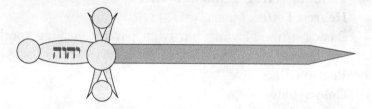

The Element of Air – the emblem of the Mind

Air is a symbol of Divine Spirit, free-moving and unconfined, penetrating everywhere. It is the Element of reconciliation and so links the human mind with the spiritual worlds. Fire transforms, Water purifies, and Earth confines, but Air is predominantly the Reconciler. It is the vital Spirit passing through all things, giving life to all things, moving and filling all things.

Elemental Air is a masculine Element referring to the power of the mind, the force of the intellect, inspiration, visualization, and imagination. It is the Element of ideas and knowledge. Symbolically, Air is related to the Creative Breath or the Word. The spoken word is much valued in Hermetic magic because it was the Word that brought about creation, and Elemental Air relates to the spoken word as speech is sound carried on breath. It is therefore connected in many mythologies with the idea of Creation as the medium for movement and the emergence of life processes. Air is a projective Element, considered to be the offspring of Fire and Water; and it is the Reconciler between these two opposing Elements, balancing their extremes. Air is movement, freshness, communication and the Ruach, human intelligence.

The Archangel Raphael

Raphael is the Archangel of Air whose name means "The Healing Power of God." The Hebrew word *rapha* means "doctor" or "healer," and it is thought that Raphael was given this name due to the story in the Book of Enoch where it is said that he healed the earth when it was defiled by the sins of the fallen angels. It may be difficult to see Raphael, who is a healer, with a Dagger until we discover that he specializes in healing wounds that are normally made with sharp edges. However, Raphael's healing domain is all encompassing: physical, mental, emotional, and spiritual.

As well as a healer, Raphael is known as the Patron of Travelers because of his help with Tobias and his travels. Therefore, this Archangel will aid the Magician with inward spiritual journeys, assisting in searches for truth and guidance. It is said that part of Raphael's healing work involves the releasing of spirits and space clearing as he often works with Michael to exorcise discarnate entities and escort away lower energies from people and places. Raphael is an angel who will aid the Magician in fine-tuning clairvoyance, bring a sense of unity to individual life, and aid those who feel out of touch with their spirituality.

Raphael typifies the dawning of the Inner Light, and his work is instructing humanity and also healing injuries and wounds (not diseases). He is a Teacher of the Hermetic Arts, for in another form he is the Great Hermes or Thoth, and rituals designed to aid in the magical arts would fall under his purview.

The Dagger

The Dagger is a means of controlling the Element of Air, and here associations to the blade of the Dagger are important: its flashing quickness, its piercing qualities, and its brightness are all symbolic of the intellect, communication, and the mental faculties. Daggers can be seen in keen observations and pointed remarks. They can penetrate surfaces, decide issues, cut through knots, compel obedience, challenge stupidities and defeat them, uphold honor, and accomplish a great many actions along these lines.

One of the significances of the Dagger symbol is freedom of spirit, but this has to be fortified by the conquest of any Airy faults such as frivolity, idleness and indecision. To win this freedom, the virtues of consistent purpose and concentration are required, the very qualities represented by the Dagger.

One may consider the Dagger as a tool for purifying emotional perceptions into clear insights because the Dagger can be used as a counter-balance to the emotions by analytical reasoning. This is another reason why the Cup and Dagger are opposite each other upon the Altar.

All cutting implements are to be classed under the Dagger category: scythes, which help harvest grain, knives which cut up food, saws and chisels which work with wood, the scissors of the housewife, and the shears of the shepherd. They are also surgical scalpels cutting away disease. The Dagger symbol applies to any such physical category and also to all mental or spiritual equivalents. This has to be carefully considered during exercises with the Dagger when trying to translate its inner meaning into consciousness.

Correspondences for Elemental Air

Divine Name	YHVH	יהוה	YHVH
Archangel	Raphael	רפאל	RPhAL
Angelic Choir:	Hadarim	הדרים	HDRYM
Angel	Chassan	חשן	ChShN
Ruler	Aral	אראל	ARAL
King	Paralda		
Elementals	Sylphs		

- **Qabalistic World:** Yetzirah
- **Letter of Tetragrammaton:** Vau
- **Hebrew Letter:** Aleph א (A)
- **Basic Nature:** Inspiring, moving, fresh, intelligent, suspending.
- **Energy:** Projective
- **Color:** Yellow
- **Part of the self:** Mind
- **Direction:** Microcosmic: East; Macrocosmic: West
- **Values and virtues:** Intellect, judgment, humanity
- **Sephiroth:** Kether, Tiphareth, Yesod
- **Planets:** Sol and Luna
- **Rituals:** Knowledge, visions, travel, instruction, study, and

freedom.

- **Ritual Forms:** Visualization, fans, high places in general, positive thinking.
- **Herbs:** Fragrant, with any flowers. Pungent, as in culinary herbs such as dill. Leaves generally. Acacia, Benzoin, Orange Bergamot, Caraway, Citron, Clover, Hops, Lavender, Lemon-grass, Lemon Verbena, Marjoram, Mastic, Mint, Pine, Sage, and Star Anise.
- **Stones:** Light stones such as Pumice. Transparent stones such as Mica. Aventurine, Jasper (Mottled), Sphene.
- **Incenses:** Light, airy scents, such as Frankincense, Benzoin, Citron, Lavender, Lemongrass, and Mastic
- **Metals:** Tin
- **Season:** Spring
- **Time:** Dawn
- **Point in Life:** Infancy
- **Astrological Signs:** Gemini, Libra, Aquarius
- **Tarot Card(s):** The Fool and the Suit of Swords
- **Sense:** Hearing, smell.
- **Symbols:** Feather, fan, incense smoke, fragrant flowers

THE ELEMENT OF EARTH – THE PENTACLE

The Element of Earth – the emblem of the Body

We usually take Earth to signify our state of real and stable solidity, but it is no more stable or solid than its associated Elements. In actuality, Elemental Earth might not be considered an Element at all in that it is the container and manifestation of the previous Three Elements. Elemental Earth is the energy through which the occult Forces condense into concrete forms of energy-expression. Here, we meet with objectivity, solidity, gravity, weight, fertility, mass, incarnation, and definition.

Earth is to Fire what Water is to Air—a counterpoise and a control. Take Fire out of Earth and Water out of Air, and no life could inhabit this planet. With no Earth to retain Fire and no Water to vaporize into Air, life would be impossible. Earth is placed at the North of the Magic Circle, opposite Fire to which it is magically married. However, by itself Elemental Earth is cold and sterile, only acting as a kind of reservoir (like the Cup) for the forces which condense into it.

We cannot establish the energies of Fire, Water or Air without the means of Elemental Earth because it makes manifestation possible between individual units of existence by allowing them to differ from each other dimensionally. This is necessary magically as well as materially. Earth has the property of conformability and resistance, offering the necessary inertia to other energies for their inter-relationship and manifestation. It is a mistake to think of inertia as a state of "deadness" or powerlessness. To the contrary, inertia is very much a power which keeps everything in proportion with everything else, and this is a magical value of Elemental Earth.

On inner levels, it is essential to master the Earth-principle if we expect our consciousness to remain in a state of constancy with itself. It is Earth which allows us to make any number of different things, and yet relate them to one another proportionally, to a common center, so that they stay together as an expression of wholeness.

The Archangel Uriel

Uriel is the Archangel of Earth, whose name means "God is Light." Uriel is considered one of the wisest Archangels because of her intellectual information, practical solutions and creative insights, and she is often shown holding a Book of Wisdom. She is to be regarded as "Light" in the sense of Knowledge and Experience. From the Book of Enoch, we read that Uriel controls the forces of the Earth's behavior in the cosmos. She is the intelligence who links our consciousness with Earth so that we may penetrate its secrets and enter its amazing treasure house. The Earth symbol is a seed holding within itself all life preceding it and all the life that will come forth from it. Uriel is the teacher of the methods for manifesting these seeds.

Uriel is said to have brought the knowledge and practice of alchemy. She illuminates unknown situations and gives prophetic information and warnings, and her expertise is divine magic, problem solving, spiritual understanding, studies, alchemy, and weather. She is also said to be the Archangel who helps with earthquakes, floods, fires, hurricanes, tornadoes, natural disasters and earth changes.

The Pentacle

Essentially, the Pentacle is a shield and a surface. It may also be referred to as a Pantacle, which means "all keys" rather than Pentacle which means "five keys." The fundamental ideology of this symbol is protection and preservation by means of shelter. It was the Shield which was anciently placed between oneself and one's aggressor. In theory, the Shield applies to anything with a protective purpose. The Pentacle is a sign of Protective Power that shields one from potential spiritual dangers. The main purpose of all Pantacles is for materializing occult Forces into concrete types of energy so that we may deal with them objectively. With the Pentacle, we can evoke these Forces and make intelligible communication with them. It will also work in reverse and dematerialize unwanted forces and shield us from energies likely to cause us harm.

The Pentacle can act in magic just as the Earth acts in our outer world. It affords stability, protection, a currency for exchanges of communication, and a focus for all forces to materialize. The Pentacle is the field of action for any force, and magically, it represents the field of whatever operation is taking place.

Fire is not matter at all; Water is a combination of elements; Air is almost entirely a mixture of elements; and Earth contains them all. So it is with the Pentacle, the symbol of Earth. As the Cup holds Water, so does the Shield hold Earth by acting as a surface, which is what Earth amounts to and why the Pentacle is its symbol.

Correspondences for Elemental Earth

Divine Name	Adonai	אדני	ADNY
Archangel	Uriel	אוריאל	AVRYAL
Angelic Choir:	Teraphim	תרפים	ThRPYM
Angel	Phorlakh	פורלאך	PVRLAK
Ruler	Kerub	כרוב	KRVB
Queen	Ghob		
Elementals	Gnomes		

- **Qabalistic World:** Assiah
- **Letter of Tetragrammaton:** Heh Final
- **Basic Nature:** Fertile, nurturing, stabilizing, grounding.
- **Energy:** Receptive
- **Color:** Black (or Green)
- **Part of self:** Body
- **Sephiroth:** Malkuth
- **Planets:** Saturn
- **Direction:** Microcosmic: North; Macrocosmic: South
- **Values and virtues:** Practical skill and experience, respect for the body
- **Rituals:** Manifestation, construction, employment, home, fertility, stability, grounding
- **Ritual Forms:** Burying, planting, making of a physical image, ritual action on physical plane.
- **Herbs:** Earthy-smelling plants, such as Patchouly and Vetivert. Mosses and Lichens, dry and stiff plants, heavy, low-growing plants such as Ivy. Roots generally. Alfalfa, Barley, Corn, Fern, Horsetail, Oats, Oleander, Potatoes (most root vegetables) Rye, and Wheat.
- **Stones:** Heavy or opaque as in coal. Green as in Emerald and Peridot. Green Agate, Moss Agate, Alum, Green Calcite, Brown jasper, Jet, Kunzite, Malachite, Olivine, Salt, Stalagmite, Stalactite, Black Tourmaline.
- **Incenses:** Dark and earthy scents, such as Dittany of Crete, Patchouly, Cypress, Fern, Mugwort, Narcissus, Oakmoss, Vervain, and Vetivert.
- **Metals:** Iron. Lead.
- **Season:** Winter
- **Time:** Midnight
- **Point in Life:** Advanced Age.
- **Astrological Signs:** Taurus, Virgo, Capricorn
- **Tarot Card(s):** The Suit of Pentacles
- **Sense:** Touch
- **Symbols:** Salt, bread, clay dish, soil, rocks, sheaves of wheat, acorn.

In Conclusion

I direct your attention once again to the arrangement of the Elemental Implements upon the altar. The Elements of Air and Fire are projective while the Elements of Water and Earth are Receptive, and the Implements of these forces are situated opposite each other as a type of balance. They collectively represent force and form in their creative aspects. The feminine energies are all potential, but inert, while the masculine symbols are pure energy, limitless and tireless, but incapable of doing anything if left alone. When projective force acts upon receptive force, its energy is gathered up and set to work. When receptive force receives impulse from the projective, its latent capacities are energized, interlocking this dynamic force and stabilizing it. One cannot function without the other on the material plane.

The Wand is opposite the Pentacle; the Cup is opposite the Dagger, and there seems to be a balance here of the human and Divine energies. The Wand can be seen to exemplify the Inner Robe of Glory, the Light of Spirit, which is the Inner Light inherent in humanity. The Pentacle can be seen to represent the Outer Robe of Concealment, the human body as the veil of the Inner Robe of Glory, which conveys the concept of the body ensouled by Spirit. The Cup is the soul, the spiritual container of the human consciousness represented by the Dagger.

If we combine these ideas, we shall see the concept of force embodied in form and form ensouled by force. And here, we are dealing with the Principle of Polarity, the subtle interaction of the life force between two parts, the flow and return, the stimulus and the reaction. The Principle of Polarity runs through the whole of creation and is the basis for manifestation.

In closing, I would like to provide the Prayer of Osiris in its entirety. This is a prayer often spoken before the partaking of the Repast.

For Osiris, who has been found perfect before the gods hath said:

These are the Elements of my Body, Perfected through suffering, glorified through trial.

For the scent of this Dying Rose is as the repressed Sigh of my Suffering.

And this Flame Red Fire is as the energy of mine undaunted Will.

The Cup of Wine is the pouring out of the blood of my heart,

Sacrificed unto Regeneration, unto the Newer Life.

The Bread and Salt are as the Foundations of my Body, which I destroy in order that they may be renewed.

For I am Osiris Triumphant, even Osiris Onnophris the Justified One

I am he who is clothed in the body of flesh

Yet in whom is the Spirit of the Great Gods.

I am the Lord of Life, Triumphant over Death

Those who partaketh with me shall arise with me

I am the Manifestor in Matter of those whose abode is in the invisible

I am purified

I stand upon the Universe

I am its reconciler with the Eternal Gods

I am the Perfector of Matter

And without Me the Universe is not.

Sources

777 and Other Qabalistic Writings of Aleister Crowley, ed. Israel Regardie

Attainment Through Magic, William G. Gray

Book Four, Liber Abba, Magick, Aleister Crowley

Foundations of High Magick, Denning & Philips

Golden Dawn Ritual Tarot, Chic and Sandra Tabatha Cicero

Inner Traditions of Magic, William G. Gray

Magical Ritual Methods, William G. Gray

Mystical Qabalah, Dion Fortune

Ritual Magic, Donald Tyson

Secrets of a Golden Dawn Temple, Chic and Sandra Tabatha Cicero

Self Initiation into the Golden Dawn Tradition, Chic and Tabatha Cicero

Temple Magic, William G. Gray

Transcendental Magic, Eliphas Levi

The Golden Dawn, Israel Regardie

The Kybalion, by Three Initiates

The Tree of Life, Israel Regardie

Three Books of Occult Philosophy, Henry Cornelius Agrippa

ABOUT THE AUTHOR

Jayne Gibson has been a student of the Western Mystery Tradition for over 20 years, and she is a Senior Adept of the Hermetic Order of the Golden Dawn.

She co-authored the book *Astrological Magic, Basic Rituals and Meditations* with Benjamin Dykes, creating the original rituals published in the book.

She was a regular contributor to *Hermetic Virtues* magazine, and she is a writer of many occult compositions, the main focus of which has been the art of ritual.

Ma'aśeh Bere'shith

A Jewish treatise on the Heavens, Earths, and Hells

Translated and Introduced by J. P. Feliciano

The *Ma'aśeh Bere'shith* ('Work of Genesis', henceforth MB), also known as *Seder Rabbâ de Bere'shith* ('Great order of Genesis') is a Jewish mystical treatise from the Geonic period (500-1000 AD), classifiable under the genre of pre-qabbalistic 'creation mysticism'. The most renowned work in this category is the contemporary *Sefer Yetzirah*, although the two texts are not directly related.

Creation mysticism was largely theoretical, aiming to exegetically unveil the esoteric meanings of creation and the universe. Its practical complement was Merkabah (chariot) mysticism, which consisted of formulae, hymns and ascetic methods to enable one's ascent through the seven palaces[1] (*Hêkalôt*) of the highest heaven in order to behold the chariot-throne of God, as well as techniques to commune with archangels. Medieval Qabbalah would later absorb much of this material into its cosmogony, integrating the Heavens, Palaces, and Chariot-Throne into the new system of the Tree of Life.[2] Most of the old magical formulae from the Hekaloth texts were also integrated into the *qabbalah ma'aśit* ('practical qabbalah') in the Middle Ages.

Editions

The MB is extant in several printed and MS recensions. The prototypical version is included as part of the Sefer Raziel,[3] whence

1   Contemporary Pagan & Gnostic parallels focused on transcending the seven planetary spheres, to reach the Ogdoad, the sphere of the fixed stars
2   See Nathan Wolski, *The Zohar Pritzker Edition, Volume Twelve* (Oxford, 2017), an invaluable compendium of Zoharic Hekaloth/Merkabah texts
3   *Sefer Razi'el ha-Mal'ak*, available in many Hebrew editions, several of which are freely available on Hebrewbooks.org

the present translation is taken. Two other recensions in MS Oxford 1531 were included in Peter Schafer's *Synopse zur Hekhalot Literatur,*[4] 743-820 & 832-853. I referred to them for variant spellings for the angelic names and a few missing fragments. An older English translation of the Raziel version was published by David Meltzer in 1976.[5] My translation has a more literal focus, and retains the original Hebrew names of the Heavens, Earths, and Hells for greater ease of reference.

Structure & Content

The Ma'aseh Bere'shith starts off as a short esoteric commentary on the first verse of Genesis, creatively reinterpreting the meaning of 'in the beginning.' This is quickly followed by a description of the purgative trials that sinners undergo after death, while transitioning through the Seven Hells, from *Sha'arê Tzelmôt* (Gates of the Shadow of Death), to *She'ol* (the Underworld), spending a period of 12 months in each plane. Their journey ends in the earth *Arqa*, described as a place from which no one reascends, located beneath the river that flows from under the Throne.

The text then moves on to a basic description of the regions above, enumerating some of the other Earths each divided by *Tohu*, *Bohu* and waters, describing *Tébel* and *Ḥeled* separately, the former as a plane of hills and mountains, the latter as the physical plane wherein humans and animals dwell. Some of the heavens are then described: *Wilon*, the veil that closes and opens each day, *Shamayim*, and *Raqi'a* separated from *Shamayim* by an ocean, with waters above it. Between these waters and *Raqi'a* are the sun, moon, planets and stars. A series of archangels appointed over the four quarters of this region (presumably *Raqi'a* or perhaps *Shamayim*) are enumerated, then another description of the sun, moon, and stars above *Raqi'a* and another series of quarter archangels that probably rule the region above it.

A section follows on how God sealed the firmament with the

---

4 Peter Schäfer, *Synopse zur Hekhalot Literatur* (Mohr Siebeck, 1981)
5 David Meltzer, *The Secret Garden: An Anthology in the Kabbalah* (Seabury, 1976)

seal of his divine name, which is succeeded by a commentary on the seven days of creation and how the Heavens mirror the Earths, proceeding then to explain how the Hells are structurally linked to the whole scheme, and enumerating the depth of each, as well as the intensity of their fire.

After describing how the angels ascend and descend, and a small section on the measurements and shape of the world, the text moves on to a description of the Water of Tears or Weeping Waters, elucidating their meaning. This is followed by a more thorough listing of the Earths and Heavens and how they are stratified. The text then describes the Hayoth ha-Qodesh and God's Throne as located in the lowermost Earth (*Aretz ha-Tahtonah*), explaining that God's Shekinah is found both above and below. The 18,000 worlds are then said to encompass the Shekinah, 4500 at each quarter. The westernmost world abounds in reified qualities, which are in turn surrounded with fire and water, after which three angels are stationed. The worlds as a whole are compassed by storms, quaking, lightning, rivers, darkness, fire, and water, &c, the whole further encircled by three other angels appointed over the entrances of the east. Five archangels appointed to the west are then enumerated. This is followed by a description of *Shahaqim* above *Raqi'a*, and the archangels of its four quarters. *Makôn* and *Ma'ôn* are then described with their archangels. *Zebul* and *'Araboth* are then described, though no archangels are ascribed thereto. Detailed descriptions of the choirs in *'Araboth* follow, then back down to *Raqi'a*, *Makôn*, and *Ma'ôn*, culminating in a grandiose description of God's sapphire Throne, which concludes the text.

The Ma'aseh Bere'shith and the Golden Dawn

The MB is an important complement to the Qabbalah of the Theoricus and Practicus grades of the Golden Dawn. In the 2=9 grade initiation, the Seven Earths and Hells are introduced in a diagram, which shows them mirroring each other, encompassed by the Water of Tears, the Water of Creation, the Ocean, and the False Sea. Though classically referring to spiritual planes, the Earths and Hells are best interpreted as inner human states and behaviours, which can either lead us to spiritual heights, or away from the light into personal hells. They also reflect the seven lower Sefirot, Malkuth to Hesed.

The diagram mirrors the Tree of Knowledge of Good and Evil, shown in the Eden Before the Fall diagram and equated with Malkuth; its branches are 14, symbolizing the dual polarity of the planetary forces, seven are positive and lead us upward, while the other seven branches sink downward into materiality and ultimately the averse Sefirot. As such, overlaying reflected planetary qualities onto the Earths and Hells is a useful means of elucidating their meaning within the GD. The planetary duality is also seen in the Seven Branched Candlestick of the Zelator grade, in whose description specific opposing traits of each planet are enumerated (based on the double letter qualities in Sefer Yetzirah).

By alternatively viewing the Hells in their traditional Jewish sense, we see the various afflictions that befall us during our journeys, illusions that must be shattered lest our growth be hindered, blessings in disguise that contribute to our development, &c. The Hells are also symbolic of negative qualities that arose during the nights of Creation. A similar alternate way of interpreting the Earths and Hells is to study the former as positive emotions, passions, desires, &c, which nonetheless can simply distract or numb us without furthering our growth, while the Hells are arduous trials and calamities that bring us to our knees initially, but ultimately strengthen us.

There are several variant sets of Earths and Hells in the extant sources, diverging in order and names of some of the planes. The Golden Dawn version of the Earths (derived from the Zohar) shows significant differences:

MB Earths	GD Earths
Aretz ha-taḥtonah (lowermost earth)	*Aretz*
Adamah ('earth')	*Adamah*
Arqa ('earth' in Aramaic)	*Giya* ('Valley')
Ḥarabah (desert)	*Nešiyah* (Oblivion)
Yabašah (dry land)	*Tziyah* (Dryness)
Tebel (world, cosmos)	*Arqa*
Ḥeled (world, span of life)	*Tebel* or *Ḥeled*

The Hells are nearly identical, save for the order of *Be'er Šaḥat* and *Ṭiṭ hayyawen*, which is interchanged, as well as the name of the penultimate Hell, which is simply *Tzel Môt* (Shadow of Death) in the GD version, but the MB has *Ša'arêy Tzel Môt*, 'Gates of the Shadow of Death.'

The Waters of Tears or Weeping Waters echo the tragedy of the Fall, and humankind's separation from the Shekinah, alluding to Adam and Eve's grief at being cast out of Eden. The Waters of Creation symbolize an imperfect creation bereft of divine oversight, whence the Shells and physical beings arose. The Ocean Waters contain the duality of good and evil, while the False Sea is the astral realm of illusion and deception. These four divisions are flawed reflections of the four rivers of Eden, and they sustain the Earths and Hells, much like the four rivers water the seven lower Sefirot.

Constant allusion is also made in the MB to *Tohu* and *Bohu*, the 'formless and void' of Genesis Chapter 1, which were elucidated in the Qabbalah. *Tohu* generally alludes to primordial, chaotic matter, raw and shapeless, while *Bohu* is akin to form and structure. In the MB, they act as dividers between abysses that delineate the various planes.

The Seven Heavens, introduced in the Practicus grade,[6] are traceable to the earliest days of Jewish mysticism. When they entered the Qabbalah, they became associated with the world of 'Asiyah. The Seven Palaces of the Hekalot literature are alternate versions of them, although some texts imply that these palaces are divisions of the highest heaven ('Araboth). The Seven Palace concept was also adapted into the Qabbalah, and greatly expanded in the Zohar, with sets of Palaces for different worlds, subdividing the Sefirot.

The standard set of heavens (seven main ones, plus an eighth one) is consistent throughout most texts, from the MB, to the Zohar and the Golden Dawn, though the order differs:

	MB	GD
0	*Wilôn* ('veil')	*Šamaym*
1	*Šamaym* ('heavens')	*Wilôn*

---

6 See Pat Zalewski, *Golden Dawn Rituals & Commentaries* (ROGD, 2011), 249. This diagram was erroneously omitted from most published GD sources.

2	Raqi'a ('firmament')	Raqi'a
3	Šaḥaqim ('fine clouds')	Šaḥaqim
4	Makôn ('site, foundation')	Zebul
5	Ma'ôn ('dwelling')	Ma'ôn
6	Zebul ('habitation')	Makôn
7	'Arabôt ('clouds')	'Arabôt

An additional 18,000 worlds are said to exist below Shamaym wherein Shekinah and Metatron are said to dwell (the MB states these worlds actually encircle the Shekinah), followed by *Tebel*, and finally our own world, poised between Eden and Gehenna.

Qabbalistically, the seven higher heavens are associated with the lower Sefirot, *'Araboth* relating to Hesed, Makôn to Geburah, &c. They are separately associated with the planets, with *'Araboth* relating to Saturn, down to Shamaym which is Luna (*Wilon* being omitted here). For planetary attributions, the preferable scheme is the MB one. The Golden Dawn uses a nearly identical set for the planets (based on the grimoire tradition[7]), but interchanges Makon and Ma'on. The heavens are an ideal framework for pathworking and astral projection, as in the old Hekalot texts, but using the safer methods of the GD.

You can use the Hebrew name of the heaven as a base, either in black on white paper, or using the corresponding Sefirotic (Queen scale) or planetary flashing colours. After apropriate preliminary work (e.g. invoking the Sefirah or corresponding planet of the Heaven), sit before the name and vibrate the name of the archangel ruling the heaven as many times as necessary to link in to it, then vibrate the name of the heaven seven times, and begin to scry.

The sets of archangels given in the MB do not cover all the heavens, so I give here their ruling archangels as listed in 3 Enoch:[8]

Heaven	Archangel
'Araboth	**Mika'ēl**
Makôn	**Gabri'ēl**
Ma'ôn	**Shataqi'ēl**

7 Joseph Peterson, *The Sixth and Seventh Books of Moses* (Ibis, 2008), 165
8 H. Odeberg, *3 Enoch: the Hebrew Book of Enoch* (Cambridge, 1928), chapter XVII

Zebul	Shaḥaqiʾēl
Shaḥaqim	**Baradiʾēl** or **Badariʾēl**
Raqiʿa	**Baraqiʾēl**
Wilon	**Pazriʾēl** or **Sidriʾēl**

The MB sets of archangels are rather impractical for a scrying invocation, being distributed according to the quarters and not vocalized (besides the incomplete and confusing attribution to the heavens), but this very arrangement is perfectly suited to rudimentary tables of practice for scrying the heavens (like the Almadel in the Lemegeton); I propose a simple square board, with the Hebrew names of the archangels ruling the heaven on each of the 4 sides for each quarter (preferably in Malachim script). Have two candles on either side, and in the very midst the paper or board with the name of the Heaven, or alternatively your preferred scrying medium (black mirror, &c.).

My translation of Maʿaseh Bereʾshith now follows.

MAʿAŚEH BEREʾSHITH: TRANSLATION

In the beginning (*berêšit*), God created the heavens and the earth. However, you must read this not as *berêšit* ('in the beginning') but rather *barā' šit* ('he created six'). And thus shall you observe that these letters of *brašyt* are those whereby the heavens and the earth were created, whereof it is said that 'for in YH YHWH, is the rock of eternity' (*tzur 'olamîm*, Isaiah 26:4): **YH** - two (letters), **YHWH** - 4, totalling six. So you have learned that by these 6 letters God created heaven and earth. Should you say that 'Only the heavens and the earth were created by these 6 letters,' as it is written (*in the previously quoted verse*) understand likewise that two worlds were created by these six letters: the present one, and the world that is to come.

It was said: 'In the beginning.' What was there in the beginning? With one letter, God created the heavens and the earth, and he sealed them with fire (*lit.* 'from fire'). And what is this one letter whereby the heavens and earth were created? It is *Hê*, for it is said: 'These are the origins (or 'generations') of the heavens and the earth when they were created.' It should not be read 'when they were created' (*be-habra'am*), but 'by *Hê* did He create them' (*ba-hê' bara'am*). By means of this letter God created the heavens and the earth, the present world and the world to come. And He sealed them with the fire of Gehinnom, which is composed half from hail and half of fire. And the sinners were judged with burning hail, scorched with fire, and judged with fire that consumes them like hail. And upon them descend angels of destruction, keeping their souls within their bodies, as it is said 'their worm shall not die' (Isaiah 66).

Angels of destruction come upon them on certain days, and on others there descends upon them the angel of death, driving them from hail to fire, and from fire to hail, like a shepherd driving his flock from one mountain to another, as it is written 'Like sheep they are laid in *šeʾol*; death shall feed on them' (Psalm 49:14).

The angels of destruction come down and judge them in *Gehinnon* for 12 months. After the 12 months, they descend to *Ša'arêy Tzelmôt* (gates of the shadow of death).

At *Ša'arêy Tzelmôt*, they are judged for 12 months. After those 12 months, they must descend to the *Ša'arêy Môt* (Gates of Death).

At the gates of death, they are judged for 12 months. After the 12 months, they descend to *Ṭiṭ-hayawen* (Muddy clay).

In *Ṭiṭ-hayawen* they are judged for 12 months. After 12 months, they descend to *Beʾr Šaḥat* (Well/Pit of ruin).

In *Beʾr Šaḥat*, they are judged for 12 months. After those 12 months, they descend to *Abaddôn*.

In *Abaddôn*, they are judged for 12 months. At the end of those 12 months, they descend to the bottommost *Šeʾol* (Hell).

In bottommost *Šeʾol*, they are judged for 12 months, whereupon all the righteous ones behold them, and say to those whose mercy is upon all their actions: 'Let the trial begin' (?).

The Holy God then says: 'No, my soul is not yet calm, for they have destroyed my house and murdered my children, as it said: 'The fierce anger of YHWH shall not return, until He has done it, and until He has performed the intents of His heart.' (Jeremiah 30:24)

And following the 12 months, they must descend into *Arqa* ('earth') under the river which originates beneath the Throne of Glory, as it is said: 'Behold, the whirlwind of YHWH goeth forth with fury, a continuing whirlwind: it shall fall with pain upon the head of the wicked.' (Jer. 30:23). Whatever descends into *Arqa* does not reascend, as it is said: 'The Gods who did not take part in forming the heavens and the earth perish upon leaving *Arqa*'. This is the fifth abyss.

Above *Arqa* there is an abyss; above the abyss there is *Tohu*; above *Tohu* there is *Bohu*; above *Bohu* is a sea; above the sea are waters; above the waters there is a world (*Tébel*) wherein are mountains, hills and their inhabitants, as it is said: 'The mountains quake at him, and the hills melt.' (Nahum, 1:5). This is the sixth abyss. Above this world is another abyss; above the latter is *Tohu*; above *Tohu* is found *Bohu*; above *Bohu* a sea, above the sea there are waters. And above these is Ḥeled ('world, universe'), humankind, domestic animals, beasts of the field, sky and birds, fish of the sea, Torah, good actions, and fear of heaven, as it is said: 'Hear this, all ye people; give ear, all ye inhabitants of the world (*Ḥéled*)'. This is the 7th abyss.

Above *Ḥeled* there is a veil (*Wilôn*) which closes at evening and opens at dawn each day, renewing the work of creation daily.

Above the veil there are heavens (*Šamaym*), as it is said: 'he stretcheth out the heavens as a curtain' (Isaiah 40:22). Wherefore are they called heavens? Because the Holy Blessed One mingled fire and water, spreading out one with the other, creating the heavens therewith, as it is said: 'Mine hand also hath laid the foundation of the earth, and my right hand hath spanned the heavens'. Do not read 'heavens' (*šamaym*) but 'fire and water' (*'eš wa-maym*).

Above the heavens there is a sea, wherein there is wheat, new wine, and pure oil. When the Holy blessed One wishes to bless the earth, he does so periodically by bringing down dew and rain.

Above the sea there are waters, and below the waters a firmament (*Raqi'a*). Between the waters and the firmament hang the sun disk, the moon, the stars and the constellations, whence the whole world receives its light. They rule over every abyss and their light descends to the lowermost earth, as it is said: 'and God placed them...'.

Above the sea are waters. Between the waters and the sea, there are sparks of hail, lightning flashes ... and walls of fire encircling them, as it is said: 'the heaven, and the heavens of heavens'.

716- At the gates of the heavens of the north wind, archangels (*śarim*) are appointed. These are their names: **ALAL, ALYAL,**

ALKWS (or **ALBWS**), **ALLKWS**, **BL'YAL** (or **BL'AL**), **BSLAL** (or **BGLAL**). The entrances of the north wind are entrusted to them.

At the gates of the south wind, archangels are appointed. These are their names: **DWRNYAL**, **DRKYAL**, **HMWN**, **DWNAL** (or **HNNAL**), and **NANYAL** (or **HNYAL**).

The entrances of the south wind are entrusted thereto.

Over the gates of the east wind, archangels are appointed. Their names are: **DWRNYAL, GBRYAL, GDRYAL, 'DRWAL, MWDYAL, RHMYAL, HNYAL.**

The entrances of the east wind are entrusted to them.

At the gates of the west wind, archangels are appointed. They are: **AL SYN** (or **ALWT, ALYNN**), **SWQYAL, ZNSYAL, BHYAL, BQTMYAL** (**BHTMYAL**), **TRPNYAL** (or **KRPNYAL, KWRPLYAL**).

The entrances of the west wind are entrusted thereto.

717- Above the firmament (*raqi'a*) there are heavens whereon are affixed the sun, the moon, and the constellations. The edges of the firmament resemble a vault. The sun, moon, the stars, constellations, and the edges of the firmament govern every abyss. Their light descends to the lowermost earth (*Aretz ha-tahtonā*), as it is said: 'And God set them in the firmament of the heavens.'

Over the gates of the north wind of the firmament, archangels are appointed. These are their names: **TWAL** (**TYAL**), **YD'AL, YNAL, NNAL, HLQWS** (**HLQWM**), **HNNAL.**

The entrances of the north wind are entrusted to them.

At the gates of the south wind, archangels are appointed. They are: **KLAH** (**BLAH**), **BHLYAL, KLBYAL, SWAL** (**LYAL**), **YLYAL, NQRYAL** (**ZRQRYAL, YWQRYAL**). The entrances of the south wind are entrusted thereunto.

Over the gates of the east wind, archangels are appointed. They are: **MSYM, KRMYAL** (or **KRMWAL**).

Over the gates of the west wind, archangels are appointed. They are: **QWRYAL, PDAL, SNDKYAL** (or **SDNYAL**), **'NYAL, 'NNAL, 'NYAL, AL, AL.**

It is sealed with a ring. **AHYH AŠR AHYH**[9]. Why is it sealed thus? For had He not sealed it with His seal, each creature would have

---

9   The context suggests "The ring *of* AHYH...," but this is not grammatically possible, as 'ring' lacks the required case ending.

been unable to understand His letters as a result of the consuming fire. And whoever would not understand His letters would be immediately overcome by fire. Therefore He smothered it with His letters and sealed it with His seal.

Thus it was said: 'in the beginning'. What happened in the beginning? First he created the heaven and the earth; He set abodes and the abysses issuing thence, He formed 7 abodes above, corresponding to 7 abysses below.

He stretched the heavens above, and mirroring them founded the earth (*adamā*) below; He let out the storm clouds (*Šaḥaqim*) above and mirroring them founded dry land (*Yabašā*) below; He fixed an abode (*Maʿôn*) above and mirroring it He established the earth (*Arqa*) below; He stretched out an abode (*Zebul*) above and mirroring it founded the world (*Tebel*) below; He stretched out ʿArabot above, and mirroring it earth (*Aretz*) below; He let out His throne above and mirroring it, stretched a part of His glory below. These are the works of the 1st day.

On the 2nd day He parted the waters. He placed some of them below, and some above, as it is said: 'And God made the firmament and cleaved the waters'.

The 3rd day He gathered the waters in one place, showed forth dry land, and called it 'earth' (*Aretz*). And He brought forth trees from it, and herbs, all species of seeds, trees and fruit, all species of saplings with branches and fruit, as it is said: 'Let the earth bring forth grass, the herb yielding seed after his kind.'

On the 4th He created the luminaries to distinguish the day from night. He set the sun to rule the day and the moon and stars the night, as it is said: 'God created the two luminaries.'

The 5th day, He created fish and all the aquatic reptiles, and the bird that flies above the face of the earth, as it is said: 'Let the waters swarm with swarms of living creatures, and let birds fly above the earth.' (Genesis 1:20)

On the 6th he created domestic, wild animals, and insects, as is said: 'Let the earth bring forth living souls after their kind.' After all this, he created man to rule over all of them.

And he established his hosts, commanding them to serve him, and placed a great angel at their head. Then the tempest and the storm encircled all of them. Those who exclaimed 'holy' and those who said 'blessed' arranged themselves in a circle, as it is said: 'the earth is abundant with his praise'.

This is the lower abyss. And above the abyss there is *Tohu*; above *Tohu*, *Bohu*; above *Bohu* there is a sea; above the sea, waters; above the waters, a desert (*haraba*), and in the desert are rivers, and the furrows of the abyss, as it is said: 'I will change the rivers into desert'.

This is the 3rd abyss. Above the desert there is an abyss; above the abyss, *Tohu*; above *Tohu*, *Bohu*; above *Bohu* there is a sea; above the sea, waters.

And upon the waters there is dry land, and upon the dry land there are oceans, rivers and every body of water, as it is said: 'The sea is his, and he made it: and his hands formed the dry land.' (Psalm 95:5)

This is the 4th abyss. Above the dry land there is an abyss; above the abyss there is *Tohu*; above *Tohu*, *Bohu*; above *Bohu* there is a sea; above the sea, waters; above the waters are more waters, and upon them there is *Arqa*, and on *Arqa* there are: the lower *Še'ol*, *Abaddôn*, *Be'eršahat*, *Ṭiṭ-hayawen*, *Ša'arê Môt*, *Ša'arê Tzalmôt*, and *Gehinnôm*.

As for the sinners who are in them, angels of destruction are appointed thereto.

The highest division is the bottommost *She'ol*, its depth is 300 years long.

The 2nd division is *Abaddôn*; its depth is 300 years long.

The 3rd division is *Be'eršahat*, its depth is 300 years long.

The 4th division is *Ṭiṭ-hayawen*; its depth is 300 years long

The fifth division is *Ša'arê Môt*; its depth is 300 years long

The 6th division is *Ša'arê Tzalmôt*; its depth is 300 years long

The 7th division is *Gehinnôm*; its depth is 300 years long.

The fire of bottommost *Še'ol* is 61 times stronger than the fire of *Abaddôn*; the fire of *Abaddôn* is 61 times stronger than the fire of *Be'eršahat*; the fire of *Be'ershahat* is 61 times stronger than the fire of *Ṭiṭ-hayawen*; the fire of *Ṭiṭ-hayawen* is 61 times stronger than the fire of *Ša'arê Môt*. The fire of *Ša'arê Môt* is 61 times stronger than the fire of *Ša'arê Tzalmôt*; the fire of *Ša'arê Tzalmôt* is 61 times stronger than the fire of *Gehinnôm*.

And **ARYAL** (or **KGBYAL**) is at the head of those archangels who praise, sing, and laud with sweet songs from their throat. He makes a way through them and opens up inroads for them. Each (archangel) says unto the other: 'what shall we do?' A radiant angel teaches them to set up ladders whereby they ascend and descend, that is, by ascending they speak praise, and by descending they bestow peace on the world.

The length of the world is 508 (or 502) years long, and its width is 518 years. It is circular and a great sea encircles it completely. The whole forms a vault, and it stands wholly erect. The whole world stands upon the fin of Leviathan. And Leviathan sits in subterranean waters, in the waters of pure fish, in the midst of the sea.

The subterranean waters are upon the waters of creation, like a small fountain at the edge of the sea; and the waters of creation stand upon the waters of creation, (again) like a small fountain at the edge of the sea. And the ocean stands upon the weeping waters like a small fountainhead at the edge of the sea.

Why are they called 'weeping waters'? For when the Holy Blessed One divided the waters, he took one part of them and placed it above, and the other part he set below. The waters which are set below are agitated and wail, shout and cry out: 'We are unworthy of being near the One who formed us.' And what do they do? They sallied forth and cleaved the abysses seeking to ascend to the heights, until the Holy Blessed One rebuked them and drove them back beneath his feet, as it is said: 'Thus saith YHWH, which maketh a way in the sea, and a path in the mighty waters' (Isaiah 43:16), and after: 'YHWH on high is mightier than the noise of many waters, yea, than the mighty waves of the sea.' (Psalm 93:4). Do not read 'waves' (*mšbry*) but 'from the voice of song', that the waters shall exclaim. Then the higher waters shall beseech and proclaim: 'YHWH on high is mightier'. And this is the reason why they are called 'weeping waters.'

The weeping waters are suspended and stand above the lowermost earth (*Aretz ha-taḥtonā*); the lowermost earth is sprawled over the waters; the waters stand upon pillars of *Ḥashmal*; the pillars of *Ḥashmal* stand upon mountains of hail; the mountains of hail stand upon treasuries of snow; the treasuries of snow stand upon the waters, and the waters over the fire, and these stand over the abyss.

And the abyss stands upon *Tohu*. *Tohu* stands upon *Bohu*; and

Bohu stands upon the wind. The wind hangs from the storm and is bound to the vault of *Adamā*.

Adamā hangs from the storm (*Sa'arah*) and is bound to the vault of the desert (*Ḥarabā*).

Ḥarabā hangs from the storm and is bound to the vault of *Yabašā* (dry land).

Yabašā is suspended from the storm and is bound to the vault of *Arqa*.

Arqa hangs from the storm and is bound to the vault of the world (*Tebel*)

Tebel hangs from the storm and is bound to the vault of *Ḥeled*.

Ḥeled hangs from the storm and is bound to the vault of *Šamaym*.

Šamaym hangs from the storm and is bound to the vault of *Raqi'a*.

Raqi'a hangs from the storm and is bound to the vault of *Šaḥaqim*.

Šaḥaqim hangs from the storm and is bound to the vault of *Makôn*.

Makôn hangs from the storm and is bound to the vault of *Ma'ôn*.

Ma'ôn hangs from the storm and is bound to the vault of *Zebul*.

Zebul hangs from the storm and is bound to the vault of *'Arabôt*.

'Arabôt hangs from the storm and is bound to the mighty arm of the Holy Blessed One, as it is said: 'The pillars of heaven tremble and are astonished at his reproof.' It is also said: 'O YHWH, how manifold are thy works! In wisdom hast thou made them all.'

Then the fire and waters encircle the lowermost earth; and then the tempest and storm encircle the fire and waters. Afterward, the tempest and storm encircle those who make a great tumult. These are then encircled by the Kerubim who fly about; then the Kerubim are encircled by the image of the *Ḥayot*; then those bearing the image of the *Ḥayot* are encircled by those who go forth and return; then those who say 'holy' and 'blessed' encircle those who go forth and return.

And in the lowermost earth are the *Ḥayôt Ha-qodeš* and the Throne of glory. The latter is the footstool of the Lord (*Adôn*) of the whole earth, as it is said: 'The heaven is my throne, and the earth is my footstool'; and further it is said: 'Now as I beheld the living creatures (*Hayot*), behold one wheel (*Ofan*) upon the earth...' (Ezekiel, 1:15).

And as His Shekinah is found on high, so she is likewise found below, as it is said: and the name of the city from that day shall be, YHWH is there.'

18,000 worlds encircle her, as it is said: 'It was roundabout 18,000'; 4500 at the north wind, 4500 at the south wind, 4500 at the west wind, and 4500 at the eastern wind, totalling 18000 worlds all around.

The world of the north wind is laden with exultation, glory, strength and power, praise and melody.

The world of the south wind is laden with exultation, glory, strength and power, praise and melody. It is also full of splendour, majesty, joy, honour, pride and grandeur.

The world of the east wind is replete with holiness and purity, strength and righteousness, victory and power.

As for the world of the west wind, it is full of beauty and wreath (sic), crown and kingdom, and a voice of pristine silence. And they are circumscribed by fire and water. After the fire and water are: ṬHRYAL, NWRYAL, and KGBYAL.

The 18 (sic) worlds are then compassed by fire and water; these are then encircled by the tempest and the storm. The tempest and storm are then encircled by quaking and trembling; these are in turn encircled by terror and fear; then thunder and bolts of lightning encircle the terror and fear; the wings of the wind encircle the thunder and lightning bolts; the wings of the wind are encircled by rivers of fire; these are in turn encircled by the rivers of the sea, rivers of waters then encircle the rivers of the ocean.

Past the rivers of water there is naught but endless darkness, without number, measure or nature, ineffable, as it is said: 'He made darkness his secret place; his pavilion round about him.' (Psalm 18:11)

Those who encircle these are: NWRYAL, NWRYAL, GBRYAL. The entrances of the east wind are entrusted to them.

Over the gates of the west wind archangels are appointed. Their names are: QRYAI, PDAL, SKNYAL, 'NAL, 'NYAL. The entrances of the west wind are entrusted to them.

Above Raqia is found Šaḥaqim, wherein are found treasuries of snow, hail, dew, manna, and the spices of the resurrection of the dead, as it is said: 'and on the clouds (*šaḥaqim*) in his majesty' (Deuteronomy 43:26).

Over the gates of *Šaḥaqim*, toward the north wind, archangels are appointed. And these are their names: **PNAL, PNYAL, RPAL, RMYAL, DRMYAL.** The entrances of the north wind are entrusted to them.

Over the gates of the south wind archangels are appointed. And their names are: **PRWAL, ṢRYAL, QNYAL, ŠSTNYAL, ŠM'YAL, ŠM'AL.** The entrances of the south wind are entrusted thereto.

Over the gates of the east wind archangels are appointed. Their names are: **ṢDQYAL QDYŠAL, TYRṬAL, TRNYAL, TWRT.** The entrances of the east wind are entrusted thereto.

Over the gates of the west wind archangels are appointed. Their names are: **ṬWRNYAL, QRNYAL, RYNYAL, MLṬYAL, PLṬYAL.** The entrances of the west wind are entrusted thereto.

Above *Šaḥaqim* is found *Makôn*, wherein a sanctuary was built, an altar of incense, and an altar of sacrifice. And **MYKAL**, the great archangel, stands and burns incense on the altar, and presents an offering on the altar of sacrifice, as it is said: 'in the place (*makôn*), O YHWH, which thou hast made for thee to dwell in, in the Sanctuary, O YHWH, which thy hands have established.' (Exodus 15:17)

Over the gates of *Makôn*, toward the north wind, archangels are appointed. These are their names: **RḤWMYAL, ḤNWNYAL, BHYAL, ŠRPYAL, MSYAL, ŠRAL.** The entrances of the north wind are entrusted to them.

Over the gates of the south wind archangels are appointed. These are their names: **ṬHWRYAL, MḤNYAL, GDYAL, ḤWŠYAL, 'NNAL, QŠYAL.** The entrances of the south wind are entrusted thereto.

Over the gates of the east wind archangels are appointed. Their names are: **ṬRPYAL, BHLYAL, BGGAL, RMMAL, QLBS** (or **QLBM**), **AṬRWN** (or **ASRWN**). The entrances of the east wind are entrusted thereto.

Over the gates of the west wind archangels are appointed. These are their names: **ALMHQNAL, ASTQNAL, LWBQYS, SWMKS, YHLA.** The entrances of the west wind are entrusted thereto.

Above *Makôn* is found *Ma'ôn*, wherein are angels and legions and the entire host of the firmament, as it is said: 'The eternal God (*elohê qédem*) is thy refuge (*me'ônā*)' (Deut. 33:27, *also read as* 'to the dwelling of the former Gods')

Over the gates of *Ma'ôn*, toward the north wind, archangels are appointed. These are their names: **AHYAL, ANYAL, HZQYAL, MDGPYAL** (or **MDGBYAL**), **ŠTPYAL, MTNNAL**. The entrances of the north wind are entrusted to them.

Over the gates of the south wind, archangels are appointed. These are their names: **KBRYAL** (or **NKBDYAL**), **NPLYAL, QDŠYAL, HWDRYAL, NHMYAL, MLKYAL**. The entrances of the south wind are entrusted thereto.

Over the gates of the east wind archangels are appointed. Their names are: **ŠMŠYAL, BRQYAL, YR'SYAL, TDRYAL, ŠRPYAL, YHLQ** (or **YHNQ**), **RBA**. The entrances of the east wind are entrusted thereto.

Over the gates of the west wind archangels are appointed. These are their names: **ANHAL, PLLAL, PLLAL, ṢWRṬQ**[10] (*Tzurṭaq*), **ŠM QDWŠ, ṬYŠPH, PYLLAL KAL ŠM HŠM**.

Above *Ma'on* is *Zebul*, whereof it is said: 'Look down from heaven, and behold from the habitation (*zebul*) of thy holiness and thy glory' (Isaiah 63:15). Above *Zebul* is found *'Arabôt*, as it is said: 'Sing unto God, sing praises to his name: extol him that rideth upon the clouds (*rokeb ba-'arabôt*)' (Psalm 68:4). In *'Arabôt* is found justice, charity, judgment, treasuries of life, of blessing and peace, and the souls of the righteous ones, and the dew wherewith the Holy Blessed One revives the bodies of the dead for the future times, as it is said: 'for thy dew is as the dew of herbs, and the earth...' (Isaiah 26:19)

The arches of the bow sit upon *'Arabôt*, high and exalted with thousands of myriads of measures; they stand before the 'Irin and Qadišin ('watchers and holy ones'). Above them are the wheels of the Ofanim, sat upon the bow. High and exalted with thousands of myriads of measures; they stand before the Śerafim, the Ofanim, and the legions. Above them are the legs of the *Hayyot*, set upon the wheels of the Ofanim. High and exalted with thousands of myriads of measures, they stand before the great archangels.

And the upper parts (*lit.* 'shells') of the bow rest upon the

---

10 This is an important name of power, called the 'Great Seal' in the Hekaloth Rabbati, and used extensively in Jewish magic

heads of the *Ḥayot*, whence emanate rays of splendour. And *Raqi'a* is resembles an awesome speculum, spread out over the rays of splendour. High and exalted with thousands of myriads of measures; it stands before the princes (*or* 'thousands', ALPY) of *šin'ān*. Above it is *Makôn*, and a refulgent vision, and it sits upon the awesome speculum. High and exalted with thousands of myriads of measures <as it is said>: The chariot of God is of myriads, even thousands...' (Psalm 68:17)

Above it is *Ma'ôn*, whose likeness is tremendous. It rests upon the refulgent vision, and it exalted with thousands of myriads of measures; it stands before the rays of splendour, and its carriage is glory. Above it is a sapphire throne, resting upon the tremendous vision. Lofty, exalted and immeasurable; exceedingly strong and mighty.

Above it is the throne of glory, resting atop a sapphire stone. It is lofty, exalted and immeasurable. It is (as) the Lord of the whole world, and His glory rests upon it, as it is said: 'and I saw YHWH seated upon a lofty and exalted throne' (Isaiah 6:1). It is furthermore said: 'and there was under his feet as it were a paved work of a sapphire stone.' (Exodus 24:10). And the entire world hangs from His mighty arm like a talisman, as is said: 'and beneath His feet....,' and further said: 'and underneath are the everlasting arms' (Deuteronomy 33:27). The splendour of sapphire and emerald encircles it, concealing it from the eye, as it is said:

The throne is encompassed by shimmering sapphire, and emerald which conceal it from view, as it is said: 'No eye shall see me' (Job 24:15) <and> 'For I will publish the name of YHWH: ascribe ye greatness unto our God'. (Deut. 32:3).

About the Author

J. P. Feliciano (b. 1982) is the Praemonstrator of the Horus-Hathor temple (Order of the Golden Dawn) in Montreal, Canada. He also heads the Canadian lodge of the Hermetic Federation, an order that explores Greco-Egyptian magic. He has written for the *Journal of the Western Mystery Tradition*, *The Hermetic Tablet*, and *A Silver Sun and Inky Clouds: A Devotional for Djehuty and Set*.

He began his esoteric journey at the age of 13 after stumbling across the occult section of his local library. He remained a solitary practitioner until the age of 22 when he was initiated into the Golden Dawn, subsequently making forays into other fields, such as Hoodoo & Martinism. His current practices & research revolve around the Golden Dawn, the Greek Magical Papyri, and Jewish mysticism.

AS WITHIN, SO WITHOUT

A GOLDEN DAWN PERSPECTIVE ON THE RELATIONSHIP BETWEEN DIVINITY AND HUMANITY

by Chic Cicero and S. Tabatha Cicero

"For the True Order of the Rose Cross descendeth into the depths, and ascendeth into the heights—even unto the Throne of God Himself, and includeth even Archangels, Angels and Spirits."

— From the Adeptus Minor Ceremony[1]

An essential feature of magical work involves the active invocation of Deities, Angels, Archangels, and other Spiritual Entities. Every aspect of the magical work of a Golden Dawn magician is intricately associated with: (1) the idea of a transcendent, ineffable Deity or the highest concept of Divinity, and (2) the idea that between the world of humans and the Absolute Unity of God exists a myriad of Spiritual Entities. More often than not, the entities that magicians work with are Angels and Archangels. The word *angel* comes from the Greek *angelos*, which is itself a translation of the Hebrew word *melakh*, meaning "messenger." Angels have been described as "messengers of the soul." A more precise definition from Golden Dawn scholar and G.H. Chief Adam P. Forrest states that an Angel is "an intermediate Intelligence between the human and the One in the Great Chain of Being."[2]

The magician is also part of this "Great Chain of Being," or divine hierarchy headed by the Ultimate Divinity. In our tradition Initiates follow a strict hierarchical order when invoking Spiritual Beings.

1 Regardie, *The Golden Dawn*, 303.
2 Forrest, "This Holy Invisible Companionship," *The Golden Dawn Journal: Book Two: Qabalah: Theory and Magic*, 188.

Godnames are called upon before any lesser aspects of Divinity or celestial Deities. Then Archangels, Angels, and other Intelligences are invoked. The magician works primarily with Archangels and Angels as "divine intermediates" in both directions of the hierarchical ranks, requesting them to command the lesser Spirits, Rulers, and Elementals to carry out the goal of the magical working.

The mere existence of Spiritual Entities has always been a matter of great debate among the general public, especially in today's secular world. Golden Dawn magicians rarely if ever question whether God, the Gods, Archangels, Angels, and Spirits exist, because our practice depends upon establishing a personal, working relationship with Divine Beings. It would certainly be difficult to perform an invocation of the God Thoth or a consecration of a talisman dedicated to the Archangel Raphael if you doubted the reality of these entities! For us, the truth of these Spiritual Beings is a given. Where magicians sometimes disagree is on the exact nature of Gods, Angels, and Spirits. The crux of the argument often lies between two stubborn, rival viewpoints: those who take an absolutist medieval view of the Spiritual Hierarchies, and those who take a completely unyielding psychological perspective. The former sees Deities, Angels, and Spirits as entirely separate from human beings, while the latter views them exclusively as denizens of the human psyche. Do these entities dwell amidst the empyrean realms beyond us, or are they simply archetypes and mental structures completely contained within the confines of our minds? Do these forces reside only within the Heavens above, or are they only found within the consciousness of man? Is there no balance to be struck between these perspectives? Or, as the Golden Dawn teaches, is there a third scenario? A middle way between these two opposing forces?

Within the teachings of the Second Order there is a paper described by Israel Regardie as a "supremely important document." This manuscript, entitled "The Microcosm—Man," contains fundamental information required to perform Golden Dawn magic. The knowledge it encompasses provides the key for turning over the engine to all manner of the Order's work. It touches upon everything from magical correspondences of the elements, planets, and Sephiroth to the Four Qabalistic Worlds, to astral work, visualization, energized will power, vibration, the health of the human aura, Divine Consciousness, and the Higher Self. But the most essential aspect of this paper is that it gives a full explanation of the Order's teachings on the connection between two opposite concepts—Microcosm and Macrocosm—how they relate to each other, and how knowledge of this relationship is used in Golden Dawn magic.

The Macrocosm is the "Greater Universe" or the totality of all that exists within the Divine Cosmos. The Microcosm or "Lesser Universe" is man, or humankind, the totality of the human individual, and a miniature version of the Greater Universe. These two comprise a unified dyad: Creator and creation, Divinity and humanity. To be more precise, the Microcosm refers to both the internal human soul and its astral outer shell—the aura. Often called the "sphere of sensation," the aura itself is a mirror of the physical body. The Order teaches that through understanding the Greater Universe, one can understand the Lesser Universe and vice-versa, for both are inherently and intimately linked. The Divine World of Spirit and the physical world of matter are two halves of a symbiotic whole, therefore everything that exists out in the Greater Universe also exists within the soul and psyche of humanity. And because our Divine Universe is comprised of various connected realms, such as the material and the spiritual, whatever affects one will affect the others. *As above, so below.*

We hold that the Order document referenced above fully answers the questions raised here. Spiritual Entities exist in both the Greater *and* Lesser Universes, and magical work on lower levels will echo and reverberate on higher ones because they are bound together. The Middle Path of Balance seems to be the natural choice here. Yet there will certainly be some who disagree and fall on one side of the argument or the other. So here we will take a closer look at these "two contending forces."

Separation: So Without

In many ancient civilizations religion and magic shared a fundamental origin and unity. One of the differences between the magical traditions of the East and the West is this: within the Western world, a split eventually developed between the concepts of "magic" and "religion," caused by the ascendancy of the Christian faith. No such grand divorce occurred in the faiths of the East. In reality there was no real split in terms of method. The prayers and miracles of Christian believers were essentially the same as the invocations and magical feats of ancient pagan worshipers. Only the Deity names and words were changed to be acceptable to the new faith. As a result, the origins of medieval magic are linked with the Christianization of the Roman Empire.

Fueled by the inherent dualism of influential religions such as Zoroastrianism, combined with a rejection of the all-too-human and temperamental gods of the Romans, early Christianity battled its own internal impulses and the various sects that espoused them, until at length one faction defeated the others. By the 4th century C.E., one sect completed its grip on power. This new church demonized the other Mediterranean faiths, resulting in the separation between medieval and ancient perceptions of magic. It was forbidden to worship any Deities other than the Judeo-Christian God. All other Gods were seen as demonic and the invocation of Deities and Spirits, the practice at the core of ancient magic, was branded idolatrous and feared. Magic of all stripes became taboo. The divorce papers were signed, so to speak.

The 12th and 13th centuries saw major intellectual and in-stitutional developments. First was the reintroduction of ancient Roman jurisprudence, the systemization of law, and the expansion of legal institutions. Next came the intellectual annexation of ancient Greek, Islamic, and medieval Jewish philosophical reflection, and the formation of institutions that examined such things as the reality and the morality of magic. The study of magic escalated in scholarly circles of the High Middle Ages, along with great concern for its repercussions. Clerical and secular authorities alike viewed magic as consorting with demons and other banned heretical practices. Frightful new legal measures, such as the inquisitional method of investigation and judicial torture, made the discovery, indictment, and punishment of magic much simpler and heinously effective.[3]

3 Collins, 410–422.

The period dating from the 14th through 16th centuries brought a new discussion as to how magic was viewed, at least by scholars, humanists, philosophers, and magicians—*magic as a natural phenomenon*. The Aristotelian view of the universe, prevalent at the time, theorized that the earth was at the center of a three-fold cosmos. Beyond the earth was the heavenly realm of God and the Angelic powers. Between heaven and earth was the area of the celestial spheres—the stars, planets, and luminaries of the Sun and Moon. The heavenly powers were thought to control the motions of the planetary spheres, which, in turn, influenced the earth below. The forces of the heavenly realm were considered the domain of the church alone. But the powers of the celestial spheres and their influence upon the earth were considered part of the natural world.[4]

FIGURE 1: Woodcut illustration from an edition
of Pliny the Elder's *Naturalis Historia*, (1582).

Marsilio Ficino (1433-1499), often called the Father of the Renaissance, translated the *Corpus Hermeticum*, the ancient wisdom

4 Cicero, *The Essential Golden Dawn*, 75-77.

texts attributed to Hermes Trismegistus. He was drawn to the magical elements contained within these texts and began to experiment with them. Ficino undoubtedly understood the connection between God, Spiritual Entities, and the human soul:

> All the Intelligences, whether They are Those of the highest rank and superior to the Souls, or Lower and part of the Souls, are so interconnected that, beginning with God who is Their Head, they proceed in a long and uninterrupted Chain, and all the higher ones shed Their rays down on the lower.[5]

But such thinking could be perilous. Realizing that he was treading on dangerous ground as far as the church was concerned, Ficino very carefully and emphatically stated that the magic that he was concerned with was *natural magic* and not *angelic* or *daimonic magic*. Whether or not he truly believed that the two fields were entirely separate was not as important as the fact that the church thought it so and tolerated its existence.

> The work that he did we should regard today as the beginnings of simple psychotherapy and quite harmless. But Ficino realized that his researches could possibly be misunderstood and condemned as the conjuration of spirits. [...] The powers of heaven were definitely the elusive prerogative of the church and jealously guarded. However, the powers of the planetary spheres upon the things of earth was another matter, partaking entirely of the natural world. Hence Ficino's emphasis on *natural* magic. It was held that the seven visible planetary bodies that moved erratically against the stable backdrop of the fixed stars were representative of seven types of influence. It was therefore possible to regard things as under Solar, Lunar, Mercurial, Venusian, Martian, Jovian, or Saturnian influence—or a mixture of all or any.[6]

---

5 Forrest quoting Ficino, "This Holy Invisible Companionship," *The Golden Dawn Journal: Book Two: Qabalah: Theory and Magic*, 188.
6 Knight, 89-90.

With the bifurcation of magic into two sections, one natural and the other supernatural, Western Magic was divided against itself once again. Natural magic was tolerated somewhat by the church, even as the infamous witch-hunts were putting people to death all over Europe. Beginning in the 16th century, scholars debated the difference between religion and magic: according to their findings, the fundamental component of religion is that it supplicates God or the Gods, and the primary feature of magic is that it coerces Spiritual Beings.[7] Of course, this way of differentiating religion from magic seems ridiculous to practicing magicians today, and likely wouldn't have made much sense to ordinarily people in the Middle Ages and the early Renaissance either. However, it does touch upon two methods, supplication and coercion, which were both used in the magical practices of the time.

At this time there was a glut of unemployed and semi-employed clerics. According to author Richard Kieckhefer, "many were ordained to lower orders and continued to claim the privileges of clergy although they had no clerical employment."[8] Clerics and unemployed clergymen were responsible for writing the majority of the magical grimoires from this period. Many of these books crisscrossed the church-sanctioned line of demarcation between natural and angelic/demonic magic. Nevertheless, the world-view in which they existed was one of separation between God and nature.

Medieval magicians employed the trappings of the clerical profession they knew well: liturgical prayers, magical gestures, methods of purification, and the like. They appealed to God and Angels to aid their rites. But their interactions with lower spirits and demons was often dominated by coercion, since they viewed these entities as adversarial "fallen spirits." The rituals they created sometimes contain elements that are transactional in nature: each party gives something and gets something in return. It was in essence a kind of age-old tradition of contract law for spirits. Kieckhefer describes such a transaction:

> The Munich manual has the necromancer invoking the
> spirits at a crossroads with "the sacrifice of a white cock,"

7 Kieckhefer, *Magic in the Middle Ages,* 14-15.
8 Ibid., 154.

which he beseeches them to accept. Another experiment requires taking a captive hoopoe along to the place of conjuration; at one stage in the proceedings the demons will ask for this bird, and when they have sworn to obey the necromancer he will give it to them.[9]

This type of "transaction" is different from a devotional oblation. Making offerings to one's patron God, Gods, or favored Spirits has been an important part of religious practice since time immemorial. Throughout the world people offer all manner of gifts to Deities and other Spiritual Beings out of love, fervent worship, or in hope of specific benefits or circumstances. Such entities are often treated as beloved ancestors or as respected teachers who have a special relationship with their devotees. But the example cited in the Munich manual feels more like a business agreement between two interested parties who each get sometime of value out of the arrangement.

The magicians of this era did not view demons as having any internal, psychological connection with the soul of the magician. A person could be possessed by a demon, or could fall under the influence of a demon, but demons were not thought to be part of the mental structure of a human being. The same was true of Angels and Archangels. There is nothing unusual about this approach, and in fact many magicians and ordinary folk in the ancient world undoubtedly thought along the same lines.

It's All in Your Head

For centuries the power of organized religion has been used to bludgeon people into blind obedience to one orthodox dogma or another. But just as every reaction results in an equal and opposite reaction, there have always been pockets of resistance to established doctrines. In more recent times when churches began to lose their political and social power, aided in no small way by advancements in science, many have chosen to eschew religion altogether. As a result, more people now claim to be atheists than at any other time in human history. For atheists, there is no God, Gods, Angels, Spirits, or magic, and those who believe in such things are basically delusional. The

9 Ibid., 162.

impulse to attribute *all* supernatural beings as belonging exclusively to the confines of the human mind is nothing new. "It's all in your head" has been used to denigrate the spiritual experience of millions past and present. By its very nature, mystical experience is ethereal and personal; it is not easily quantified using the traditional methods of science. So, as science gained ascendancy, a new science emerged to explain the spiritual world—modern psychology.

The publication of William Battie's *Treatise on Madness* in 1758 foreshadowed the birth of modern psychology, the true beginnings of which date to the mid-19th century experiments of Hermann von Helmholts and Wilhelm Wundt. Psychology emerged as an empirical, accepted science in the 19th century, but its two most notable figures arrived in the first half of the 20th century, Austrian psychologist Sigmund Freud (1856-1939) and his Swiss counterpart Carl Gustav Jung (1875-1961). Both were pioneers of psychotherapy or the treatment of mental disorders.

Freud developed the earliest form of psychotherapy, which he called *psychoanalysis*. He discovered that the corporeal symptoms of patients suffering from hysteria often disappeared after seemingly forgotten material was brought into the realm of consciousness. From this Freud conjectured one of the most fundamental theories—that within the human psyche there exists a powerful segment known as the *unconscious* which influences all of our actions, yet functions with material or content that cannot be recalled or remembered by normal processes.

Freud developed the theory that the conscious mind is only a small part of our composition, and our motivations are caused, for the most part, by factors that we are unaware of. Freud postulated that the psyche is divided into three distinct factions: the *id*, the *ego*, and the *super-ego*. According to Freud, the *id* is the division of the psyche that is completely unconscious and which functions as the origin of instinctual impulses and demands for instant satisfaction of primal needs. It is the reservoir of unconscious drives, ruled by the pleasure principle and instant gratification. The *ego* is that portion of the psyche which is conscious, most directly governs thought and behavior, and most concerned with outer reality. The ego mediates between the id, the super-ego, and the stipulations of reality or society. The *super-ego*, primarily unconscious, is that which is created by the internalization of moral standards from parents and society— it is the *conscience* and the ego ideal, a moralizing faculty, which monitors and censors the ego. Because of society, parental guidance, and peer pressure, humans experience a process of repression from the day of birth. Thus the id and the super-ego are usually in conflict in most people since, as Freud thought, repression was necessary in order for humanity to live within the bounds of civilization.

Freud's tools for exploring the human psyche included hypnosis, dream analysis and a new technique that he termed "free association." The goal of Freudian analysis was to release repressed memories, and provide an increase in self-knowledge that would release trapped energies and result in a more satisfying existence for the patient.

Freud appreciated his Jewish heritage and had an on-going interest in religion. He wrote several books on the topic including *Totem and Taboo* (1913), *The Future of an Illusion* (1927), *Civilization and Its Discontents* (1930), and *Moses and Monotheism* (1939). Nevertheless, he considered himself an atheist. His views on religion and spirituality were very clear, as he stated in his book *New Introductory Lectures on Psychoanalysis* (1933) where he writes "religion is an illusion and it derives its strength from its readiness to fit in with our instinctual wishful impulses" and in more damning terms in *The Future of an Illusion*, Freud wrote that "religion is comparable to a childhood neurosis."[10]

Through the influence of Freud and his peers, the clinical model of modern psychology methodically discarded any notion that the human soul was spiritual in nature. In other words, "It was all in your head." To many in the modern era, it doesn't matter if a person believes that sacred Gods and Angels are separate from human beings or whether these Holy Beings are connected to us via the human psyche. To medieval mages and modern magicians alike, secular society proclaims "a pox on both your houses!"

Analysis: As Within

The works of Swiss Psychologist C. G. Jung can be seen as part of the apex of the Occult Revival of the late 19th and early 20th century.

10 Cherry, "Sigmund Freud's Theories About Religion."

More than any other thinker of the modern age, Jung affected the manner in which esotericism, sometimes branded by its detractors as "rejected knowledge," found acceptance in scholarly discourse.

One early influence on Jung was French philosopher Lucien Lévy-Bruhl, who posited that humankind had developed two ways of thinking, one primitive, which was non-logical yet characterized by "participation," and the other modern, logical, and ruled by the laws of cause and effect. These seemingly separate and distinct mentalities proved to be more entangled than Lévy-Bruhl first imagined, however, and by the end of his life he concluded that both mentalities were universal to the human mind.[11]

Jung's work was heavily influenced by the concept of "two ways of thinking," as proposed in German Mesmerist circles, particularly the idea of two complementary avenues of consciousness associated with a dyad of opposites: night and day, light and dark, heart and mind, dream and reason, internal and external, symbolism and discursive language, nature and society, rational consciousness and collective unconscious.

> The psychology of Carl Gustav Jung was grounded in German Romantic mesmerism to a much larger extent than is usually appreciated, and he adopted an approach to history on Romantic and Idealist foundations. According to Jung's account, which has exerted an enormous influence on popular notions of 'esotericism' after World War II, a continuous spiritual tradition could be traced from Gnosis and Neoplatonism in late antiquity, via medieval alchemy to Renaissance traditions such as Paracelsianism, and from there to German Romantic mesmerism and, finally, modern Jungian psychology. Jung formed the centre of what has become a highly influential tradition of modern thought in which psychology is combined with a fascination for myth and symbolism, in deliberate reaction against the dominant trend of rationalization and disenchantment of the world.[12]

11 Hanegraaff, "The Globalization of Esotericism," *Correspondences 3*, 55-91.
12 Hanegraaff, *Western Esotericism: A Guide for the Perplexed*, 66-67.

It was also during this time period that the theory of evolution was becoming a dominant paradigm in scientific thought and shaking up the existing branches of knowledge, such as biology, geology, theology, and cultural studies. But it was closely mingled with the newly-emerging study of psychology, wherein ideas of the Divine Spirit "could easily be psychologized and thereby transformed into narratives about the evolution of the human spirit, or human consciousness as such."[13]

Jung's definition of the *psyche* included not only that which we call the soul but also the intellect, the spirit, and the totality of all psychic processes. The psyche is as real as the body is real, and all psychic phenomena are real, since the psyche is indistinguishable from its manifestations. The psyche expresses itself in images that are full of meaning and purpose—it creates reality every day. It has its own peculiar structure and form.

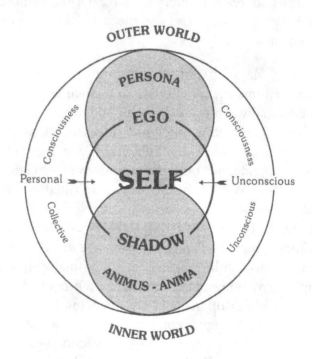

FIGURE 2: Jung's Model of the Psyche.

---

13 Ibid, 84.

For the psyche as it presents itself—as it is experienced by us—is inseparable from our physical being. But this by no means implies a biological 'dependency'. The psyche deserves to be taken as a phenomenon in its own right; there are no grounds at all for regarding it as a mere epiphenomenon, dependent though it may be on the functioning of the brain. One would be as little justified in regarding life as an epiphenomenon of the chemistry of carbon compounds.[14]

Jung employed Gnostic ideas to illustrate the objective of psychological self-knowledge as an "interior sun" or the process of inner illumination of the psyche by which human beings are able to reach a numinous, transpersonal spiritual reality. But the concepts and images of alchemy, with its emphasis on the transmutation from base matter into gold, or from darkness to light, was an ideal fit for expressing Jung's process of *individuation*, the method of self-discovery by which a person confronts archetypal images from the subconscious mind until at length he or she achieves a state of self-realization or wholeness.

What had once been veiled in occult jargon and symbolism, and thus viewed as superstition and nonsense by the public at large, was now expressed in such a manner that psychologists and other intellectuals sat up and took notice. Jung's exploration of psychology, in conjunction with his study of the paranormal, made him the crucial link between psychology and magic.

The difference between Freud's and Jung's approaches to psychology was primarily due to the fact that Jung viewed the human psyche as a whole organism, and Freud did not. Freud extrapolated a rather disorderly picture of the psyche wherein autonomous components of the mind battled for dominance. Jung saw the psyche as being complete in itself from birth, the various elements of which attempted to work harmoniously together—whose natural inclination was toward unity. While both men recognized two basic halves of the psyche (conscious and unconscious), Jung further divided the unconscious into two levels—personal and collective. And Jung's interest in the occult was one of the primary reasons for

14 Jacobi quoting Jung, 8-9.

his ultimate break with Freud.

Falling at the end of the 19th century, Jung's theories were perfectly timed to reach a new audience hungry for a modern approach to existential questions. The terminology of magic began to permeate psychological discourse. The gods and angels of magic were described by the science of mind as archetypes, while demons were converted into neuroses. But Jung also wrestled with the non-spiritual zeitgeist of the modern age and endeavored to transform psychology into a science of the *soul*. His work epitomized the need to reach beyond the dry labelings of science and find spiritual meaning so essential to human health and wellbeing. In the words of Petrarch: "For what, pray, will it profit to have known the nature of beasts, birds, fishes and snakes, but to be ignorant of, or to despise the nature of man— why we are born, whence we come and whither we go."[15]

Jung explored the depths of his own dreams and visions for what they had to teach him, and recorded the results in his *Red Book*. Unlike Freud, Jung was not prepared to consign spirituality to the dustbin—a sign hanging above Jung's office door read: *Avocatus Atque Non-Avocatus Deus Aderit,* "whether or not he is called, the God will be present." (Surprising to some, a good number of scientists also display a mystical side and a sense of awe at the workings of the universe.)

Jung's theories of individuation, the collective unconscious, and *synchronicity*—meaningful coincidences with no apparent causal relationship—would have a huge impact on influential author-magicians such as Israel Regardie.

The Third and Middle Way

It was Regardie's belief that magic was a forerunner of psychology, and could be regarded as a subdivision of the science of the mind. He sought to tear down the artificial walls that divided spirituality from psychology. Taking his cues from Jung, Regardie understood that the various schools of magic and their extensive teachings comprised an enormous body of ancient wisdom that had huge implications for modern psychology. His studies and ritual work in the Hermes Temple of the Stella Matutina confirmed this for him. According

---

15 Whitfield, 44.

to Regardie, the goal of both magic and psychotherapy is the well-being of the individual—his or her growth and health on every level: physical, mental, and psychological. Magic, however, also includes *spiritual* well-being. His book *The Middle Pillar*, published in 1938, gave step-by-step instructions on how to perform practical exercises of ceremonial magic. Going even further, Regardie reasoned that psychotherapists could use the techniques of magic, such as the Lesser Ritual of the Pentagram and the Middle Pillar Exercise of the Golden Dawn, in a clinical setting for the benefit of patients. He held that the ancient art of magic can give back to the modern science of psychology that which it has so unwisely neglected—a systematic practice for addressing the spiritual factor in humans, in a manner that is in accord with modern psychological principles. A third and middle way.

> If life is sorrow, then the only thing to do is to end this sorrowful existence by getting off the perpetually revolving wheel of existence. Life follows life, incarnation follows incarnation—and all of them spell anxiety and sorrow. For these sages, it was apparent that it might be millions of years before the masses of humanity would develop enough insight to be able to terminate the sorrowful cycle of existence. But for the illuminated individual who will apply himself to a specific psycho-spiritual discipline, escape might come aeons sooner than for the average member of mankind.
>
> This release, they learned, comes only through the achievement of a higher consciousness by the individual. Call it cosmic consciousness, the mystical experience, communion with God—all spell the same message— *release*, None may know it for another. Each man must himself attain *for himself* awareness of his own oneness with infinite life—the consciousness that a state of separateness exists only within his own mind.
>
> Not until man does recognize that he is himself a microcosm of the macrocosm, a reflection of the universe, a world within himself, ruled and governed by

his own divinity, can he escape from the wheel. It is the achievement of this one realization which all schools of mysticism, magic and various forms of occult teaching refer to as the Great Work.[16]

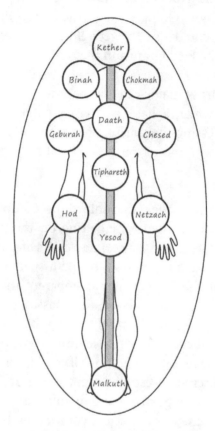

FIGURE 3: The Middle Pillar against the Human Body.

The third and middle way alludes to the Pillar of Mildness on the Tree of Life, also known as the Middle Pillar. It is that with reconciles and mediates between two opposite forces or positions. For the sake of this brief essay, it refers to the path of reconciliation between two opposing viewpoints: do Spiritual Entities exist completely outside of us, or do they exist only within our minds? It is our position that neither of these perspectives is correct, for each view is only half of the

16 Regardie, *The Middle Pillar*, xxv-xxvi.

AS WITHIN, SO WITHOUT

equation. The Truth lies in the balance between these two extremes in a panentheistic understanding that the Divine permeates and interpenetrates every part of the universe and also extends beyond space and time. The heavenly hosts are not artificially segregated from human beings like distant potentates. Likewise, visionary work and internal dialog with the Divine are not simply mental flights of fancy. Heaven and the human psyche are intimately connected mirrors of each other.

Some may assume that the modern Golden Dawn's outlook on this topic is not rooted in the historical record; that it developed out of Jung, Regardie, and other psychologists and magicians of their era. We contend that there is plenty of evidence for our views, dating at least back to the Gnostics, the Hermetics, and Middle Platonists, and continuing through the teachings of the medieval Qabalists and the renaissance philosophers.

Same as it Ever Was

Critics of the Golden Dawn system often claim that the psychological dimension of magic is purely a modern phenomenon, that the older traditions had no such internal dimension, that working with Spiritual Entities is simply a matter of give and take between completely independent but interested parties. Contract law for Spirits. Are they correct? Or is there any evidence stemming from the ancient world that supports the Golden Dawn's view of a third and middle way that straddles the external versus internal divide?

Ancient texts and scriptures do provide proof for the Middle Way. Gnosticism, in particular, points to the Sacred Source within. The origins of Gnostic Christianity place it inside Judaism, as a kind of apocalyptic reaction movement that had developed inside the Hebrew faith by the time Christianity emerged. It was also influenced by Middle Platonism.[17]

Gnosticism affirmed that direct, personal and absolute knowledge of the authentic truths of existence is accessible to human beings, and that the acquisition of such knowledge is the supreme achievement of human life. To the Gnostic, a person who fully achieved Gnosis

---

17 Erhman, 119.

165

was "no longer a Christian but a Christ."[18] It was only natural that Gnostics who held this view were not inclined to recognize the supreme authority of church, priest, or dogma. This spiritual outlook distinguishes Gnosticism from orthodox Christianity, which sought to silence it.

Some early Gnostic and Christian texts affirm the concept of the Sacred Within, such as the New Testament Gospel of Luke (17:20-21):

> And when he was demanded of the Pharisees, when the kingdom of God should come, he answered them and said, The kingdom of God cometh not with observation: Neither shall they say, Lo here! or, lo there! for, behold, *the kingdom of God is within you.*[19]

This parallels a section in the Gnostic Gospel of Thomas, which tells us:

> Jesus said, "If your leaders say to you, 'Look, the (Father's) kingdom is in the sky,' then the birds of the sky will precede you. If they say to you, 'It is in the sea,' then the fish will precede you. Rather, *the kingdom is within you and it is outside you.*[20]

The above passage clearly indicates what we have described as the middle way between external and internal Divinity in perfect equilibrium. Interestingly, the Gnostic Gospel of Thomas, which contains many of the sayings of Jesus in a basic and uncomplicated form, is now thought by many scholars to have been written prior to the canonical gospels, sometime around 50-70 C.E., and was composed even earlier than the Gospel of Mark.[21] The passage

---

18 Pagels, 134.
19 Italics are ours.
20 Patterson and Meyer. Italics are ours.
21 "Also concurring with Jenkins and Cameron, the members of the Jesus Seminar–Robert W. Funk, John Dominic Crossan, Burton Mack, Stevan L. Davies, Stephen J. Patterson, and John Kloppenborg–suggest that the "work is wholly independent of the New Testament gospels; most probably in existence before they were written. It should be dated AD 50-70." Remson, 14.

indicated also suggests a metaphysical interpretation of the Kingdom of Heaven as being contained within the human mind and body. This Kingdom is not confined to human consciousness, however. It is present everywhere. Moreover, the quest for internal self-knowledge is paramount to understanding the universal truths of Divinity. Gnostic belief holds that the exploration of human experience is concurrent with Divine reality. This approach was embraced by those in the ancient world who were influenced by Gnostic and Neoplatonic thought. Second century Christian apologist Justin Martyr described a conversation he had shortly before converting from Platonism to Christianity when he was asked:

> What affinity, then, is there between us and God? Is the soul also divine and immortal, and a part of that very regal mind? Speaking as a disciple of Plato, Justin answered without hesitation, "Certainly."[22]

This idea was also seen in the teachings of reputed Gnostic magician Simon Magus as reported by second-century theologian Hippolytus of Rome who wrote that Magus taught that every individual was a dwelling place for the Divine:

> man who is born of blood is (the aforesaid) habitation, and that in him dwells an infinite power which he affirms to be the root of the universe.[23]

Gnostic theologian Valentinus and his followers taught that *Anthropos* ("humanity") manifests divine life and divine revelation; and that *Anthropos* was the underlying nature of the "collective entity, the archetype, or spiritual essence, of human being" as opposed to the more mundane collective meaning of the term "humanity" as we have come to know it. Valentinus held that "when God revealed himself, He revealed himself in the form of Anthropos." Some Gnostics believed that

the primal father of the whole, the primal beginning,

---

22 Pagels, 122.
23 Coxe, 75.

and the primal incomprehensible, is called *Anthropos*...
and that is the great and abstruse mystery, namely, that
the power which is above all others, and contains all
others in its embrace, is called *Anthropos*[24] [para] For
this reason, these gnostics explained, the Savior called
himself "Son of Man" (that is, Son of *Anthropos*).[25]

Author Elaine Pagels states that many Gnostics would have agreed
in principle with 19th century psychologist Ludwig Feuerbach's
view that "theology is really anthropology." "For gnostics, exploring
the *psyche* became explicitly what it is for many people today
implicitly—a religious quest."[26] She affirms that Gnosticism shared
certain affinities with modern psychotheraputic methods for
exploring the self. "Both gnosticism and psychotherapy value, above
all, knowledge—the self-knowledge which is insight. They agree
that, lacking this, a person experiences the sense of being driven by
impulses he does not understand."[27]

Yet for all the similarities shared between Gnosticism and
psychotherapy, most modern-day psychotherapists "follow Freud in
refusing to attribute real existence to the figments of imagination.
They do not regard their attempt to discover what is within the
psyche as equivalent to discovering the secrets of the universe."[28]
This is where contemporary magicians are able to bridge the gap.

Gnosticism and psychotherapy also share an emphasis on the
symbolic use of language to describe and comprehend internal
qualities of spiritual experience. Valentinus taught that all of creation
originated from a vast "depth" or "abyss." Jung understood this as
representing the unconscious mind in the jargon of psychoanalysis.
He interpreted this creation story as a mythic account of the origin
of human consciousness.[29]

Pagels goes on to state that Gnosticism and psychotherapy share
another major premise in that both agree, counter to orthodox

24 Irenius, *Against the Heresies*, Quoted in Pagels, 122-123.
25 Pagels, 123.
26 Ibid. 123.
27 Ibid. 124.
28 Ibid. 134.
29 Ibid. 133.

Christianity, that the human psyche contains *within itself* the potential for liberation or destruction, as indicated by a saying attributed to Jesus in the Gospel of Thomas:

> When you come to know yourselves, then you will be known, and you will realize that you are the sons of the living Father.[30] [...] If you bring forth what is within you, what you bring forth will save you. If you do not bring forth what is within you, what you do not bring forth will destroy you.[31]

Those who resisted the divine impulse to gain self-knowledge were characterized by the Gnostics as being asleep, unconscious, drunk, or filled with darkness, just as the Hiereus warns the Neophyte in the Ceremony of the Zelator: "The foolish and rebellious gaze upon the face of the created World, and find therein nothing but terror and obscurity. It is to them the Terror of Darkness and they are as drunken men stumbling in the Darkness."[32] The Gospel of Thomas even describes what modern magicians know as the Dark Night of the Soul, a temporary period of depression that often occurs during the normal course of spiritual development wherein the student experiences a feeling of the loss of the presence of God. This difficult period must be endured before the student can advance to higher levels of spiritual growth:

> Jesus said, "Let him who seeks continue seeking until he finds. When he finds, he will become troubled. When he becomes troubled, he will be astonished, and he will rule over all things.[33]

The Gospel of Thomas rejects the idea that the coming of the Kingdom of God is an actual historical occurrence that will follow a predetermined chronological sequence of events. Once again the text points to an exalted state of consciousness:

---

30 Quoted in Pagels, 128.
31 Quoted in Pagels, 126.
32 Regardie, *The Golden Dawn*, 172.
33 Quoted in Pagels, 127.

[The Disciples] said to him, "Shall we, then, as children, enter the Kingdom?" Jesus said to them, "When you make the two one, and when you make the inside like the outside and the outside like the inside, and the above like the below, and when you make the male and the female one and the same ... Then you will enter [the Kingdom].[34]

Similar wording is found in the Gospel of Philip from the Nag Hammadi Library:

[The Lord] said, "I came to make the things below like the things above, and the things outside like those inside. *I came to unite them in one place."*[35]

These last passages evoke the well-known Hermetic Axiom from the Emerald Tablet of Hermes Trismegistus: "As Above, so Below." A rather lovely adaptation of this passage speaks to the heart of our argument: *"As above, so below, as within, so without, as the universe, so the soul..."*[36]

FIGURE 4: Hermes Mercurius Trismegistus from Pierre Mussard, Historia Deorum fatidicorum, Venice, 1675.

---

34 Quoted in Pagels, 129.
35 Robinson, 141. Italics are ours.
36 Simms, 120.

In line with this discussion, there is a beautiful passage in the Hermetic writings that echos the expanded visualization of the Lesser Pentagram Ritual given by Israel Regardie.[37]

> If then you do not make yourself equal to God, you cannot apprehend God; for like is known by like. Leap clear of all that is corporeal, and make yourself grown to a like expanse with that greatness which is beyond all measure; rise above all time and become eternal; then you will apprehend God. Think that for you too nothing is impossible; deem that you too are immortal, and that you are able to grasp all things in your thought, to know every craft and science; find your home in the haunts of every living creature; make yourself higher than all heights and lower than all depths; bring together in yourself all opposites of quality, heat and cold, dryness and fluidity; think that you are everywhere at once, on land, at sea, in heaven; think that you are not yet begotten, that you are in the womb, that you are young, that you are old, that you have died, that you are in the world beyond the grave; grasp in your thought all of this at once, all times and places, all substances and qualities and magnitudes together; then you can apprehend God.
>
> But if you shut up your soul in your body, and abase yourself, and say "I know nothing, I can do nothing; I am afraid of earth and sea, I cannot mount to heaven; I know not what I was, nor what I shall be," then what have you to do with God?[38]

Returning to the famous quotation from the Emerald Tablet that is most common to the ears of Golden Dawn magicians:

> True, without falsehood, certain and most true, that which is above is as that which is below, and that which is below is as that which is above, *for the performance of the miracles of the One Thing.*[39]

---

37 Regardie, *The Middle Pillar*, 54.
38 Copenhaver, 41-42.
39 Italics are ours.

Two opposing forces combining into a third which makes the system whole. The third and middle way. The recurring theme we are seeing here is that of a universal triptych; an unfolding of spiritual reality into a Divine Triune that is inherently and inarguably unified. While they can be separately *defined*, they cannot be separated in essence. Why three? Because three is the primary number of manifestation.[40] Three parameters are needed to determine the position of an object in physical space. Three lines form the triangle. Since ancient times the triangle's strength and stability has been used in architecture and engineering. It is the only lineal figure into which all surfaces can be reduced, because every other polygon can be divided into triangles by drawing lines from its angles to its center. This makes the triangle the first true polygon and the most rigid and predicable of the regular geometric figures: if you know the lengths of the three lines that comprise a triangle, you know what the angles must be; and if you know what two of the angles are, you know what the third angle must be.[41] This is an analogy for any pair of opposites because there is always a third way, a middle path that reconciles them. This is explained by the Hierophant in the Ceremony of the Neophyte:

> On the altar is a white triangle to be the image of that immortal light, that triune light, which moved in darkness and formed the world of darkness and out of darkness. There are two contending forces and one always uniting them; and these three have their image in the threefold flame of our being and in the threefold wave of the sensual world.[42]

The number three is a fundamental concept in the various religions and spiritual traditions the world over. In his book on the occult power of numbers, Westcott tells us:

> It was considered the Mistress of Geometry because the triangle is the principal of Figures [...] Indeed it is impossible to study any single system of worship

---

40 Cicero, "Sacred Geometry: Magical Polygons and Polygrams, Part 1," 22.
41 Greer, *Techniques for Geometric Transformation*, 46.
42 Regardie, *The Golden Dawn*, 157.

throughout the world, without being struck by the peculiar persistence of the triple number in regard to divinity. Whether as a group of deities, a triformed or 3-headed god, a Mysterious Triunity, a deity of 3 powers or a family relationship of 3 Persons, such as the Father, Mother and Son of the Egyptians, Osiris, Isis and Horus.[43]

Dr. George W. Plummer, one of the founders of the Societas Rosicruciana in America elaborates on the Universal Trinity in his Seminary of Biblical Research:

Man has always held to the concept of a Divine origin. ONE and ALL-INCLUSIVE in its essential nature and character, yet expressing in a threefold manifestation composed either of the Father-Mother-Offspring attributes, or else of three special individualistic phases. [...] To Christian Mystics, this world and all that therein is, is of the same substance as the Cosmic Trinity, because it is composed of "Emanations" of that Trinity.[44]

Some argue that similarity alone neither proves nor disproves a Christian copying of ancient pagan Deity triads, and that because of their time and place ancient pagan faiths were unlikely to have been the source material for the Christian doctrine of the Holy Trinity.[45] Many Church Fathers who were influential in the development of Trinitarian doctrines were actually immersed in the teachings of the Stoics, Aristotle, and other aspects of Greek philosophy. The most direct influences were Middle Platonism and Neoplatonism, through the teachings of such philosophers as the Jewish theologian Philo of Alexandria, Neopythagorean philosopher Numenius, early church father Justin Martyr, and the Neoplatonist teacher Plotinus.[46] During the late 2nd century, the doctrine of the Trinity was taking shape in Christian thought, no doubt influenced by scriptural passages such as the Gospel of John (1 John, v; 7, 8), which will be very familiar to

43 Westcott, 20.
44 Plummer, 4-5.
45 Tuggy, <https://plato.stanford.edu/archives/win2016/entries/trinity/>
46 Ibid.

Golden Dawn adepts:

> For there are three that bear record in heaven, the Father, the Word, and the Holy Ghost, and these three are One. And there are three that bear witness in earth, the Spirit, and the water, and the blood: and these three agree in One.[47]

Union: Contained Within

As the first true enclosed polygon, the triangle is also the first true figure of a container. This is one reason why the "Triangle of Art," a symbol used to facilitate the manifestation of spiritual entities, is also used to *contain* Spirits in ceremonial evocations.

FIGURE 5: The Triangle of Art.

Through its number, three, the triangle corresponds to Binah, the third Sephirah, associated with the idea of the Great Mother—the Divine Feminine. Ample evidence has come down to us from ancient sources regarding the Great Goddess as Great Container. Prehistoric female-shaped vessels of pottery apparently refer to this concept. The ancients could certainly see that the mother contains the child, and

47 Regardie, *The Golden Dawn*, 301.

gives it life and nourishment. They likely surmised that the Great Mother was the metaphysical "Ground of Being" that contains all things as well as the manifested "Place of Being" wherein we exist.[48]

> The names of Goddesses such as the Egyptian Isis, Nuet, and Hathor—two of Whom are prominent in the Order—also contain hints of this ancient conception of Goddess. As many readers will know, the name Isis, Iset in Egyptian, means throne. But *iset* can also mean chamber, tomb, womb, or simply place; and all these either contain or establish. Nuet's name is spelled with the pot hieroglyph, another container, and has to do with place, especially a town or settlement. An interpretation of Hathor's name as House of Horus (Hwt Hor) reveals that She is the Sky Goddess Who contains the Hawk God, Horus.[49]

One image that has been used to represent the mother is the vesica, a figure made by linking two circles together, bringing the outside edge of each to the midway point of the other.

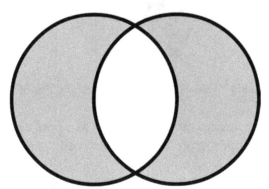

FIGURE 6: The Vesica formed between two Circles.

In the Hermetic Qabalah of the Golden Dawn, the vesica is seen as a transitional figure that connects various levels of the Sephiroth on the Tree of Life, and is the subject of meditation for the Practicus. When drawing the Tree of Life with a straightedge and compass, the

---

48 Forrest, "The Goddess and the Golden Dawn."
49 Ibid.

Sephiroth are formulated at the points where the circles intersect, and vesicas are formed in the common areas claimed by two interlinked circles.

FIGURE 7: Vesicas formed in Drawing the Tree of Life.

The image of the vesica can easily be seen as a grail or chalice. When viewed standing upright on one of its two points, the vesica becomes a different sort of passageway: the birth canal. The pointed oval is a universal symbol of the Divine Feminine in its capacity to surround and contain life within, until that life is ready to emerge.

There is another aspect of the vesica (and its straight-lined sibling, the rhombus) which relate to its function as a passageway between different levels of Being: the Four Qabalistic Worlds of Atziluth, Briah, Yetzirah, and Assiah. Representing four levels of spiritual density and manifestation, the Four Worlds are sometimes pictured on a single Tree of Life, with Kether occupying the Divine

World of Atziluth, Chokmah and Binah falling in the Creative World of Briah, and so on. But another diagram shows four connected Trees of Life, one for each world, sometimes stacked on top of one another in a kind of Jacob's Ladder formation. Three liminal vesicas mark the inflection points of transition between the worlds, indicating where Tiphareth of Assiah becomes Makuth of Yetzirah—and where Kether of Yetzirah becomes Tiphareth of Briah as well as Malkuth of Atziluth, etc.

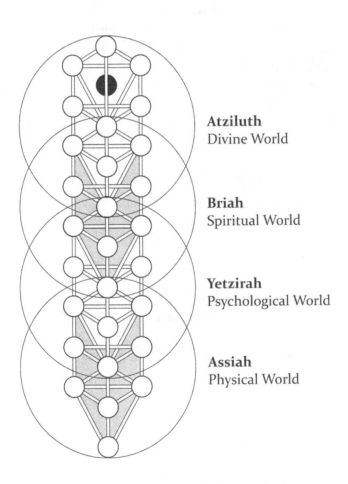

Atziluth
Divine World

Briah
Spiritual World

Yetzirah
Psychological World

Assiah
Physical World

FIGURE 8: The Four Worlds of the Qabalah
in the "Jabob's Ladder" Formation.

This diagram perfectly portrays the connection between the Divine Mind in Atziluth and the human soul in Assiah. There is no question here that the two are intimately linked. Furthermore, the Order teachings tell us:

It is said that Kether is in Malkuth, and again, that Malkuth is in Kether but after another manner. For downwards through the Four Worlds the Malkuth of the less material will be linked unto the Kether of the more material. From the Synthesis of the Ten corruscations of the AOUR (Light) proceedeth the influence unto EHEIEH, the Kether of Atziluth. And the connecting thread of the AIN SOPH is extended through the worlds of the Ten Sephiroth and is in every direction. As the Ten Sephiroth operate in each Sephirah, so will there be a KETHER in every MALKUTH, and MALKUTH in every KETHER, thus:

Adonai Melekh
This will be the Malkuth of Atziluth.
Metatron
This will be the Kether of Briah.
Sandalphon - Metatron - Nephesch ha-Messiah
These will be the Malkuth of Briah.
Chaioth ha-Qadesh
This will be the Kether of Yetzirah.
Aschim
This will be the Malkuth of Yetzirah.
Rashith ha-Gilgalim
The Kether of Assiah.
Cholem Yesodoth
The Malkuth of Assiah.
Thaumiel
The Kether of the Qlippoth.

The symbol of the connection between MALKUTH of YETZIRAH and KETHER of ASSIAH will be of a form somewhat resembling that of an hour glass. The thread of the AIN SOPH before alluded to, traversing the centre thereof, and forming the AIN SOPH connection between the Worlds.[50]

The teachings of Jewish mystic Isaac Luria (1534-1572) were an important influence on the Qabalah of the Golden Dawn. In addition to the well-known diagram of the Tree of Life, there is a teaching in Lurianic Qabalah which depicts the ten Sephiroth as a series of concentric circles surrounded by the three veils of negative existence: *Ain* ("nothing") the outermost veil, *Ain Soph* ("limitless") the middle veil, and *Ain Soph Aur* ("limitless light") the innermost veil. Insofar as it is possible to describe the indescribable, it is said that the main characteristic of Ain is to give or bestow of its own essence or Light.

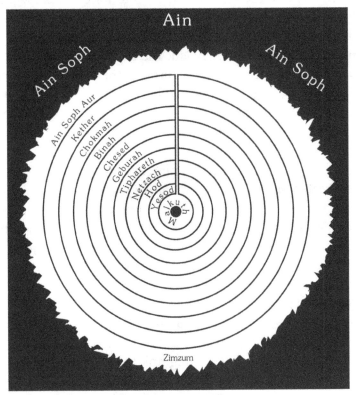

FIGURE 9: The Sephiroth in Concentric Circles.

---

50 Regardie, *The Portable Complete Golden Dawn System of Magic*, Vol. 9, 74.

179

The main attribute of Ain Soph is to take in the essential Light of Ain and transmit it. Ain Soph is envisioned as an infinite sphere in which a smaller sphere of empty space comes into being through the process of *tzimtzum* or "contraction" of Ain Soph from the surrounding Light—not unlike an empty set of lungs inhaling to gather in and contain (and therefore limit) the surrounding air. According to the tradition, Ain Soph formed into an empty circle which was surrounded by a circle of Light. A line or ray of the Divine Light penetrated the empty circle to its center, resulting in a succession of concentric circles marking the divisions of creation. The primary point of Light at formed at the center of Ain Soph is Ain Soph Aur, the Limitless Light from which the Universe was created, and it is within the center of Ain Soph Aur that the emanations of the ten Sephiroth layer in concentric circles. The first and outermost of these is Kether and the tenth and most interior circle is the physical realm of Malkuth.

The symbolism of the line of Light entering the circle of space was important in Lurianic Qabalah. The circle symbolized all natural cycles of creation: the seasons, the orbit of the planets, the phases of the moon, etc. The line represented humanity. Luria held that there were two aspects of the emanation of the Divine Light. One was linear, in the form of *Adam Kadmon*, the "heavenly man" or "body of god."

This was the prototype of humanity, as well as the first and highest created being: the first definitive form that appeared before all else in the sphere of creation. The second aspect of the emanation was circular, wherein the Sephiroth took form within the body of the Adam Kadmon in a series of concentric circles. By joining the symbols of line and circle, Luria was joining humanity with the Divine Nature.[51]

Conceived prior to but still a part of the world of Atziluth, Adam Kadmon mediates the Divine Light into the Four Worlds below him. "From his eyes, mouth, ears and nose, the lights of the Sephiroth burst forth."[52] He is an intervening link between the Ain Soph and the order of Qabalistic Worlds yet to come into manifestation. This Heavenly Man is the consciousness of the Divine, containing within

51 Magee, 230.
52 Scholem, 265.

itself everything that is needed to create the manifest Universe as a reflection of the Divine Universe. He contains within his being Will (Atziluth), Intellect (Briah), Emotion (Yetzirah) and the capacity for action (Assiah).

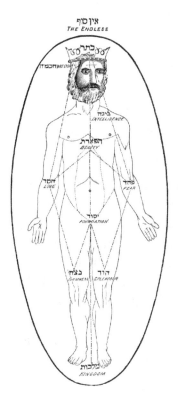

[FIGURE 10: Adam Kadmon against the Tree of Life.]

According to Lurianic tradition, the light of the Sephiroth streaming forth from Adam Kadmon was gathered in separate "containers." At this early stage, the Sephiroth were not yet separate, but bound together as a series of lights or points. These Sephirotic Lights were then given "vessels" or fields of containment in which to organize their substance and operate. Those belonging to the three Supernal Sephiroth were sturdy enough to receive the Light but the lower seven Sephiroth were not. When the Light struck the next six spheres from Chesed to Yesod it did so with such potency that the vessels shattered one by one, sending fragments falling. Malkuth also cracked but did not shatter. The result was an imperfect material order wherein nothing was how it should be.

> It all sounds like a cosmic accident, but according to Luria it was all predestined. If this is the case, then God's contraction and the subsequent creation of the imperfect universe are events that *had* to occur; in some way God needed them to happen. [...] Indeed, Scholem remarks that "Luria is driven to something *very* much like a mythos of God giving birth to Himself; indeed, this seems to me to be the focal point of this whole involved and frequently rather obscure and inconsistent description.[53]

Adam Kadmon is the mirror of reflection that is used by the Divine to *experience itself* through the Four Worlds of the Qabalah; for only a descent into all four Worlds will enable the Divine to experience all aspects of Divinity. However, once Adam Kadmon descends into the Active World of Manifestation, he must be reflected back to the original Atzituthic Source. This image of the primordial man is a perfect symbol for the Hermetic axiom "As Above, So Below." To be sure, this image has to be considered in a non-corporeal sense. "Adam Kadmon is an Aristotelian *final* cause: he is logically prior to the rest of creation, and simultaneously the end toward which creation is moving."[54]

Macrocosm and Microcosm

Secular society has little use for subjective experiences of consciousness. The bias of the "It's all in your head" faction has become a yoke that is difficult to throw off in the modern age. Golden Dawn magicians transcend this barrier and embrace the idea that consciousness is not limited to the cells in our brains. The principle of Macrocosm and Microcosm, summarized in the phrase "As Above, So Below," is integral to the philosophy and mechanics of Western Magic, precisely because the Greater and Lesser Universes are in a

53 Magee, 230.
54 Ibid.

certain way equivalent, and the primary patterns of our experience of the universe and the primary patterns of our experience of ourselves are one and the same.[55] In the same way that every human being exists on all levels of experience, everything that exists around us in the material world also exists on all levels of experience. The reflection of these patterns between the Divine is not exact in every way, however, particularly on the physical realm, because "the universe" doesn't have fingers, toes, and noses like human beings do. Nevertheless, the Qabalistic Tree of Life, often seen as an abstract image of Adam Kadmon, is the perfect metaphor-map for explaining the relationship between Divinity and humanity, and the various ways we can access magical forces that exist in both. For the Tree is a symbolic blueprint of the Divine Universe as well as a diagram of the human soul. Any pattern, quality, or energy that exists in one, also exists in the other. Both are connected, and what affects one will affect the other.

This brings us back full circle to the Golden Dawn manuscript cited at the beginning of this essay, "The Microcosm—Man":

> Thou shalt know that the whole Sphere of Sensation which surroundeth the whole physical body of a man is called "The Magical Mirror of the Universe." For therein are represented all the occult forces of the Universe projected as on a sphere, convex to the outer, but concave to man. This sphere surroundeth the physical body of a man as the Celestial Heavens do the body of a Star or a Planet, having their forces mirrored in its atmosphere. Therefore its allotment or organization is the copy of that Greater World or Macrocosm. In this "Magical Mirror of the Universe," therefore, are the Ten Sephiroth projected in the form of the Tree of Life as in a solid sphere. A man's physical body is within the Ten Sephiroth projected in a sphere.
>
>
>
> The divisions and parts of the body are formed from the Sephiroth of the Tree of Life [...] In the Magical Mirror of the Universe, or the Sphere of Sensation, Man is placed between four pillars of the Tree of Life as

---

55 Greer, *Circles of Power,* 14.

projected in a sphere. These keep their place and *move not*.[56]

The *Sphere of Sensation* is a phrase used in the Golden Dawn to describe the aura. Among the subtle bodies of layered energy that envelop the physical body of every human, the aura is a division of the etheric body composed of *ether* or life-force energy. It is a layer of astral substance, an egg-shaped sphere of light energy that expands out about two or three feet from the physical body. "The Microcosm—Man" document tells us that the human aura contains a complete star-map of the heavens, or a thorough blueprint of all the divine forces within the Universe, including the Tree of Life and all of its associated energies: elemental, Sephirotic, planetary, zodiacal, etc.

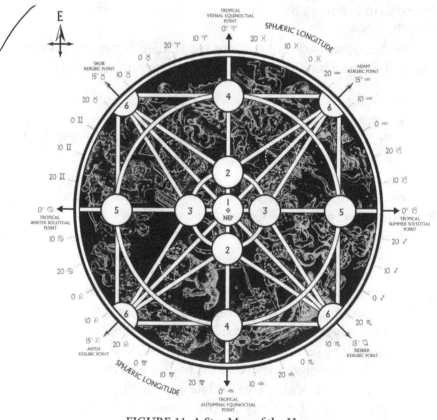

FIGURE 11: A Star Map of the Heavens.

---

56 Regardie, *The Golden Dawn*, 125.

In its teaching on the Celestial Tarot, the Order superimposes charts of the constellations onto the Sphere of Sensation as a structural basis for all types of astrological magic.

The Tree of Life as projected in a solid sphere is also discussed in a Second Order paper written by Mathers, where he states that everything in the created universe contains a mirror image of the Tree in miniature, set against a celestial map polarized on the plane of the ecliptic rather than on the earth's equator (making the North Pole as that of the Heavens and not that of Earth):

> When the Tree of Life is considered not as being a plane but as a solid figure, and when it is projected in the Sphere, the North Pole of the Sphere will coincide with Kether, and the South Pole with Malkuth.
>
> As we have before sufficiently learned the Ten Sephiroth are repeated not alone in each whole figure, but also in the parts thereof, so that every material thing created, will have its own Sephiroth and Paths.[57]

The Middle Pillar Exercise, wherein the magician connects the Universal Pillar of Mildness *without* to the Middle Pillar *within*, activates each Sephirah within her or her soul. This simple rite is a perfect example of how Golden Dawn magicians use the connection between the Greater and Lesser Trees of Life to charge the Sphere of Sensation with Divine Light. The Exercise of the Middle Pillar has many expanded variations, including a version that activates the internal Archangels of the interior Sephiroth.[58]

The idea of the Ten Sephiroth projected in a Sphere is also discussed in relation to the Celestial Tarot and the Enochian Tablets in certain ZAM and ThAM-level teachings by Mathers, where the correlation between the Greater and Lesser Universes and the spiritual forces contained therein are also mentioned:

> It is demonstrated in the Tarot manuscripts that when the 10 Sephiroth in their grouping which is called the Tree of Life are projected in a Sphere (Kether coinciding

---

57 Ibid., 760. Italics are ours.
58 Cicero, *Experiencing the Kabbalah*, 220-227.

with the North Pole, Malkuth coinciding with the South Pole, the Pillar of Mildness with the Axis) then the Pillars of Severity and of Mercy are quadrupled, i.e. there are five Pillars instead of three Pillars.

The same scheme is therefore applicable to the Celestial Heavens, and the mode of the governance of these Tablets in the Heavens is also set forth in the Tarot manuscripts. But as before and as there is said, the rule of these Four Tablets, *Terrestrial as well as in the Heavens,* is in the Spaces between the 4 Pillars. That is, between the double Pillars of Severity and Mercy. In these vast spaces at the ends of the Universe are these Tablets placed as Watch-Towers, and therein is their dominion limited on either side by the Sephirotic Pillars, and having the great central cross of each Tablet coinciding with one of the 4 Tiphareth points in the Celestial Heavens. Therefore even in the small squares into which each Tablet is divided, *each represents a vast area of dominion, having the correlation thereof in the Universe, in the Planets, in our Earth, in the Fixed Stars, and even in Man, in animals, vegetables, and minerals.*[59]

"The Microcosm—Man" paper goes on to discuss how certain parts of the human anatomy correlate to elemental and planetary forces.

But a primary focus of the document is on one of the most important teachings on the Tree of Life, the magical anatomy of the human psyche, otherwise known as the Qabalistic Parts of the Soul (*Neshamah,* the *Ruach,* and the *Nephesh)* and how these forces illustrate both the mind of Deity in the act of creation-involution, and the psychic soul of humanity as a mirrored reflection of the Divine Mind (and the soul of the magician in the act of spiritual aspiration-evolution).

The highest of these, the Neshamah, encompasses the Sephiroth of Kether, Chokmah, and Binah. This corresponds to the highest aspirations of the soul. The greater Neshamah is further sub-divided into three parts: The *Yechidah,* the *Chiah,* and the *Neshamah.* The

59 Regardie, *The Portable Complete Golden Dawn System of Magic,* Vol. 10, 31. Italics are ours.

Yechidah, centered in Kether, is our true *Divine Self*, the root essence of our spiritual nature. The *Chiah*, or life force, located in Chokmah, is the highest active principle in the human soul. It is our divine will, our inquisitive urge to become more than human. The sub-division of the *Neshamah* (as distinct from the greater Neshamah), is the intuitive soul located in Binah, although it lends its name to the other Supernals as being generally descriptive of the soul's greatest aspirations. The Neshamah in Binah initiates various ways by which the self can be defined as being unique to the individual as well as limitless in archetypal manifestation.

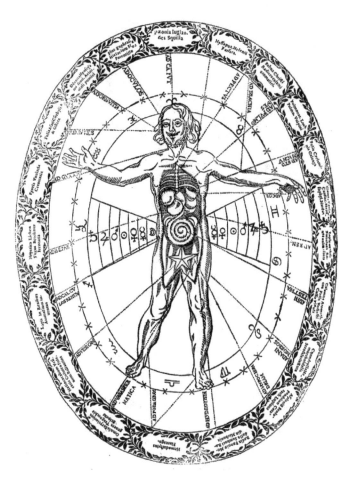

FIGURE 12: Chart showing the relationship between the human body and the exterior universe. From Kircher's *Œdipus Ægyptiacus*.

The middle soul or Rational Self, the *Ruach*, is located in the five Sephiroth from Chesed to Yesod, although it is centered in Tiphareth. Five faculties are to be found in this pentad of spheres: memory (Chesed), will (Geburah), imagination (Tiphareth), emotion (Netzach), and intellect (Hod). The Ruach also overlaps, to a lesser extent, Daath and Yesod. This is the conscious mind and reasoning powers—the conscious part of our being which is the abode of the ego.

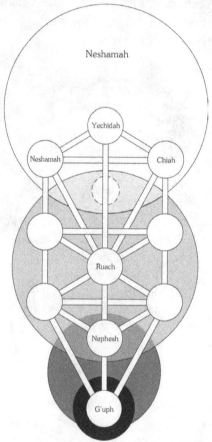

FIGURE 13: The Qabalistic Parts of the Soul.

The Lower part of the soul, the *Nephesh* is located in Yesod and also overlaps Malkuth (which it shares with the *G'uph*, a low level of psycho-physical functions). The Nephesh is essential to the workings of magic, because it is the seat of the personal unconscious as well as the seat of the aura, the Sphere of Sensation.

As to the functioning of this soul meta-system, "The Microcosm—Man" tells us:

From Malkuth is formed the whole physical body under the command and presidency of the Nephesch. The Nephesch is the subtle body of refined astral Light upon which, as on an invisible pattern, the physical body is extended. The physical body is permeated throughout by the rays of the Ruach, of which it is the material completion. The Nephesch shineth through the Material body and formeth the Magical Mirror or Sphere of Sensation. This Magical Mirror or Sphere of Sensation is an imitation or copy of the Sphere of the Universe. The space between the physical body and the boundary of the sphere of Sensation is occupied by the ether of the astral world; that is to say, the container or recipient of the Astral Rays of the Macrocosm. [...]

This spiritual consciousness is a focus of the action of *Neschamah*. The lower will-power should control the descent of this spiritual consciousness into the *Ruach*, and thence into the *Nephesch*, for the consciousness must descend into the *Nephesch* before the images of the Sphere of Sensation can be perceived. For it is only the rays of this consciousness permeating the *Ruach* that can take cognizance thereof. This faculty of the spiritual consciousness is the seat of Thought. *Thought* is a *Light* proceeding from the radiation of this spiritual consciousness, traversing the *Ruach* as Light traverseth Air, and encountering thereafter the symbols reflected in the sphere of Sensation, or magical mirror of the Universe. These symbols are by its radiation (i.e. that of the Thought) reflected again into the Spiritual Consciousness where they are subjected unto the action of the *Reasoning Mind* and of the *Lower Will*. That is, in the ordinary natural man when awake, the thought acteth through the *Ruach*, subject when there to the action of the Lower Will, and submitted to the reasoning power derived as aforesaid from Chokmah and Binah. […]

All thought action in the spiritual consciousness originateth in radiation, and radiation is as inseparable from the spiritual consciousness as it is from Light.

This Spiritual Consciousness is the focus of the action of *Neschamah*. The spiritual consciousness is, in its turn, the Throne or Vehicle of the Life of the Spirit which is *Chiah;* and these combined form the Chariot of that Higher Will which is in *Kether.* Also it is the peculiar faculty of *Neschamah* to aspire unto that which is beyond. The Higher Will manifests itself through *Yechidah.* The *Chiah* is the real Life Principle, as distinct from the more illusionary life of the Physical Body. The Shining Flame of the Divine Fire, the *Kether* of the Body, is the Real Self of the Incarnation. Yet but few of the sons of men know it or feel its presence. Still less do they believe in or comprehend those Higher Potencies—Angelic, Archangelic or Divine, of which the manifestation directly touching *Yechidah* is the Higher Genius.

This *Yechidah* in the ordinary man can but rarely act through the spiritual consciousness, seeing that for it to do so the King of the Physical Body, that is the Lower Will, must rise from his Throne to acknowledge his superior. That is the reason why, in some cases, in sleep only doth the Higher Will manifest itself by dream unto the ordinary man. In other cases it may be manifested; at times through the sincere practice of religious rites, or in cases where the opportunity for self-sacrifice occurreth. In all these cases the Lower Will hath for a moment recognised a higher form of itself, and the YHVH of the man hath reflected from the Eternal Lord of the Higher Life. This *Yechidah* is the only part of the man which can truly say-EHEIEH, I am. This is then but the Kether of the Assiah of the Microcosm, that is, it is the highest part of man as Man. It is that which toucheth, or is the manifestation of a higher and greater range of Being.

This Yechidah is at the same time the Higher Human Self and the Lower Genius, the God of the Man, the Atziluth of his Assiah, even as Chiah and Neschamah form his Briah, and Ruach his Yetzirah. This is the Higher Will and the Divine Consciousness, as Daath is the Spiritual Consciousness, Tiphareth the Human Consciousness, and Yesod the Automatic Consciousness.

It is the Divine Consciousness because it is the only part of man which can touch the All-potent forces. Behind Yechidah are Angelic and Archangelic Forces of which Yechidah is the manifestor. It is therefore the Lower Genius or Viceroy of the Higher Genius which is beyond, an Angel Mighty and Terrible. This Great Angel is the Higher Genius, beyond which are the Archangelic and Divine.[60]

All of this points to the Jacob's Ladder effect we discussed in the section on the vesica and the Four Qabalistic Worlds.

It is the same principle of the transition of energies and images up and down the various levels of the soul, from the Spiritual Consciousness of the Neshamah to the Automatic Consciousness in Yesod. As the Magical Mirror of the Universe, the Sphere of Sensation is the conductor of mental images as well as an instrument through which these images can be used to affect magic, reflecting the workings, goals, and energized thought-forms upwards into higher levels of the Divine Ladder. All mental imagery is copied from the human psyche onto the concave bowl of the Sphere of Sensation and then mirrored out into the universe. This is the most essential implement in the magician's toolbox. With it we are able to perform all types of divination, talisman consecrations, Spirit Vision work, and other forms of magic. Its use enables us to mold consciousness using images selected and charged with energized willpower. By working with the astrological charts and other energies mapped onto the Sphere of Sensation, magicians are able to "dial in" to their Macrocosmic counterparts.

From the Ultimate Divinity to the Angels, Spirits, and humans, as well as the lower spirits and elementals—all are links in Ficino's "long

---

60 Regardie, *The Golden Dawn*, 128-131.

uninterrupted chain." Angels in particular are seen as companions on the Theurgist's path, working together in the Great Chain of Being. Deities, Archangels, Angels and Spirits also exist on different levels of experience and are associated with the various energies that comprise the celestial charts embedded within the human aura. These Beings exist within the Microcosm just as they exist in the Macrocosm. They are as real as their heavenly doubles. The magician is able to create, enliven, and work with mental images that can be projected onto the canvas of their personal Sphere of Sensation, connecting the Microcosmic force or Angel with its Macrocosmic counterpart by means of a direct line of communication though the vesica passageways that exist between the worlds. Golden Dawn magicians seek to bring a particular spiritual energy within the human soul in an alignment with that same force as it exists in the greater universe.

Science has come to accept that everything in the universe is made up of energy. We know that all matter is vibratory energy. So, when we invoke a Divine or Angelic name in a *vibration* of that particular name, we take advantage of a physical phenomenon known as *harmonic resonance*, which shows that if one object starts to vibrate strongly enough, another object nearby will begin to vibrate or resonate with the first, *if both objects share the same natural vibratory rate*. The magician vibrates a Godname in order to effect a harmonic resonance between a Spiritual Entity as it exists within the psyche and as it exists out in the greater universe. The aim is to have the psyche "resonate" in perfect clarity with the Divine. But this is just one of several tools that are available to the magician.

In his discussion on how modern psychology has influenced contemporary esoteric thought, Wouter Hanegraaff describes the "double phenomenon of the psychologizing of religion combined with a sacralization of psychology."[61] Influenced by Jungian psychology, the human mind itself is presumed to have a sacred dimension. However, the spiritual is not reduced to psychology alone. Instead, the spiritual and psychological realms are discovering and recovering ways of bridging the artificial gaps between them. Whether the Divine is "real" or merely "in the mind" is ultimately a

61 Hanegraaff, "The New Age Movement and the Esoteric Tradition," *Gnosis and Hermeticism: From Antiquity to Modern Times.* 378.

pointless question, because it assumes a false dualism between inner and outer realities.

From here we circle back around to our original question: Do these Divine and Angelic forces reside only within the Heavens above, or are they only found within the consciousness of man? Once again the Third and Middle Way strikes the balance between opposing viewpoints—these forces abide in both Macrocosm and Microcosm. How could it be otherwise? And if you could acknowledge and combine the best of both worlds, ancient spiritual practice and modern esoteric insight, why would you not take advantage of all the tools available to you?

> Whoever has not known himself has known nothing, but he who has known himself has at the same time already achieved knowledge about the depths of all things.[62]

---

62 Robinson, "Book of Thomas the Contender," *The Nag Hammadi Library in English*, 189.

Sources

An Introduction to Gnosticism and The Nag Hammadi Library. URL = <http://www.gnosis.org/naghamm/nhlintro.html/> (accessed May 25, 2020).

Battie, William. *Treatise on Madness, London*: Whiston & White, 1758. URL = <https://play.google.com/store/books/details?id=F6J bAAAAQAAJ&rdid=book-F6JbAAAAQAAJ&rdot=1/> (accessed May 16, 2020).

Cherry, Kendra. "A Historical Timeline of Modern Psychology Landmark Events in History from 1878 to Today," URL=<https://www. verywellmind.com/timeline-of-modern-psychology-2795599/> (accessed May 16, 2020).

_____. "Sigmund Freud's Theories About Religion," URL = <https://www.verywellmind.com/freud-religion-2795858/> (accessed May 16, 2020).

Cicero, Chic and Sandra Tabatha. *The Essential Golden Dawn: An Introduction to High Magic*, St. Paul, MN: Llewellyn Publications, 2003.

_____. *Experiencing the Kabbalah, A Simple Guide to Spiritual Wholeness.* St. Paul, MN: Llewellyn Publications, 1997.

_____. *Golden Dawn Magic: A Complete Guide to the High Magical Arts.* Woodbury, MN: Llewellyn Publications, 2003.

Cicero, Sandra Tabatha. "Sacred Geometry: Magical Polygons and Polygrams, Part 1," *Hermetic Virtues Vol. III, Ed. 3,* Winter Solstice 2009.

Collins, David. "Magic in the Middle Ages: History and Historiography." *History Compass. Vol. 9, No. 5.* Blackwell Publishing 2011.

Copenhaver, Brian P. (Translator/Editor) *Hermetica: The Greek Corpus Hermeticum and the Latin Asclepius in a New English Translation, with Notes and Introduction,* United Kingdom: Cambridge University Press, 1995.

Coxe, A. Cleveland. *Ante-Nicene Fathers, Volume V: Fathers of the Third Century.* Edinburgh: T&T Clark, 1885.

The Emerald Tablet of Hermes URL = <https://www.bota.org/resources/emtablet.html/> (accessed May 25, 2020).

Erhman, Bart. *Lost Christianities: The Battles for Scripture and the Faiths We Never Knew,* New York: Oxford University Press, 2003.

Flint, Valerie. *The Rise of Magic in Early Medieval Europe.* Princeton, NJ: Princeton University Press, 1991.

Forrest, Adam. "This Holy Invisible Companionship, The Golden Dawn Journal: Book Two: Qabalah: Theory and Magic. St. Paul, MN: Llewellyn Publications, 1994.

Forrest, Isidora. "The Goddess and the Golden Dawn." Unpublished Lecture.

Greer, John Michael. *Circles of Power: Ritual Magic in the Western Tradition,* Paul, MN: Llewellyn Publications, 1997.

_____. *Paths of Wisdom: Cabala in the Golden Dawn Tradition.* London: Aeon Books, 2017.

_____. *Techniques for Geometric Transformation.* St. Paul: Llewellyn Publications, 2002.

Hanegraaff, Wouter. "The Globalization of Esotericism," *Correspondences: Online Journal for the Academic Study of Western Esotericism,* Vol 3, 2015. URL = <https://correspondencesjournal.com/volume-3/> (accessed May 25, 2020).

_____. *Western Esotericism: A Guide for the Perplexed,* London: Bloomsbury, 2013.

Jacobi, Jolande. *The Psychology of C.G. Jung.* New Haven: Yale University Press, 1973.

Kieckhefer, Richard. *Forbidden Rites: A Necromancer's Manual of the Fifteenth Century,* University Park, PA: Pennsylvania State University Press, 1997.

_____. *Magic in the Middle Ages,* United Kingdom: Cambridge University Press, 2000.

King James Bible Online. URL = <https://www.kingjamesbibleonline.org/> (accessed May 25, 2020).

Knight, Gareth. *Magic and the Western Mind: Ancient Knowledge and the Transformation of Consciousness.* St. Paul, MN: Llewellyn Publications, 1991.

Magee, Glenn Alexander. *Hegel and the Hermetic Tradition,* Ithica, NY: Cornell university Press, 2001.

Pagels, Elaine. *The Gnostic Gospels.* New York: Random House, 1979.

Patterson, Stephen, and Marvin Meyer. *The "Scholars' Translation" of the Gospel of Thomas,* URL = <http://earlychristianwritings.com/text/thomas-scholars.html/> (accessed May 25, 2020).

Plummer, Dr. George W. "The Universal Trinity," *Instructions in Christian Mysticism,* Seminary of Biblical Research, Societas Rosicruciana in America, 1927.

Regardie, Israel. *The Golden Dawn: An Account of the Teachings, Rites and Ceremonies of the Order of the Golden Dawn,* 7th ed. Woodbury, MN: Llewellyn, 2015.

_____. *The Middle Pillar: The Balance Between Mind and Magic*, 3rd ed., annotated. St. Paul, MN: Llewellyn, 1998.

_____. *The Portable Complete Golden Dawn System of Magic*, Las Vegas, NV: New Falcon Publications, 2013.

Remson III, Richard. "The Gospel According to Thomas: Authoritative or Heretical?" (2007). Religious Studies Honors Thesis, Paper 6.

Robinson, James M. The Nag Hammadi Library in English, San Francisco: Harper & Row, 1977.

Scholem, Gershom. *Major Trends in Jewish Mysticism*, New York: Schocken Books, 1967.

Simms, Maria Kay. *Circle of the Cosmic Muse*, St. Paul, MN: Llewellyn Publications, 1994.

Tuggy, Dale. "Trinity," *The Stanford Encyclopedia of Philosophy* (Winter 2016 Edition), Edward N. Zalta (ed.), URL = <https://plato.stanford.edu/archives/win2016/entries/trinity/>, (accessed May 25, 2020).

Van der Broek, Roelof and Wouter J. Hanegraaff. "The New Age Movement and the Esoteric Tradition," *Gnosis and Hermeticism: From Antiquity to Modern Times*. Albany, NY: State University of New York Press, 1998.

Westcott, W. Wynn. *Numbers: Their Occult Power and Mystic Virtue*. London: Theosophical Publishing Society, 1890.

Whitfield, J.H. *Petrarch and the Renascence*, New York: Haskell House, 1966.

ABOUT THE AUTHORS

Charles "Chic" Cicero was born in Buffalo, New York. An early love of music, particularly of the saxophone, resulted in Chic's many years of experience as a lead musician in several jazz, blues and rock ensembles, working with many famous performers in the music industry. His interest in Freemasonry and the Western Esoteric Tradition resulted in research articles on Rosicrucianism and the Knights Templar, printed in such publications as *Ars Quatuor Coronatorum and the 1996-2000 Transactions of the Metropolitan College of the SRIA*. Chic is a member of several Masonic, Martinist, and Rosicrucian organizations. He is a Past Grand Commander of the Grand Commandery of Knights Templar in Florida (2010–2011) and is the current Chief Adept of the Florida College of the Societas Rosicruciana in Civitatibus Foederatis. A close personal friend and confidant of Dr. Israel Regardie, Chic established a Golden Dawn temple in 1977 and was one of the key people who helped Regardie resurrect a legitimate branch of the Hermetic Order of the Golden Dawn in the United States in the early 1980s, with initiatory lineage that dates back to the original Order of 1888. He met his wife and co-author, Sandra Tabatha Cicero, shortly thereafter. Chic served as the G.H. Cancellarius of the Hermetic Order of the Golden Dawn from 1985 to 1994, and as G.H. Imperator of the Order from 1994 to the present day.

Sandra "Tabatha" Cicero was born in rural Wisconsin. A lifelong fascination with the creative arts has served to inspire her work in the magical world. After graduating from the University of Wisconsin-Milwaukee with a Bachelor's Degree in Fine Arts in 1982, Tabatha worked as an entertainer, typesetter, editor, commercial artist, and computer graphics illustrator. In 2009 she obtained a degree in Paralegal Studies. She met Chic Cicero in in 1983 and the Golden Dawn system of magic has been her primary spiritual focus ever since. Tabatha spent five years working on the paintings for *The Golden Dawn Magical Tarot* which she began at the encouragement of Israel Regardie. Tabatha is a member of several Martinist and Rosicrucian organizations, and is the current Imperatrix of the Societas Rosicruciana in America (www.sria.org). She has served as the G.H. Cancellaria of the Hermetic Order of the Golden Dawn from 1994 to the present day.

Both Chic and Tabatha are Chief Adepts of the Hermetic Order of the Golden Dawn as re-established by Israel Regardie (www. hermeticgoldendawn.org), the oldest continuously operating Golden Dawn Order in the United States, as well as an international Order with temples in several other countries.

THE MACGYVER GOLDEN DAWN TEMPLE[1]

by Frater D

I am not by any stretch of the imagination a master builder. But Hiram Abiff or not, many of us doing the work of the Golden Dawn, and particularly those pioneering new temples, often have to find a way to make very specific items, often in the face of very real challenges such as a lack of skills, lack of money to hire skilled craftspeople and buy expensive materials, and a lack of storage space for all of these items.

I set myself a challenge of finding a way to acquire the major accruements of a Golden Dawn temple, setting four basic criteria:

- The production of the temple equipment should require no specialist skills.
- The production of the Temple equipment should require no specialist or expensive tools.
- Materials should be cost effective.
- Equipment should be storable in a small space or double as inconspicuous household items.

For the purposes of this article, I have limited the scope to the equipment needed for the Neophyte ritual and the Equinox ritual, as these are the rituals that will be performed most by a pioneering temple. This allows time and potentially dues to acquire additional equipment. As I am based in Europe, pricing has been tracked and recorded in Euros. Measurements have also been made in metric as centimetres (cm).

As it is contrary to both my own custom, and the custom of many Golden Dawn temples to share images of regalia, I've included images of some of the equipment in early stages of development, but not the finished items.

---

1 MacGyver, for those not in the know, was a wonderful 1980's TV show about a genius protagonist who often resorted to innovative solutions made from unlikely materials.

Part 1: Major Equipment

Pillars and Banner Stands

The pillars of the temple, if made to be solid and permanent, made from drainpipes or carpet rolls, can be clumpy, difficult to transport and very conspicuous if left around your household. I was also aware that many of the more makeshift solutions for this problem did not make allowances for the tetrahedrons atop of the pillars. I looked at several different options for pillars before settling on an elegantly simple solution that both stores small and which can be integrated into a household as regular items.

To solve this conundrum, I ordered uplighters from Ikea. These uplighters, at €8 a piece, would form the basis for pillars that would be physically imposing, appear solid and support the tetrahedrons.

These uplighters stand at 175cm tall, with the upplight shade having a diameter of 28cm, and the foot of 26cm would do nicely. It came is a small box as the shaft of the uplighter came as a series of short metal lengths that screw into one another so it both can be used, when not being a pillar, as an uplighter in the home, and comes into small pieces for easy transport.

As I had these, along with other items, delivered from Ikea, I got lots of strong cardboard, from which I cut three circles of a 28cm diameter, two to sit atop the uplighter shade (with bulb removed) and one to expand the diameter of the foot, affixed (and removable) with sticky hook and hoop pads. For the pillar cover, I chose to use black and white fabric respectively. I then calculated the circumference using the formula Pi/π multiplied by the diameter of the circle (14cm), giving a result of approximately 88cm. To this measurement I added an additional 2cm at each side, giving a width of 92 cm. For the length/ height, I took the actual height of 175 cm, adding 2 cm for the top. I then cut a circle of 32cm to cover the top of the cardboard atop the uplighters. The sides and top of the fabric were sewn together to an exact size, the seams turned inside.

As well as allowances at the top of the material, an extra ten centimetres were added to the length for the bottom, giving a total length of 187cm. The bottom of the pillar sleeves had a narrow width elastic sewn into it, so the sleeves would pass over the cardboard base and gather tightly at the bottom, under the base. This ensured the pillar material was held taut, giving a nominal appearance of solidity, both visually and to the touch.

Uplights form the basis for the pillars and can easily be reintigrated into the home

Fabric pillar sleeves can be customised using print on demand fabric with the Egyptian motifs

In terms of cost, the uplighters cost €16. Fabric cost an additional €5 a metre, a cheap polycotton, taking 2.5 metres per pillar or 5 metres in total, meaning another €25. The offcuts would also later be used for collars for lamens. As I sew, I had elastic and thread. Additional embellishment is also possible, for example adding ' and ⊐ for the pillars of Solomons temple in felt, costing about €2 for two squares. Alternately, the offcuts could be used by a more adept sewer to add J and B, or to countercharge the pillars with adornment in the opposite colour at top and bottom.

As an advanced level of enhancement, it is possible to print custom fabric beginning at €10 a metre. This would allow inclusion of the Egyptian images, back and front for the pillars. As this custom material would not need to be on the caps of the pillars, 4 metres of fabric totalling €40. This level of customisation obviously needs to be size specific and requires digital design. This puts the cost of the pillars between €50 and €70 depending on customisations.

The banner stands have essentially the same solution, with the same uplighters bought and the lampshade removed. The flexes are also cut off. One is painted white and the other left black, the flared tops resembling a lotus, and which can also be painted gold. To hang the banners, hooks can be glued on. Alternately, using a bit for drilling metal, drill a hole through the stem of the uplighter near the top, putting a bolt through and adding one bolt to hold in place and another at the end to stop the banner from falling off the end when dipped. The bolts and nuts are also painted. This puts the cost at €16 for the two uplighters, another euro or two for the hooks or bolts, and an additional €10 for paint (gold also being used elsewhere later).

Banners of the East and West

The Banners of the East and West can be included in the fabric design if printing custom Egyptian pillars. Alternately, they can be ordered on their own, with a set fitting on about ½ a metre, with a cost of €5-10. They can be cut out, with the edges secured using bias binding tape (a metre of black and white costs a few Euro on eBay or in habadasheries). I already had this. The tops of the banners are folded over towards the back and a channel sewn for a dowel. A dowel is inserted and ribbon or cord added for hanging. Red tassels can be bought on ebay for a euro or two. Art for the banners can be found online, and additional materials such as dowel, tassels and cord can be bought for perhaps an additional €15.

The Double Cube Altar

For the double cube altar, I again use items that can be reintegrated into a household as side tables without raising eyebrows. Again going to Ikea, I found Lack square tables at €6 each, of which I ordered three. The legs on these unscrew for ease of transport. The tables measure 55cm by 55cm, with a height of 45cm. To get the shape of a double cube two tables are stacked, with the top off an additional table added to make up for the shortfall in height, giving an accurate double cube to navel height for me, a 5'10" man. As a stack this is a rather precarious balancing act, so I advise using hook and loop sticky pads to join this stack together, or if in situ, gluing it together. To give the double cube a solid appearance, a fabric wrap is created, 110cm in width, and 230cm in length, the ends joined together using hook and loop/ Velcro sewn to the fabric. The offcuts can be used for the collars again. Cost is €18 for the tables, an additional €15 for fabric, and an additional €5-10 for hook and loop/Velcro length to close off.

The double cube altar comes apart afterwards and can be used in a household as side tables or bedside tables.

| Double cube altar without the wraparound cover | Uplighters without shades ready to be transformed into banner stands |

Banners of the East and West, custom
printed on fabric and awaiting finishing

Part 2: Officer Equipment

Mantles of the Three Superior Officers

In this instance I went to eBay and bought three cheap fantasy cloaks
in black, red and white velvet at €10 each. I got the longest lengths
possible so I could use the extra material for overlayering caplets
reaching to the shoulder. As they were hooded, hoods were removed.
Other than the cost of the cloaks and thread, the only other cost was
3 small sheets of felt for the cavalry crosses on the left breast of each.
While it would have been possible to use the material from the hoods
at no additional cost, because felt has no selvedge edge, its easier for
those with elemental sewing skills. Felt sheets cost an additional €3.

Collars and Lamens

For the collars I used leftover fabric from the altar and pillars and
leftover velcro from the double cube altar. I only had to purchase
fabric for a red collar. The lamens were printed from digital artwork

at a local print shop on glossy paper and glued to thick cardboard (thanks to Ikea again). The cost, in this instance was about €10 for the lot.

Wands and Sceptres

For the sceptres I bought three wooden broom handles for the Hierophant, Hegemon and Kerux wands at €6 each. They were cut to a more reasonable size. I fashioned heads and rings using polymer clay costing €25, built on the broom handles before being removed for oven cooking. Polymer clay has shrinkage of about 2%, making it ideal for building directly on the sceptres over a layer of paper to allow for shrinkage. Sceptres were painted with acrylic paints and varnished. I already had acrylic paint and varnish, but I'd allow a budget of another €20 for this, bringing the cost for all three sceptres to around €65.

Other Officer Equipment

There was no workaround for the swords of the Sentinel and Hiereus, but I was fortunate to find masonic swords at €80.

The cup of the Stolistes came from a thrift or charity shop and the censer of the Dadouchos cost €20. The lantern of the Kerux was also found in a thrift shop and painted red.

Part 3: Other Supplies and Sundries

Cross and Triangle

I had a cross and triangle so it was not necessary to make this, but it is a relatively easy thing with wood, a mitre saw, wood glue, paint and varnish. I have seen these well produced online starting at €40.

Items for the Mystic Repast

Items for the Mystic Repass such as goblet, candle, vase and plate were wholly acquired by looking around the house.

Tetrahedrons

I still haven't found the best way to make tetrahedrons, or at least its something I'm still working through, though simple versions can be made using acetate used in theatre lighting and electric candles underneath. At its cheapest this should be achievable for under €20.

Part 4: Costs

Looking overall at costs, the following totals were achieved.

Pillars		€50
Banner Stands		€26
Banners		€25
Altar		€43
Mantles		€33
Collars and Lamens		€10
Sceptres		€65
Swords		€80
Cross and Triangle		€40
Tetrahedrons		€20
	TOTAL	€392

As this process used some preowned materials, and leaves no room for contingencies, inflation, price fluctuations or postage, or for extra bits I may have overlooked, I would recommend a contingency margin be added of an additional 25%, bringing the total to just under €500. I have also been blessed with a lot of serendipity in undertaking this project and cannot guarantee others will be equally blessed, but perhaps with my methods and roadmap, a similar level of improvised but functional temple equipment can be achieved.

Conclusion

Because the banner stands, pillars and altar pack flat, it's theoretically possible to transport all the equipment in two to three suitcases. As many of the items double as household items, they can also take pride of place around the home rather than being something you need to explain away in an embarrassed manner. The tools used are sewing machine, saw, drill, paint brushes. Nothing too unreasonable, in my opinion. While an ability to sew to some degree is needed, it does not require adept level skills to achieve a workable result.

The overall cost is under €500, meaning that cost, if split between a few members, or covered with a year's advanced dues, is wholly achievable. More importantly though, it puts the work of setting up a Golden Dawn temple or working the Golden Dawn system more easily in the reach of a different demographic of people, quite different from the wealthy members that made up much of the initial membership of the original Golden Dawn.

I began by saying I am no master builder, no Hiram Abiff, nor even a Chic Cicero, who as we all know set the bar for beautiful temples very high, but perhaps I, and others aspiring to the Golden Dawn tradition, can be MacGyvers.

ABOUT THE AUTHOR

Frater D has spent the last 15 years in service to various esoteric impulses including the A.'.A.'., the Golden Dawn and Rudolf Steiner's anthroposophy. His Work is withdrawn and focused in those organisations of which he is a member. In his muggle life he is a potter, visual artist and social sculpture.

Astrological Dignities from the Neophyte Knowledge Lecture

by Frater Manu Forti

At the end of the Neophyte Initiation Ceremony of the Order of the Golden Dawn, the newly obligated Neophyte is introduced to a quintet of basic subjects to memorize perfectly before being eligible to attain the rank of Zelator.[1] These subjects cover the basic building blocks of the Hebrew alphabet, the Kabbalistic Sephiroth and Astrological symbology. In this article, I will delve deep into some of the astrological information present, which at first may seem arbitrary to the newly obligated Neophyte. Specifically, I will provide a rationale for the essential dignities of the Seven Traditional Planets by examining their roots in Western Astrology. Furthermore, I will touch upon astrological information present in the Elemental Knowledge Lectures to support these rationales.

In summary, the Neophyte must memorize the following astrological information:

a) The symbols, names and the duplicated conditions of the four classical elements,

b) The symbols and names of the Twelve Signs of the Zodiac,

c) The attribution of Twelve Zodiac Signs to the Four Classical Elements,

d) The symbols and names of the Seven Classical Planets and

e) The three most powerful Essential Dignities of the Seven Classical Planets.

---

1 These subjects were listed towards the end of the Neophyte Initiation ceremony of the Original Order of the Golden Dawn and the Alpha & Omega. See Farrell, Nick, *Mather's Last Secret*, pg. 64.

A Little History

The astrology presented in the Knowledge Lectures of the Outer Order of the Golden Dawn was probably influenced by, if not lifted directly from, the works of astrologers such as William Lilly (1602 – 1681 AD) or Raphael (1795 – 1832 AD). Lilly in particular was an influential seventh century astrologer who wrote one of the first comprehensive astrological texts in the English language, titled *Christian Astrology*. He was heavily influenced by such traditional authors as Dr John Dee, Johannes Kepler and Cornelius Agrippa. Furthermore, he had access to astrological texts from the Hellenistic period, such as the *Tetrabiblos* by Claudius Ptolemy (90 – 168 AD).

The tradition Lilly was drawing from spans over two millennia and contains a wealth of philosophical and theoretical information used to construct astrology as we know it today. It is widely believed that Western Astrology has its roots in the astrological religions of the Mesopotamians, the Persians, the Assyrians, and of course the Ancient Egyptians. These different astrological traditions more than likely came face to face after the conquest of Egypt, the Persian Empire and near India in the 4th century B.C.E by Alexander the Great. It was probably in the cities of Alexandria and Athens, that these traditions were systemized into the first astrological doctrines. This systemized western astrological tradition took root and flourished in the Roman Empire over a period of about 700 years in which many Hellenistic treatises on astrology were produced. The term "Hellenistic" is used because, even though it was mostly practiced in the Roman Empire, Greek was considered the educated language of the times and many of the astrological technical terms were rooted in the Greek language.

After the fall of the Roman Empire, the Dark Ages set in in Europe and Astrology went into a sharp decline. If not for the Persians and later Arabian traditions, the Hellenistic Tradition would not have survived. Astrology was then reintroduced to Europe through the crusades and flourished again during the renaissance, which is why authors such as Lilly would have access to such traditional texts.[2]

2 For a comprehensive study of the history of Western Astrology, see Campion, Nicholas, *The History of Western Astrology Volumes I and II*.

It is to these recently rediscovered Hellenistic texts that we must look to understand the rationale of many astrological doctrines still in use today.[3] One can find a wealth of information regarding the four elements in the works of Plato, Aristotle and Agrippa. Similarly, much information on the planets and the Zodiacal signs is relatively easy to come by. However, while the essential dignities of the planets are well established, it is only recently we have discovered the technical origins of these attributions.

The Dignities

In relation to the seven classical planets, the Neophyte Knowledge Lecture says that,

> "These planets are astrologically speaking considered to be more powerful in certain parts of the Zodiac respectively than in others."[4]

These "certain parts" are called dignities and can be generally broken down into two groups: the essential and the accidental dignities, of which this article focuses on the former.[5] When astrology was systemised in Hellenistic times, a series of five essential dignities were introduced, *viz*:

a) The Domiciles or Houses,
b) The Exaltations,
c) The Triplicities,
d) The Decans or Faces, and
e) The Bounds or Terms.

Furthermore, two more "debilitations" were introduced, called the "Fall" and the "Detriment."[6]

---

3 This work was spearheaded by Project Hindsight. <http://www.projecthindsight.com/>
4 Knowledge Lecture 0=0 to 1=10 (Private Collection).
5 Accidental dignities are dependent on a planets position in the Scheme of 12 Houses. This will be touched upon later and are a subject of the Fourth Knowledge Lecture of the Golden Dawn.
6 A planet's fall is the opposing sign to its exaltation while a planet's detriment is the opposing sign to its Houses.

In the Neophyte Knowledge Lecture, it says that,

> "[Planets] are most powerful in their own "Houses,"
> that is in those signs which they rule "absolutely," very
> powerful in the special sign of their "exaltation," and
> moderately powerful when in their three signs of the
> Triplicity which they rule."[7]

From this we can deduce that the chiefs of the of the Golden Dawn
only required initiates to memorize three of the Essential Dignities
of the Planets. However, the Decans become a prominent topic when
studying the Minor Arcana of the Tarot in the Grade of Zelator
Adeptus Minor.[8] For this article, I will focus on delivering an in
depth philosophical and theoretical rationale as to the assignment
of Planets to these three Dignities. Some of these Dignities from the
Alpha & Omega Knowledge Lecture are published in the *Astrology of
the Golden Dawn* from the Golden Dawn Study Series.[9]

Some Basic Concepts – The Four-fold system of Astrology

Astrology, both traditional and modern, can be broken down into a
four-fold series of topics. These include the Planets, the twelve Signs of
the Zodiac, the Houses or Places, and the Aspects or Configurations.
These form the fundamental backbone of any astrological chart and
have their roots in pre-Hellenistic astrological traditions. A basic
understanding of these concepts is required before delving deeply
into the origin of the astrological dignities.

1. Planets

Modern astrologers generally deal with a whole range of planets,
asteroids and fictitious points when casting charts. However,
astrology is rooted over 2 millennia before the invention of the
telescope. Hence astrologers have only a limited range of objects to
work with. These objects, termed "the Traditional Planets" or "the
Old Planets," formed the basis of astrological ideology. Planets as a

7   Knowledge Lecture 0=0 to 1=10 (Private Collection).
8   Regardie, Israel, *The Golden Dawn* 6th Edition, p. 541.
9   Brodie-Innes, John William, *Astrology of the Golden Dawn*, pg. 10.

whole tend to represent archetypical topics, which are subsequently coloured by their positions in the Zodiacal belt and the relationship between each.

In the Neophyte Knowledge Lecture, we are presented with the seven Traditional Planets in Chaldean Order, along with their Astrological Symbols, as shown in Figure 1. In this scheme of thinking, the Sun and the Moon are considered as planets, as they operate the same way, moving around Earth from the reference frame of the observer against the backdrop of the Sphere of the Zodiac. For more advanced students of the Golden Dawn system or Kabballah, this may remind you of the Spheres of Assiah.

Order	Planet	Symbol
1	Saturn	♄
2	Jupiter	♃
3	Mars	♂
4	Sol (Sun)	☉
5	Venus	♀
6	Mercury	☿
7	Luna (Moon)	☽

Figure 1. The Seven Traditional Planets and their Symbols

In relation to the planets, the Knowledge Lecture also introduces four additional points. The first two of these are the modern planets Uranus (♅) and Neptune (♆).[10] As these planets cannot be typically seen with the naked eye, they were not known of in Hellenistic times.[11] Hence, they were not included in the system of dignities. Modern Astrologers tend to attribute Dignities to these Planets, but that is beyond the scope of this article.[12]

The other two additional points presented are termed "*Caput*

10 At the time of the foundation of the Order, Pluto (♇), and the whole range of planetoids and asteroids, were not discovered.
11 Technically, Uranus can be seen with the naked eye, but it is a rare occurrence and evidently unknown in ancient times.
12 For those interested, modern astrologers attribute Uranus to Aquarius, Neptune to Pisces and Pluto to Scorpio.

Draconais" and *"Cauda Draconais,"* or the North and South Nodes of the Moon. These nodes are fictitious points and describe the intersection between the monthly orbit of the moon and the ecliptic. See Figure 2. The nodes are always 180° apart and move in retrograde.[13]

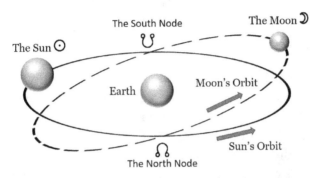

Figure 2. The Nodes of the Moon

The astrological significance of the nodes is related to the eclipses. This significance, along with a general warning, is outlined in the paper on the Hexagram Ritual given to Adeptus Minor students:

> "And be thou well wary of dealing with these forces of the North and South Nodes, or with those of Sol or Luna, during the period of an eclipse; for they are the Powers of an eclipse. For the Eclipse to take place, both the Sun and the Moon must be in conjunction with them in the Zodiac, those two luminaries being at the same time either in conjunction or in opposition as regards each other."[14]

When discussing the Dignities of Planets, two basic qualities must be considered. These are the Benefic/Malefic status and the Sect of the Planet. In the third Knowledge Lecture,[15] the Theoricus is introduced to the Benefic/Malefic status of the Planets (also called

---

13 Retrograde describes the apparent reverse motion of an astrological object from the reference frame of the observer.

14 Regardie, Israel, *The Golden Dawn* 6th Edition, p. 288

15 Farrell, Nick, *Mather's Last Secret*, pg. 135. These are published in Brodie-Innes, John William, *Astrology of the Golden Dawn*, pg. 7.

the Fortunes or Infortunes),[16] summarized in Figure 3.

	Diurnal	Nocturnal
Sect Light	☉	☽
Benefic	♃	♀
Malefic	♄	♂

Figure 3. The Benefit/Malefic and Sect status of the Planets.

The rationale behind these assignments seems to be heavily based on the visual appearances of the planets. Jupiter and Venus tend to be very bright in the night sky, while Saturn and Mars tend to be much dimmer (Jupiter is considered the Greater Benefic, while Venus is considered the Lesser. Saturn is considered the Greater Malefic, while Mars is considered the Lesser). One issue modern astrologers have with this designation is that it paints a very black and white image of astrological delineations, i.e. either good or evil. This is a very surface level view of traditional astrology, ignoring many other contributions to a spectrum of meaning. The most basic of these is planetary Sect. This concept was only recently rediscovered; hence it would not have appeared in any of the Order's teachings. However, it is a fundamental concept.[17]

Basically, each of the planets is a member of either the "Diurnal Sect" or the "Nocturnal Sect." See Figure 3. Each Sect is led by a Sect Light, which fittingly is the Sun or Moon and has two planets associated with each. Mercury is considered neutral and takes on the character of a Sect depending on whether it rises before the Sun in the

16 The Knowledge Lecture also described the North Node, the Sun and Mercury as Benefics, and the South Node and Uranus as Malefics. In certain traditional schools, the North and South Nodes were considered Benefic and Malefic. However, Modern Astrology places a lot of emphasis on the meaning of these two points. The Sun could be considered a Benefic; however, in Traditional Astrology, the Sun could be considered a Malefic if it is within 15^0 of a planet. This phenomenon is called combustion and tends to weaken the planet's significations. In Modern Astrology, Uranus tends to be associated with ideas of rebellion and large-scale change. This may be why the writers of the Knowledge Lecture considered it a Malefic. Mercury tends to be more neutral and whose temperament is heavily dependent on what planets it is associated with.
17 Valens, Vettius, The *Anthology*, 1(1), 2(2) and 3(5).

morning (Diurnal) or sets after the Sun in the evening (Nocturnal).[18] The Sect of an astrological chart is determined whether the Sun is above or below the Horizon (the Ascendant-Descendant Axis). For example, if the Sun is above the horizon, we have a Diurnal Chart and Jupiter becomes the most positive Benefic, while Mars becomes the most negative Malefic. On the contrary, if the Sun is below the horizon, we have a Nocturnal Chart and Venus becomes the most positive Benefic, while Saturn becomes the most negative Malefic. The most positive Benefic is termed the Benefic "of the Sect" while the most negative Malefic is termed the Malefic "Contrary to the Sect."

2. Signs

Probably the most well-known and popular concept in astrology is the Twelve Signs of the Zodiac. Each individual sign colours a planet placed in it in a different way. A good analogy describes the planet as an actor and the Zodiacal Sign is the role it plays; each actor playing each role in a different way. Modern astrology focuses mainly on the sign the Sun is placed in (Sun Sign Astrology common in magazines and newspapers). However, this can be easily extended to all of the planets.

In the Neophyte Knowledge Lecture, the twelve Zodiacal Signs are presented along with their anthropomorphic identities and astrological symbols. The significations and qualities of these are based on several factors, the most relevant being the Gender, Elemental Triplicity and Quadruplicity. See Figure 4.[19]

The Gender of a Sign is in relation to the Sign's tendency to be active (masculine) or passive (feminine). The use of the term "Gender" may seem a little dated, but in many ways traditional astrologers would take it literally, e.g. planets in masculine sign indicate the birth of a male. Perhaps for modern times it would be better to use terms such as active and passive, yin and yang, or to emit and receive.

---

18 Hephaestio of Thebes, *Apotelesmatika*, 1, 2:9.
19 Regardie, Israel, *The Golden Dawn*, 6th Edition, p. 50. These are also published in Brodie-Innes, John William, *Astrology of the Golden Dawn*, pg. 7.

Sign	Image	Symbol	Gender	Triplicity	Modality
Aries	Ram	♈	Male	Fire	Cardinal
Taurus	Bull	♉	Female	Earth	Fixed
Gemini	Twins	♊	Male	Air	Mutable
Cancer	Crab	♋	Female	Water	Cardinal
Leo	Lion	♌	Male	Fire	Fixed
Virgo	Virgin	♍	Female	Earth	Mutable
Libra	Balances	♎	Male	Air	Cardinal
Scorpio	Scorpion	♏	Female	Water	Fixed
Sagittarius	Archer	♐	Male	Fire	Mutable
Capricornus	Goat	♑	Female	Earth	Cardinal
Aquarius	Waterbearer	♒	Male	Air	Fixed
Pisces	Fishes	♓	Female	Water	Mutable

Figure 4. The Twelve Signs of the Zodiac

The Elemental Triplicity of a Sign is in relation to the attribution of the four Elements to the Twelve Signs of the Zodiac. The Triplicities were originally conceived as groupings of three based on a simple triangle, each sign being 120° apart. These groupings eventually became associated with the four Elements, Fire, Earth, Air and Water.[20] These elemental qualities form the basis for the second set of significations for each Sign. In summary, Fire Signs tend to be active and energetic, Earth Signs tend to be rationale and practical, Air Signs tend to be competitive and intellectual, while Water Signs tend to be emotional and sensual. In line with many of the Golden Dawn's teachings, it might be noticed that the Fire and Air Signs are the active elements while the Water and Earth Signs are passive elements.[21]

Finally, the Quadruplicity of a Sign is in relation to a grouping of the signs into sets of four based on a square, each sign being 90° apart. Cardinal Signs tend to demonstrate active expressions of their significations but run out of energy quickly. Fixed Signs show a more stubborn long-lasting nature. Mutable Signs tend to show a mix of

20 Hellenistic Astrologers referred to Triplicities as Trigons, see Valens, Vettius, *The Anthology*, 2(1).
21 This is especially evident with regard the Elemental and Spirit Pentagrams. See Regardie, Israel. *The Golden Dawn, 6th Edition*, pg. 282.

these previous qualities.[22]

The Hellenistic Astrologers developed a useful teaching tool relating the planets to the Twelve Signs of the Zodiac which will become useful when discussing the rationale of some of the dignities and related concepts. This teaching tool was called the *Thema Mundi*, or the "Nativity of the World".[23] This schematic is outlined in Figure 5.

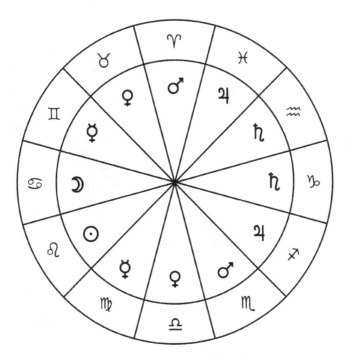

Figure 5. The *Thema Mundi*

Both luminaries (the Sun and the Moon) are assigned to Cancer

---

22 Many astrologers also relate the meaning of the Signs to particular times of the year and to the images of the associated constellations. In the Order's Equinox ceremony, we commence the Spring Equinox when the Sun enters Aries and the Autumnal Equinox when the Sun enters Libra. When the Zodiac was standardized, this was fundamentally true. However, due to an astronomical phenomenon called the Precession of the Equinoxes, from the perspective of the Earth, the Sphere of the Zodiac moves about 1° westward every 72 years. In reality, when we celebrate the vernal Equinox, it is actually the Sign of Pisces that rises above the Horizon. This essentially creates two different Zodiacs (Tropical and Sidereal), where the significations for each Sign are derived from both.

23 Maternus, Firmicus, *Mathesis*, 3, 1:8-15

and Leo respectively. Next Mercury is assigned to Virgo. The rationale behind involves Mercury's position in the sky. Each sign of the Zodiacal belt occupies 30° of the ecliptic. As Mercury is the planet most physically close to the Sun, it never strays more than one Zodiacal sign away before turning retrograde. Similarly, Venus's position in Libra is due to Venus never straying more than two Zodiacal signs from the Sun. Next Mars, Jupiter and Saturn are attributed to Scorpio, Sagittarius and Capricorn, as they are the next planets that progress in natural and Chaldaic order from the Sun.

To account for the rest of the attributions, the myth goes that the Sun moved into the Sign of Virgo and the heat was so over-bearing, Mercury moved as far away from the Sun as he could to Gemini. Next, the Sun moved to Libra and Venus moved as far away as she could to Taurus. Similarly, the Sun moved onwards, and Mars, Jupiter and Saturn moved to Aries, Pisces and Aquarius respectively.

One might wonder why, of the luminaries, the Sun is attributed to Leo and the Moon to Cancer, and not the other way around. This basic attribution could simply be derived from Leo being a Fire Sign and Cancer being a Water Sign.

One may also wonder why this system has Cancer on the eastern horizon (the Ascendant) of the *Thema Mundi* as opposed to Aries (Traditionally, the initial Zodiacal Sign in modern Astrology). There are a few theories, but I favour the theory that it is related to Cancer rising over the Eastern Horizon every year when the Nile flooded.[24]

3. Aspects

Another well-known concept in modern astrology is the Doctrine of Aspects (or configurations). Aspects were developed as a way of analysing the relationship between planets in astrological charts. The works of Hellenistic astrologers such as Antiochus of Athens[25] and Porphyry of Tyre[26] present a series of definitions regarding aspects, most notable the Greek term "*epimarturia.*" *Epimarturia* can be translated as "witnessing" or "testimony." Essentially, an aspect can

---

24 For a more in-depth discussion and origin of the Thema Mundi, see Brennan, Chris, *Hellenistic Astrology: The Study of Fate and Fortune*, pp 228 – 236.
25 Antiochus of Athens, *Definitions and Foundations*, pp. 43 – 56.
26 Porphyry, *Introduction to the Tetrabiblos*, pp 11 – 19.

be described as one planet bearing witness or testimony to another.

These aspects were derived from a series of Hellenistic contemporary optical theories, which placed heavy emphasis on affinity between astrological Signs and formation of complete polygons.[27] These affinities were previously described earlier as Gender, Triplicity and Quadruplicity-based; e.g., two Fire Signs or two Cardinal Signs share an affinity.

Furthermore, the temperament of the aspect, i.e. how good or evil the aspect is, was derived from the *Thema Mundi* in relation to the Sun, the Moon and the Ascendant in Cancer and Leo. See Figure 5.[28]

Aspects can be either viewed as Sign-based or degree-based aspects. A Sign-based aspect commences when a planet ingresses into (enters) a Sign. For example, planets that are four Signs apart share a square Sign-based aspect. It is of no concern where in either Sign the planets are. Once either of the planets leave that particular Sign, the square aspect is done. On the other hand, a degree-based aspect only becomes relevant when two planets enter an aspect within a specific degree range. In Hellenistic astrology, this range was 3° (13° when the moon was involved),[29] while in medieval and modern astrology a series of "Orbs" surrounding each planet came into play.[30] When the boundary of each planets' Orb met, the aspect commenced. A degree-based aspect was said to "perfect" when the aspect went exact. In the Third Knowledge Lecture of the Golden Dawn, the Theoricus is presented with a series of Orbs as shown below.[31]

Saturn and Jupiter - 9°

Mars, Venus and Mercury - 7°

Sol - 15°

Luna - 12°

The Cusp or Edge of any House - 5°

---

27 For more on Hellenistic optical theories see *The Optics of Euclid*.

28 Ptolemy, *Tetrabiblos*, 1, 18.

29 Antiochus, *Summary*, 8-9.

30 Lilly, William. *Christian Astrology*, pg. 107.

31 Farrell, Nick, *Mather's Last Secret*, pg. 135. However, to the author's knowledge, there is no published material from the Golden Dawn with this information.

It has been noted that the 12°/13° Orb of the Moon could be derived from the fact that the Moon travels this degree range across the sky every 24 hours. Furthermore, the 15° Orb of the Sun is highly relevant in a Hellenistic astrological doctrine termed "Under the Beams," in which any planet within 15° of the Sun is said to be somewhat debilitated.

In the Second Knowledge Lecture of the Golden Dawn, the Zelator is presented with a series of Aspects which are derived from the above considerations and are still used in modern astrology.[32] Below is a summary of the main configurations with some commentary:

Conjunction = Two planets in the same sign – Good or Evil depending on nature of the planets.

In Hellenistic astrology, the conjunction was not strictly speaking an aspect, as conjunct planets were essentially on top of each other and their significations combined. However, a conjunction technically does share affinities between gender, triplicity and quadruplicity. The Hellenistic astrologers broke the conjunction down into a series of smaller "aspects." If two planets are in the same Sign, they are considered "Copresent;" if two planets are within 15°, they are considered in "Assembly;" and if two planets are within 3° they are considered in "Adherence."[33]

Sextile = Two Planets 60° apart – always Good.

Two planets or Signs in sextile share similar genders and form a complete hexagon on an astrological chart. Analysis of the *Thema Mundi* from Figure 5 reveals that with respect to the Ascendant, the sextile has a Venusian quality,[34] the Lesser Benefic, hence the "Good" nature of this aspect.

Square or Quintile = Two planets 90° apart – always Evil.

Two planets or Signs in Square share similar quadruplicities and form a complete square polygon on an astrological chart. Analysis of the *Thema Mundi* from Figure 5 reveals that with respect to the Ascendant, the square has a Martian quality, the Lesser Malefic,

---

32 Farrell, Nick, *Mather's Last Secret*, pg. 105. These are also published in Brodie-Innes, John William, *Astrology of the Golden Dawn*, pg. 9.

33 Antiochus, *Summary*, 8-9.

34 Notice how Venus in Libra is Sextile to the Moon in Cancer, and how Venus in Taurus is Sextile to the Sun in Leo. This schematic applies to the rest of the aspects.

hence the "Evil" nature of this aspect.[35]

Trine = Two planets 120° apart – the most powerful of the Good Aspects.

Two planets or signs in Trine share similar genders and triplicities and form a complete triangular polygon on an astrological chart. Analysis of the *Thema Mundi* from Figure 5 reveals that with respect to the Ascendant, the Trine has a Jupitarian quality, the Greater Benefic, hence it is considered the most powerful of the "Good Aspects."

Opposition = Two planets 180° apart – the most powerful of the Evil Aspects.

Two planets or signs in Opposition share similar genders and triplicities and form a complete two-sided polygon (a straight line) on an astrological chart. Analysis of the *Thema Mundi* from Figure 5 reveals that with respect to the Ascendant, the Opposition has a Saturnian quality, the Greater Malefic, hence it is considered the most powerful of the "Evil Aspects."

The Knowledge Lecture also presents a series of minor aspects. These aspects were introduced in the Renaissance period by Johannes Kepler and were not present in Hellenistic Traditions.[36] In Figure 6 below, a summary of the above aspects with their appropriate symbols is shown.

Aspect	Symbol	Degrees	# of Signs Apart
Conjunction	☌	0°	0
Sextile	✳	60°	3
Square	☐	90°	4
Trine	△	120°	5
Opposition	☍	180°	7

Figure 6. The Major Aspects

35 In Hellenistic astrology, the Square aspect was shown to have a little more complicated nature. In certain circumstances, it could show a highly benefic nature, especially when a Benefic "overcame" a planet, i.e. if a Benefic squared a planet later in Zodiacal order, it was considered very auspicious.
36 Kepler, Johannes, *Harmonies of the World.*

This scheme accounts for eight Signs, leaving four unaccounted for. These four Signs are considered relatively inactive in Hellenistic Astrology, and planets in these signs are termed in "aversion." Modern astrological traditions have largely replaced the aversions with the Semi-Sextile (⚹ - 30°) and the Quincunx (⚻ - 150°).

4. Houses

The final part of the four-fold system is the Twelve "Houses" or "Places".[37] This area is probably the least known part of the four-fold system in popular astrology, although certain aspects such as the Ascendant (as I have mentioned previously) are well known. While the progression of the Zodiac is based on the annual motion of the Sun, the Twelve Houses or Places are based on the diurnal motion of the Sun in a single day. On average, a planet will spend two hours of the day in a particular house before moving on to the next. The Twelve Houses are primarily used to designate different areas of a person's life. A planet in a particular house will express its significations in that area of life.

In the Third Knowledge Lecture of the Golden Dawn, the Theoricus is introduced to the primary method of calculating the Houses.

> "The 4 cardinal points are given by the Meridian and the Horizon. The Meridian gives South and North points, or the Zenith and Nadir, and the Horizontal Line give an East, West, and these points are 90 degrees of oblique ascension, each quadrant (quarter) being then divided into 3 points, gives 12 Houses, each 30 degrees."[38]

The Horizon consists of the East and West Points, also called the Ascendant (1st House) and the Descendant (7th House). The Ascendant (Asc) is the point that rises on the Eastern Horizon at the moment of birth or an event. The Descendant (Dsc) is the point that

---

37 A confusion sometimes arises here regarding the term "Houses." Domicile "Houses" are in relation to the Zodiacal Signs, while this House system is fundamentally different, as will be explained further on.

38 Knowledge Lecture 2=9 to 3=8 (Private Collection). To the author's knowledge, there is no published material from the Golden Dawn with this information.

sets on the Western Horizon. The Meridian consists of the South and North Points, also called the Imum Coeli (IC - 4th House) and the Medium Coeli (MC - 10th House) respectively.

There are many forms of House division. When Western astrology was first being standardized in the Hellenistic tradition, a system called Whole Sign Houses was used. In Whole Sign Houses, whatever sign the degree of the Ascendant is placed at the moment of birth is considered the whole 1st House. The 2nd House occupies the next Zodiac sign, and so on until each House is associated with one Zodiacal sign only. In this system, the cusp of each House is aligned with the cusps of the Zodiac signs. This may well have been the original reason why there were twelve Houses and not some other number. This House system was relatively unknown in Western Astrology from the Medieval Period up to about the 1980s with the release of an article by James Holden reconstructing the original system.[39] Therefore, this system would have been unknown to the Golden Dawn at the time of writing the Knowledge Lectures. It is interesting to note that this Whole Sign Houses never fell out of use by the Vedic astrological tradition in India.

In the Whole Sign system, the Zenith and Nadir are not considered when calculating the 4th and 10th House cusps, as the boundaries of the zodiac signs are used instead. Therefore, the Imum Coeli (IC) and the Medium Coeli (MC) are considered sensitive points much like the lunar nodes that float around the chart.

A second category of House system was created in the Hellenistic Tradition called the Quadrant House system. This is the system described above in the Third Knowledge Lecture. It uses the Zenith and Prime Meridian to calculate the cusps of the 4th and 10th Houses while keeping the east and west points on the Horizon at the degrees of the Asc and Dsc respectively. These four points are of 90° of oblique ascension to each other and are further divided into three by various methods to create several different systems of quadrant houses, each giving a total of twelve Houses. Due to the tilt of the earth and depending on the position for where the astrological chart is cast, the cusps of the 4th and 10th Houses change positions. This is due to the earth's equator intersecting the Horizon at oblique angles.

---

39 Holden, James Hershel. *Ancient House Division*. American Federation of Astrologers Journal of Research (1982), 1.(1), pp 19-29.

Therefore, quadrant systems tend to show Houses of unequal sizes.

The original quadrant system, which can be found in the works of Hellenistic astrologers such as Vettius Valens[40] or Porphyry,[41] simply divides these quadrats into three equal sizes on an astrological chart. However, over the centuries more sophisticated mathematical models exist, calculating the House cusps. While the original Golden Dawn Order was active, the Placidus House system was in common use, hence it would be understandable that the members of the Order would use this system as most Astrological Empherides (published Tables of Houses) followed this system. However, the tradition from William Lilly that the Knowledge Lectures probably derived from used the Regiomontanus House system. It is generally up to the astrologer which system to use for study and practice.

The Significations of the Houses, which are presented to the Zelator in the Second Knowledge Lecture of the Golden Dawn[42] are derived from three main considerations:

a) The Accidental Dignities

b) Relationship to the Ascendant

c) The Planetary Joys

In the Forth Knowledge Lecture of the Golden Dawn, the Practicus was introduced to the concept of Accidental Dignity.[43] An Accidental Dignity is basically the position of a planet in a particular House. As the Asc, Dsc, IC and MC are at the cusps of cardinal points they are considered of highest importance and are called "Angular" or "pivotal." The House before each Angular House is called the Succedent House as it is the House a planet resides before it enters an Angular House. Succedent Houses are said to "rise up" towards an Angular House and are second in importance. Finally, the House after Angular is said to be "falling away" or "Cadent" and hence the weakest of the houses.

---

40 Valens, Vettius. *Anthology*, 3(2).

41 Porphyry, *Introduction to the Tetrabiblos*, 43.

42 Farrell, Nick, *Mather's Last Secret*, pg. 134. A summary of these is published in Brodie-Innes, John William, *Astrology of the Golden Dawn*, pg. 41.

43 Ibid., pg. 170.

If we recall the section above about the Aspects and Configurations, we saw that the particular Signs (and hence Houses from the Whole House system) have particular relationships to the Asc. In this scheme, the 2nd, 6th, 8th and 12th Houses are in Aversion to the Asc as they have no affinity.[44] Furthermore, Houses in opposition tend to have opposing significations.[45]

Each planet is said to have a specific House where it expresses its "Joy". A Joy is a House where a planet is strongest and gives significations to. See Figure 7 for a diagram of the Joys in the 12 Houses.[46]

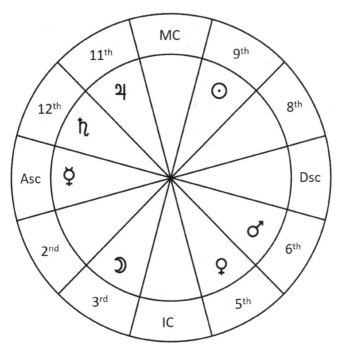

Figure 7. The Planetary Joys

---

44 These Houses in Aversion tend to show very negative significations.

45 For example: The 1st House is associated with the self while the 7th House could be associated with the partner.

46 For a broad discussion rationale on the Planetary Joys, Chris Brennan, *The Planetary Joys and the Origins of the Significations of the Houses and Triplicities.*

The Dignities

1. The Houses or Domiciles

While the term "House" is used in modern astrology, the term "Domicile" may be more apt, as it can be confused with the Doctrine of "Houses" or "Places," as mentioned earlier.

The general idea is that, each of the seven Traditional Planets has either one or two Zodiacal Signs that they feel "at home" in. These particular signs are essentially where a planet feels most comfortable and able to produce their significations naturally. They are essentially the signs where that planet expresses its nature the strongest. Furthermore, it is evident that the significations of a planet match closely with that of its ruling Houses, as they are so closely connected. In the Knowledge Lecture of the Neophyte, we are presented with a table of ruling Houses,[47] as shown in Figure 8.

Planet	Ruling Signs
♄	♑ and ♒
♃	♐ and ♓
♂	♈ and ♏
☉	♌
♀	♉ and ♎
☿	♊ and ♍
☽	♋

Figure 8. The ruling Houses of the seven Traditional Planets.

At first, this arrangement seems random and arbitrary. However, if the student studies closely, they will see this arrangement exactly follows that of the *Thema Mundi* presented in Figure 5. The

47 Knowledge Lecture 0=0 to 1=10 (Private Collection). However, these are published in Brodie-Innes, John William, *Astrology of the Golden Dawn*, pg. 10.

luminaries are in Cancer and Leo, with of the planets in order from the Sun spanning out on each side. The two final signs, Capricorn and Aquarius, are occupied by Saturn. This can lead to very basic interpretative principles based on opposing polarities. The Light of the luminaries opposes the cold darkness of Saturn. This can be extended to the other planets such as the obvious dichotomy between Mars and Venus. Even the opposing ideas of Jupiter and Mercury can be examined, such as the idea of long and short journeys.

2. The Exaltations

In the scheme of essential dignities, exaltations tend to follow the ruling Houses in importance. While an exaltation encompasses a whole sign, it is interesting to note that each one is strongest at a particular degree, e.g. the Sun at 19° Aries.[48] For this article, the whole signs as presented in the Neophyte Lecture will be discussed. See Figure 9.

Planet	Exaltation
♄	♎
♃	♋
♂	♑
☉	♈
♀	♓
☿	♍
☽	♉

Figure 9. The Exaltations of the seven Traditional Planets.

Planets in their exaltation are said to "be raised up" or "display more power." The origin of these exaltations is not fully known;

---

48 There is a general standardized series of exaltation degrees, however, not all sources agree exactly. For the most part, the whole signs are used. See Valens, Vettius. *Anthology*, 2(4), for the standard set of Exaltation degrees.

however, it has been suggested they are inherited from previous Mesopotamian traditions.[49] While the origins are obscure, there are certain interesting correlations evident in the arrangement.

First, much like that shown with the Domiciles in the previous section, we can see rudimentary pairs of opposites. This was originally outlined by Rhetorius of Egypt.[50] The light and heat of the Sun in Aries is opposed to the cold darkness of Saturn in Libra. Also, the Sun in Aries represents Winter turning into Spring, while Saturn in Libra represents Summer turning into Autumn.[51] It is well known that when the Sun enters Aries at the Vernal Equinox, the day start to get longer than the night as we approach the warm summer. Similarly, when the Sun enters Libra at the Autumnal Equinox, the night gets longer than the day as we approach the cold winter. These Equinoxes are the origin of the Equinox ceremonies of the Order of the Golden Dawn.[52] At the Summer Solstice we have Jupiter in Cancer, representing life, abundance and vitality, while at the Winter Solstice we have Mars in Capricorn, representing death and decay. Finally, we can compare Venus in Pisces' and Mercury in Virgo's opposition much the same way we can with the Sephirothic Spheres in the Qabalah with a balance of Desire and Intellectualism.[53] In the exaltation scheme, the Moon does not appear to have a diametrically opposing planet.

Another interesting correlation is regarding the *Thema Mundi* presented in Figure 5.[54] For the Diurnal planets (Jupiter and Saturn), the sign of Exaltation is Trine to one of the ruling Houses. For example, Jupiter in Cancer is Trine Jupiter in Pisces. For the Nocturnal planets (Venus and Mars), the sign of Exaltation is Sextile to one of the ruling signs. For example, Venus in Pisces is sextile to

---

49 Brennan, Chris. *Hellenistic Astrology: The Study of Fate and Fortune*, pp 247 - 249.

50 Rhetorius, *Astrological Compendium*, 8.

51 Autumn may be called Fall in some countries.

52 Regardie, Israel. *The Golden Dawn*, 6th Edition, pp. 248 - 257

53 For those unaware, in the Kabbalistic Tree of Life studies by all Initiates of the Golden Dawn, the Sphere of Hod (Mercury) on the Pillar of Severity is opposite the Sphere of Netzach (Venus) on the Pillar of Mercy connected by the Path of Mars. This is more so an interesting correspondence as it was unlikely this was the rationale behind the exaltation scheme.

54 Porphyry, *Introduction to the Tetrabiblos*, 6

Venus in Taurus.

While the origin of the exaltations is relatively unknown, it is clear from the above two considerations that there was some underlying rationale behind it.[55]

3. The Triplicities

In the Neophyte Knowledge Lecture, one is given a very basic attribution of the Planets to the four Elemental Triplicities. This attribution follows closely the Exaltations in importance. Figure 10 shows the Triplicity scheme presented to the Neophyte.

Element	Planets	Signs
Fire	☉ and ♃	♈ ♌ ♐
Earth	☽ and ♀	♉ ♍ ♑
Air	☿ and ♄	♊ ♎ ♒
Water	♂	♋ ♏ ♓

in the Neophyte Knowledge Lecture.

This scheme encompasses each Element being assigned two planets with Mars solely being assigned to the Element of Water. However, in much Occult literature, each Element is assigned one Diurnal planet and one Nocturnal planet, and the planet Venus is assigned to the Element of Water with Mars. Furthermore, a third cooperating planet is assigned to each Element. See Figure 11 for a summary of this schematic.

---

55 A recent translation of *The Great Introduction to Astrology* by Abu Ma'shar contains much information on the origin of the Exaltations.

Element	Diurnal Planet	Nocturnal Planets	Cooperating Planet
Fire	☉	♃	♄
Earth	♀	☽	♂
Air	♄	☿	♃
Water	♀	♂	☽

While the Neophyte does not need to memorize the alternative arrangement, it is interesting to study it in relation to the Golden Dawn attribution. Both arrangements can be derived from the same theoretical construct shown in Figure 7, called the Planetary Joy scheme.[56]

According to Aristotle, each element had a natural tendency to either travel upward or downward.[57] This was the basis of his doctrine of "natural place." In this schematic, Fire rises the highest with Air right below. The Earth is at the lowest point with Water resting above. This gives rise to the following order from highest to lowest: Fire, Air, Water Earth. This ordering was adopted by many philosophical schools such as in Hermeticism. Note that this Elemental arrangement is different to that of the grade structure of the Outer Order of the Golden Dawn and Zodiacal Order.

If we examine the Planetary Joys in Figure 7, much like the doctrine of Natural Place, Fire is on the top (surrounding the MC) and Earth is at the bottom (surrounding the IC) of the chart in relation to the Planetary Triplicities from Figures 10 and 11. Furthermore, the planets surrounding the Asc on the eastern side of the chart match the Planets from the Air Triplicity. At the Dsc on the Western side of the Chart, we have Mars corresponding to the Water Triplicity of the arrangement in Figure 10. Why then, is Air attributed to the East side of the chart while Water attributed to the West side? Perhaps one explanation could be in relation to the Winds from the Rituals

56 Brennan, Chris. *The Planetary Joys and the Origins of the Significations of the Houses and Triplicities.*
57 Aristotle, *On the Heavens*, II, 13-14.

of the Pentagram.[58] However, a more logical answer may be found by combining the Doctrine of Natural Places with that of the motion of the Planets through the Houses. Throughout the day, the Asc remains at the eastern horizon; however, from the reference frame of the observer, the planets move from East to West past the MC. This is essentially a clockwise motion. If we analyse this movement from the construct in Figure 7, we can see the clockwise motion of the Planets cause the Air Planets on the Eastern Horizon to "rise up" towards the MC and the Water Planet on the Western Horizon to "fall down" towards the IC. This essentially mirrors the doctrine of Natural Places.

Why then are there cooperating Planets in the alternative arrangement and why is Venus attributed to the Water Triplicity? Notice how all three Diurnal Planets (the Sun, Jupiter and Saturn) are above the Horizon, while all three Nocturnal Planets (the Moon, Venus and Mars) are below the Horizon. From this we can label the top half of the chart as diurnal and the bottom half as nocturnal.

For the Diurnal Elements (Fire and Air), the most diurnal planet is considered the diurnal ruler, while the other is considered the nocturnal ruler. Hence, for the Element of Fire, the Sun is the Diurnal Ruler (as it is the Sect Light) and Jupiter is the Nocturnal Ruler. For the Element of Air, Saturn is the Diurnal Ruler and Mercury is the Nocturnal Ruler (as it is less Diurnal than Saturn). Finally, the nearest planet in each case is considered the cooperating ruler. Hence, Saturn for the Element of Fire and Jupiter for the Element of Air.

For the Nocturnal Elements (Earth and Water), the most Nocturnal Planet is considered the Nocturnal Ruler and the other is the Diurnal Ruler. Hence for the Element of Earth, we have the Moon as the Nocturnal ruler (as it is the Sect Light) and Venus as the Diurnal Ruler. For the Element of Water, we have Mars as the Nocturnal Ruler. As Venus is the closest Planet in the clockwise direction of Planetary motion through the Houses, it assumed the role of the Diurnal Ruler in the alternative arrangement. Similarly, as with the Diurnal Planets, the closest other Planet assumes the role

---

58 This explanation only holds up for Air and Water as the MC which is associated with the element of Fire is more northern, which is not in line with the Nature of the Winds, as Fire is attributed to the South. The same for Earth.

of cooperating ruler. This would be Mars for Earth and the Moon for Water.

Practical Use of the Dignities

Not a lot of practical astrology teaching was given to members of the original Outer Order besides a few general instructions in the Knowledge Lectures. Some papers were written by adepts such as J.W. Brodie Innes.[59] For the most part, practical Astrology was probably learned externally from the Order's system as Astrology texts were for the most part available in bookshops.

For the purposes of the current article, I will elucidate a practical method to astrologically time rituals using the aforementioned dignities and a few other considerations. In traditional Astrology, this method is known as Electional or "Katarchic"[60] Astrology, a tradition where contemporary Horary Astrology probably has its roots.[61]

First, take note of a few preliminary considerations:

a) There are many rules regarding Electional Astrology, most of which I will not go into as it is outside the scope of this article. Only aspects presented in the Knowledge Lectures of the Golden Dawn will be considered.

b) There is no such thing as a perfect election. While you can make an election chart as subjectively positive as possible, Malefic Planets are always going to be somewhere annoying.

c) The perfect timing of an election may not coincide with your day to day activities such as work or family commitments.

d) Things change whether you adopt the Tropical or Sidereal Zodiacs. Furthermore, things can change depending on which House system you adopt. For this example, I will be using the Tropical Zodiac and the Whole Sign House with sign-based aspects for simplicity.

---

59 Brodie-Innes, John William, *Astrology of the Golden Dawn.* Edited by Darcy Kuntz.

60 Dorotheus of Sidon, *Carmen Astrologicum*, Book 5 (5)

61 Brennan, Chris. *The Katarchē of Horary.*

Let's take, for example, the consecration of the Rose Cross of the Adeptus Minor.[62] This symbol is associated with the Sephira of Tiphareth and hence the ritual is solar in nature. Therefore, it is desirable to time this ritual to a point when the Sun is well dignified. A planet is well dignified when it is in a sign it rules and aspected positively to other planets.

There are two different tools used to cast charts: Astrological Ephemerides[63] and Astrological software.[64] Before the invention of Astrological software, all astrologers had to cast charts by hand and Ephemerides were essential tools. Ephemerides are tables of Astrological positions throughout the year for all the main celestial objects. It is, with these Ephemerides, that we determine the initial viable timeframes. From our studies earlier, we determined the signs in which the Sun is well dignified. For the year 2020 C.E. these are shown in Figure 12.

Importance	Sign	Dignity	Time Frame
1	♌	Ruler House (+ Diurnal Triplicity)	July 23 20:04 UTC – August 23 22:06 UTC
2	♈	Exaltation (+ Diurnal Triplicity)	March 20 11:59 UTC – April 20 13:54 UTC
3	♐	Diurnal Triplicity	November 22 04:05 UTC – December 22 06:04 UTC

Figure 12. Timeframe for solar dignify for the year 2020 C.E.

The time zone UTC (Universal Time) given in the Ephemeris is essentially Greenwich Meantime, or GMT. Once the general periods have been decided from the Ephemerides, we can move on to astrological software to further narrow down the time frames. For the following considerations, consult online astrological software for each date in question.

As a triplicity rulership in Sagittarius on its own is relatively weak, we can omit this consideration. The next step is the desire to

62 Regardie, Israel. *The Golden Dawn*, 6th Edition, pp. 310 - 316
63 See <https://www.astro.com/swisseph/swepha_e.htm> for a free publicly available series of Ephemerides.
64 See <https://www.astro.com/cgi/chart.cgi> for an online astrological chart calculator.

have the Sun in good aspect with other planets in order to assist in the positive manifestations towards the Sun. We must strive for the following two conditions:

a) Positive aspects (Conjunction, Sextile and Trine) with the Benefics (Jupiter and Venus). It is highly beneficial that an aspected Benefic is well dignified by Sign as this will increase its positive influence on the target planet.

b) No negative aspects (Conjunction, Square and Opposition) with the Malefics (Saturn and Mars). It is highly beneficial that a Malefic is well dignified by Sign also as this will decrease its negative influence on the target planet.

When considering the time frame for Leo from Figure 12, analysis of a chart cast for this period shows that both Jupiter and Saturn in Capricorn are in aversion to the Sun, and Mars in Aries is Trine to the Sun. Furthermore, Venus in Gemini is Sextile to the Sun until August 8th where it enters Cancer and is in Aversion. See Figure 13 for a demonstration of this election.

For this consideration, Jupiter and Saturn are of no concern. As Mars is positively aspected to the Sun we can invoke Mars's positive qualities, such as courage or fortitude. Venus Sextile the Sun is also quite a positive aspect. Therefore, this election is most positive while the Sun is in Leo before the 8th of August.

When considering the time frame for Aries from Figure 12, analysis of a chart cast for this period shows that Jupiter in Capricorn is square to Sun while Saturn in Aquarius is sextile to the Sun. Venus in Taurus is in aversion to the Sun until April 4th when it enters Gemini and hence is sextile to the Sun. Mars in Capricorn is square to the sun until March 31st where it enters Aquarius and becomes sextile to the Sun. See Figure 14 for a demonstration of this election.

For this consideration, we can ignore the period before April 1st as Mars is square the Sun as this is a very negative aspect. From this point onwards, Mars and Saturn are sextile to the Sun. Both Malefics have a moderately positive aspect to the Sun potentially supplying both courage (from Mars) or discipline (from Saturn). Saturn itself is currently very well dignified in its own Ruling House (Aquarius) and hence increasing potential positive Saturnian qualities. In this chart Jupiter is both square to the Sun and in an afflicted Sign (Capricorn). Venus is interesting in that while in aversion it is in its ruling House but that is of no use to the Sun. It is not until Venus leaves Taurus and enters Gemini that it has a meaningful aspect, but it is no longer dignified by sign.

There are several steps to reduce the time frame further. It is common enough to choose a day based on the attributions of the planets to the day of the week. Considering the Sect of a planet was also a very common method, as it will point out which Malefic is the most negative and which Benefic is most positive. Furthermore, traditional astrologers would have also attempted to ensure the Moon is well dignified, as it is the planet closest associated with the material plane (the Sphere of Levanah). The final step would be to reduce the timeframe to a particular time of the day where the planet is most active; however, this area alone is a topic for another article. I would suggest choosing a time where the planet is in the angular (1st, 4th, 7th and 10th) Houses as these are the most active. Specifically, the 1st House as it relates to the self or the 10th House as it relates to the magician's life work.

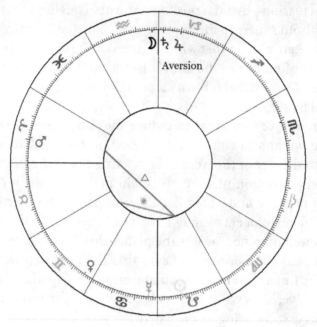

Figure 13. Potential Solar Election when Sun is Dignified in Leo

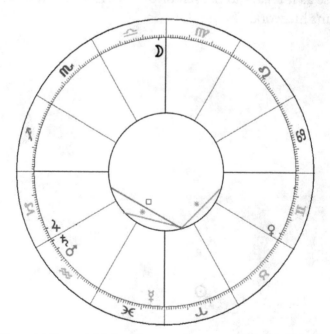

Figure 14. Potential Solar Election when Sun is Dignified in Leo

Bibliography

Antiochus of Athens, *Definitions and Foundations*. Translated by Robert Schmidt. Berkeley Springs, WV. The Golden Hind Press. 1993

Aristotle, *On the Heavens*, Translated by Thomas Taylor, Somerset, England : The Prometheus Trust, 1807.

Brennan, Chris. *Hellenistic Astrology: The Study of Fate and Fortune*. Denver, CO. Amor Fati Books. 2017.

Brennan, Chris. *The Planetary Joys and the Origins of the Significations of the Houses and Triplicities*. ISAR International Astrologer Journal (2013), 42(1), pp 27-42.

Brennan, Chris. *The Katarchē of Horary*. National Council for Geocosmic Research Journal (2007). Summer, pp 23-33.

Brodie-Innes, John William, *Astrology of the Golden Dawn*. Edited by Darcy Kuntz. Holmes Publishing Group. Lynnwood, WA. 1996.

Campion, Nicholas. *A History of Western Astrology: Volume 1 The Ancient World*. London. Bloomberg Academic. 2008.

Campion, Nicholas. *A History of Western Astrology: Volume 1 The Medieval and Modern Worlds*. London. Bloomberg Academic. 2009.

Dorotheus of Sidon, *Carmen Astrologicum*. Astrology Classics. 2005.

Euclid, *The Optics of Euclid*, Journal of the Optical Society of America (1945), 35(5), pp. 357 – 372.

Farrell, Nick. *Mather's Last Secret*. Rosicrucian Order of the Golden Dawn 2001.

Hephaestio, of Thebes. *Apotelesmatika*. Translated by David Pingree. Leipzig. 1973.

Holden, James Hershel. *Ancient House Division*. American Federation of Astrologers Journal of Research (1982), 1.(1), pp 19-29.

Kepler, Johannes, *Harmonies of the World*, Translated by Charles Glenn Wallis. Global Grey. 2014.

Lilly, William. *Christian Astrology*. London. John Macock. 1659.

Ma'shar, Abu, *The Great Introduction to Astrology*, Translated by Keiji Yamamoto and Charles Burnett, Brill Academic Publishing, 2019.

Maternus, Firmicus. *Mathesis*. Translated by James Hershel Holden. Tempe AZ. American Federation of Astrologers. 2011.

Porphyry the Philosopher. *Introduction to the Tetrabiblos*. Translated by James Hershel Holden. Tempe, AZ. American Federation of Astrologers. 2009.

Ptolemy, Claudius. *Tetrabiblos*. London, Davis and Dickson. 1822.

Raphael. *A Manual of Astrology*. London. C.S. Arnold. 1827.

Regardie, Israel. *The Golden Dawn. 6th Edition*. St. Paul, MN. Llewellyn. 2006

Rhetorius the Egyptian. Astrological Compendium. Translated by James Hershel Holden. Tempe, AZ. American Federation of Astrologers. 2009.

Valens, Vettius. *Anthology*. Berkeley Springs, WV. The Golden Hind Press. 1993.

ABOUT THE AUTHOR

Frater Manu Forti is an Astrologer and statistician living in rural Ireland. He has a PhD in Physics and currently works in the field of medical diagnostics. In 2014, he was initiated into an Order based on the Golden Dawn and has been a practicing magician since, focusing on astrology. Manu is certified in the traditional branch of Hellenistic Astrology and operates his own online blog. His other interests focus on Ceremonial Magic, Tarot and the Kabbalah.

https://manufortiastrologyblog.com

ON THE ROSE AND CROSS ON THE MEMBERSHIP ROLL

by Frater A.R.O.

The Membership Roll of the R.R. et A.C. contains several Symbols which are not mere decoration. They allude to powerful teachings and formulae, and their very presence in the Book of the Oath serves to further bind the Members of our Order to that solemn Obligation they took, and, as a sacred seal, offer a protective and guiding force to the Order as a whole.

There are several Symbols upon the Scroll, the first of which is the Rose of Ruby and the Cross of Gold, from which the name of the Inner Order is derived. This is a five-petalled Red Rose, in which is placed a Golden Cross, surrounded by green leaves and the letters R and C.

This is an ancient Symbol, which was first published in German in 1785 in *The Secret Symbols of the 16th and 17th Century Rosicrucians*, by A Brother of the Fraternity, said to be from an old manuscript.

In that volume, the Symbol in question was surrounded by the Latin words *Mea Victoria in Cruce Rosea*, which translates as: *My Victory is in the Cross of the Rose*. These are the very words that are spoken by the Candidate in the Second Point of the 5=6 Ritual of Adeptus Minor, which allow for the Pastos of our Founder, Christian Rosenkreutz, to be opened.

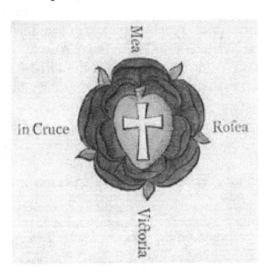

There are many Mysteries in this Symbol, and it is a powerful emblem of the triumph of Good over Evil, and the victory of Life everlasting over Death. As it is written, "So when this corruptible shall have put on incorruption, and this mortal shall have put on immortality, then shall be brought to pass the saying that is written, Death is swallowed up in victory." This is explored further in the 7=4 Grade of Adeptus Exemptus.

The Cross is made up of Six Squares, referring to Tiphereth. It is the same Cross as that of the Outer Order, except that the Red Colour of Self-Sacrifice has been transmuted into the Gold of Attainment. It is the Risen and Victorious Christ.

The Cross is contained within a heart-shaped Alchemical vial or flask. It is the Elixir of Life, through which the Alchemical transformation takes place. We are told in the 5=6 Ritual "Be thy heart the Centre of Light," and the Crux Ansata or Ankh, the Egyptian Symbol of Life, is used to impart this instruction, and is itself a form of the Rose Cross. It is also the Symbol of Venus, the planet of Love, and so we see an additional significance to the heart, and even to the door through which we enter the Vault. As it is written, "And now these three remain: faith, hope and love. But the greatest of these is love." So do we bear the Rose Cross Symbol upon our breasts, the place of the heart, the position of Tiphereth within our Sphere of Sensation.

Think also of the Initiations of the Heart, which are Sadness and Suffering. As the Chief Adept enjoins the Candidate: "They have been but the purification of the Gold. In the Alembic of thine Heart, Through the Athanor of Affliction, Seek thou the true Stone of the Wise." Here then in this Symbol do we see the Alembic of the Heart, in which can be found the purified form of the Cross of Gold. For, as we are told in the 5=6 Ritual, "The Symbol of Suffering is the Symbol of Victory."

The earlier form of this emblem shows the White Cross of Purification within a Gold Heart. In this form, they are reversed, so that the Cross of Gold is reached through the Purified Heart. As it is written, "Blessed are the pure in heart, for they shall see God." Further, the 5=6 Ritual of Adeptus Minor tells us: "Achievements are but as nothing in the sight of the Lord of the Universe, for he looketh at the Heart."

The form of the Rose here given is also seen on the Cross of Victory employed in the 5=6 Ritual of Adeptus Minor, where it represents the Five-fold division of Spirit and the Elements, divided further into its Sub-Elements, creating twenty-five in total. In that Symbol its various Colours are shown openly, while in this they are hidden. So it is with many other aspects of the Order's teachings.

It may be noticed that the Rose of Five Petals is orientated so as to represent the upright Pentagram, emblematic of the rule of Spirit over the Four Elements, and of the Five-fold Name of יהשוה, Yeheshuah, or Christ. The Red Colour alludes to the importance of Self-Sacrifice, and also to the Martial force of Geburah, the Fifth Sephirah, to which the Pentagram is especially attributed.

However, there is also another Pentagram displayed in this Symbol, and this is the inverted form hidden in the leaves or thorns. This form, symbolic of Evil, is placed beneath the flower, and it rises from the thorny stem of the Rose.

ON THE ROSE AND CROSS

We must consider this placement carefully, for the beauty of the Rose is ensured by the protective quality of the thorns, which prick the hand of any who seize it. Without these, the Rose could not survive. Here again we see the Mystery mentioned in the 5=6 Ritual of Adeptus Minor: "Even the Evil helpeth forward the Good."

This also shows the importance of the Crown of Thorns that was placed upon the head of Christ in the Crucifixion, wherefore he is crowned King over all the Qlippoth. As it is written, "I hold the Keys of Hell and of Death."

For in the Credo it is said that "He descended into Hell," and it was this descent that preceded his ultimate Resurrection and Triumph. So must we be the Kings of our own Qlippothic Kingdoms before we can attain to the Crown of the Higher.

The Green Colour of the leaves or thorns is the natural complement, or Flashing Colour, to the Red Colour of the Rose. We cannot have one without the other. Thus also, we cannot have Good without Evil, nor a true and complete Knowledge of one without the other, for to truly know Good, we must also know Evil. This is the Mystery of the Serpent of Wisdom, and hence also why the Order teaches of the Profane as well as the Sacred. The significance of the Colours Red and Green are highlighted in the Portal Ceremony in the description of the Hierophant's Lamen:

"The Two Colours Red and Green, the most Active and the most Passive, whose conjunction points out the practical application of the Knowledge of Equilibrium, are Symbolical of the Reconciliation of the Celestial Essences of Fire and of Water, for the reconciling Yellow unites with the Blue in Green, which is the Complementary Colour to Red, and with Red in Orange, which is the Complentary Colour to Blue."

The inverted Pentagram and upright Pentagram unite together to form a Ten-pointed Symbol, thus alluding to the 10 Sephiroth, in which is contained both Good and Evil. Further, the Pentagram itself is attributed to Geburah, which the Zohar tells us is the root of Evil. So do we use the Five-pointed Star to ward off Evil, and gain mastery over it, even the Evil within our own nature. We see this explored further in the 6=5 Grade of Adeptus Major.

Further still, this Ten-pointed figure is the Fourth Form of the Decagram, as shown in the 4=7 paper on the *Polygons and Polygrams*, which states:

> "It shows the operation of the duplicated ה of the Tetragrammaton יהוה and the concentration of the Positive and Negative forces of the Spirit, and the Four Elements, under the Presidency of the Potencies of the Five in Binah, the revolutions of the forces under Aima, the Great Mother."

Here we see the Positive and Negative, the dual polarity of the Magnet, which is also to be found in all aspects of Creation, for it comes from her, Binah, the Great Mother, through Malkuth, the Inferior Mother. ה, the fifth letter of the Hebrew alphabet, is the only letter repeated in the Tetragrammaton, the first alluding to Binah, the Mother in her higher aspect (the Barbelo of the Gnostics), and the second alluding to Malkuth, the Mother in her lower aspect (the fallen Sophia of the Gnostics). Without this final duplication, there would be no Malkuth, no Kingdom, no physical world. So, indeed, do we owe our physical lives to this polarity. So also must we recognise the importance of polarity to the existence of all Life. Hence also why we must have the polarity of forces present in the Symbol of the Rose itself.

The letters R and C on either side of the Symbol allude to the fifth clause—indeed, the Pentagram again—that the ancient Rosicrucian Brethren agreed to, as pointed out in the 5=6 Ritual:

> "The word R.C. to be their mark, seal, and character."

In this, the word shall be an identifying mark, not merely on the mortal self, worn as a literal sign or *signum* by the Adept, but also a spiritual inscription, indeed the character of the soul. As it is written, "he has also put his seal upon us." So then also may the Adept endeavour to look for this mark or seal before accepting anyone who professes to be a member of the Rosicrucian Order, as in the Tenth or Malkuth Clause of the Obligation, for, with the true Rosicrucian, this is an indelible, ineffaceable mark.

We might also notice that the letters R.C. are referred to not as letters, but as "the word." There are many Mysteries to this, but one alone is supreme. As it is written, "In the beginning was the Word, and the Word was with God, and the Word was God."

Together with the Cross in the centre of the Symbol, which can be seen to be the + sign, they present the simple formula of R+C, or the Rose and Cross of the ancient Rosicrucian Fraternity. Separately, these are potent Symbols, but together they become something even more, and so do they form the Rose Cross that we bear upon our breasts, and even the Cross of Victory.

The letters R and C are also shown in a more elaborate form upon the Membership Roll. The R is made up of a Red Equal-armed Cross, the form of which is symbolic of the Elements and the Name, and the colour of which represents "the Energy of the Lower Will purified and subjected unto that which is Higher." Around this Cross twines a Green Serpent, alluding to the Serpent of Wisdom. The C is made up of the stem and flower of a Lotus, the Egyptian equivalent of the Rose, with three leaves, symbolic of the Three Supernals and the Trinity, through Whom we Live, Die, and Live Again. Inside the Lotus is contained a Black Calvary Cross and Circle, or Celtic Cross, another form of the Rose Cross, which is shown upon the Lamen of the Hierophant, and those of the Dais Officers. The Black is emblematic of Putrefaction, the fifth stage of Death, and so completes the Alchemical Colours present in these Symbols.

So is the Mystery of the Rose and Cross hidden also in the Outer Order, and only after the passage of the Five Grades, the Pentagram once more, is this hidden Symbol finally unveiled.

The letters I.N.R.I. are also present between these emblems, which we know to represent many Mysteries, not least of all the Key Word of the 5=6 Grade of Adeptus Minor, the Analysis of which provides us with the very formula of the entire Second Order.

Thus far concerning the Symbols of the Rose and Cross upon the Membership Roll.

ABOUT THE AUTHOR

Frater A.R.O. is an initiate of the Golden Dawn.

The ages pass like crumpled pages in a book,
Some still pristine within the annals of our mind.
A century to come and go is all it took
For much of magic to be lost, and now we find
That somehow it is here again for us to know.
The birthright of our hungered spirit lingers still,
The fruit of inner trees we weather, nurse and sow
That we might come in contact with our higher will.
The light glows stronger now, despite time's leaden hold;
The magi stir from deep within their temple tombs—
What once was but a metal has become fair gold,
And where an ancient garden was, a rose now blooms.

— Frater Yechidah

CPSIA information can be obtained
at www.ICGtesting.com
Printed in the USA
LVHW011937131220
674086LV00023B/383

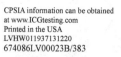

9 781908 705174